M

T

W

T

F

S ATURDAY

S UNDAY

BON APPÉTIT
Weekend entertaining

BON APPÉTIT

Weekend entertaining

from the editors of Bon Appétit

Condé Nast Books · Pantheon
New York

Table of Contents

For Bon Appétit Magazine

WILLIAM J. GARRY, Editor-in-Chief

LAURIE GLENN BUCKLE, Editor, Bon Appétit Books

MARCY MacDONALD, Editorial Business Manager

CARRI MARKS, Editorial Production Director

SYBIL SHIMAZU NEUBAUER, Editorial Coordinator

JORDANA RUHLAND, Assistant Editor

MARCIA LEWIS, Editorial Support

NAO HAUSER, Text

H. ABIGAIL BOK, Copy Editor

GAYLEN DUCKER GRODY, Research

JEANNE THIEL KELLEY, Food Research

For Condé Nast Books

JILL COHEN, President

ELLEN MARIA BRUZELIUS, Division Vice President

LUCILLE FRIEDMAN, Fulfillment Manager

TOM DOWNING, Direct Marketing Manager

CRAIG DAVIS, Direct Marketing Analyst

PAUL DiNARDO, Direct Marketing Assistant

LYNN DUFFY, Direct Marketing Assistant

Produced in association with
PATRICK FILLEY ASSOCIATES, INC.

Design and art direction
SALSGIVER COVENEY ASSOCIATES INC.

Front Jacket (clockwise from top left): *Corn, Tomato and Basil Salad (page 73); Steak Sandwiches on Garlic Baguettes with Arugula and Tomatoes (page 72); Tricolor Roasted Peppers (page 73).*

ISBN: 0-375-40250-0

Condé Nast Web Address: http://www.epicurious.com

Random House Web Address: http://www.randomhouse.com

Printed in Hong Kong by Pearl East Printing Co.

First Edition

2 4 6 8 9 7 5 3 1

Introduction

We have all come to accept the idea of a Monday-through-Friday calendar crammed with appointments, dead-lines, commitments and stress-provok-ing workloads—and "multi-tasking" as a means of getting it all done. And before we all agree to similarly hectic, jam-packed weekends (the final free-time frontier as we approach the turn of the century), we at Bon Appétit magazine would like to suggest an alternate approach to the stretch of time between Friday night and late Sunday. While the five-day week may be devoted to a to-do list longer than your arm, the weekend should be set aside for the important things: family gatherings, keeping up friendships and celebrat-ing milestones great and small.

This is a book for anyone who trea-sures family meals, dinner parties with friends and celebrations both casual and elegant—even though you may feel that you don't have the time, the energy or the know-how to pull it all together and pull it off. You do; it's simply a matter of thinking you do. We'll take it from there.

A COOKBOOK, A MENU GUIDE, AN ENTERTAINING sourcebook—these are all ways you could describe this book. But behind its multifaceted exterior beats a single, simple idea: When all is said and done, it is the getting together, the *being* together that counts.

A meal is the magnet that lures one and all to the table, to the party and the celebration. It is the thing around which everything else revolves, the focus of the festivities, whether they are of the everyday vari-ety or the once-in-a-lifetime kind. That's why this book is organized by meals, from menus that cele-brate special occasions to those that make the most of typical weekend nights. So whether you've been presented with the challenge of a daughter's wed-ding in your back yard or you simply have a few friends coming over on a Saturday night, there is a menu here to turn to, one that will offer a hand, suggest a countdown strategy, take you through the process of shopping, cooking and serving, with a memorable meal guaranteed.

OCCASIONS TO CELEBRATE

THERE ARE THREE SECTIONS TO THIS BOOK, EACH comprising ten menus. In the first, called Occasions, there are complete, foolproof party plans for the special events we most often celebrate on the weekend, from the impending arrival of a baby to a big anniversary. There are "all-purpose" menus here (for example, a lovely dinner that might honor a promotion, an engagement or a homecoming) in and among more "event-specific" menus, such as a child's birthday party. There's a romantic supper for two (if you have children, the fact that the two of you are home alone is occasion enough to celebrate); a grand, pull-out-all-the-stops party for fifty (feeding a crowd was never so easy and elegant); and several mid-size menus in between. And in keeping with that flexibility in the number of people served, the menus here (and thoughout the book) also include "Options," dishes that mix and match with the main meal, allowing you to substitute based on personal preference, seasonality, ease and such.

Key to the "doability" of these festive menus are the detailed strategies that precede each one and the do-ahead tips scattered throughout the recipes. The strategies are broken down into what can be done—in terms of both the recipes and the party particulars—weeks, days and even hours before your guests come knocking. This information is supported by the recipe tips, which detail freezing and storing information at different points throughout the cooking process. Throwing a party that's sure to become a special memory requires planning and organization, both of which are simplified for you here. Of course, despite the best-laid plans, it can't all be as perfect as the ideal (see the sidebar at right on what might happen and what you might do), as anyone with any entertaining experience will tell you. The trick, come what may, is to (a) pretend it was planned, (b) switch to plan B, or (c) laugh and open another bottle of wine.

It Will Happen

It's inevitable. Mistakes, accidents, even disasters will happen when you're entertaining. The trick is to rise above them, never letting on that you are embarrassed, mad or terrified. If you're cool, calm and collected, your guests will be too. Try any of these tactics for dealing with the unexpected.

BAD WEATHER. If you're planning an outdoor party, even in July, have a backup plan. This could be as simple as moving the group inside, or reserving a tent if it's a large event like a wedding.

KITCHEN DISASTERS. Whether the main course burns, drops to the middle of the floor or becomes the dog's treat, dinner must go on. Salvage what you can and serve it with a flourish; pick up the phone and order in Chinese; or gather everyone up and head out to a restaurant.

TECHNICAL DIFFICULTIES. When it comes to entertaining, Murphy's Law prevails. Know that the garbage disposal ("dishwasher" and "toilet" would also work here) *will* break when there are more than eight people at your house for dinner. Laugh it off, and your guests will too.

GUEST MISHAPS. When things get broken, quickly remove the evidence and go on with the party. When wine gets spilled, blot the stain with club soda, then cover it up with a napkin so that no one has to look at it. If someone gets hurt, attend to them rather than the dinner you're cooking.

PARTIES LESS PLANNED

IN THE BOOK'S MIDDLE SECTION, CALLED "Instant Entertaining," the menus speak to a more spontaneous kind of party-giving, the kind that just sort of happens when you're open to the idea of having everyone back to your place for a quick brunch, lunch, snacks or wonderfully informal dinner. Novices at entertaining may at first find the idea of volunteering for a spur-of-the-moment gathering more terrifying than a committed relationship or the prospect of parenthood; but these last-minute, come-as-you-are get-togethers can be the most fun you'll have on any given weekend (and, like relationships and parenting, they're never as impossible/awful/scary as you imagine them to be).

The trick to feeding a crowd on little or no notice is a well-stocked pantry (for a list of what to keep on hand, see the sidebar opposite); a sense of adventure and/or humor helps, too. Knowing what you have to work with in the kitchen or what you need to stop for on the drive home will make it that much easier to pull off a last-minute brunch for the neighbors you bumped into at the flea market; lunch for your in-laws, stopping by because they were "in the area"; or dinner for the friends who spent their Sunday helping you with a home-improvement project. The ten menus in this section suggest buffet meals that take just minutes to set out; your guests do the rest, helping themselves to dishes that can be "assembled" from what you provide.

The Instant Entertaining Pantry

A well-stocked pantry (a phrase we use to encompass the cupboard, the freezer and the refrigerator) makes spur-of-the-moment entertaining easy. Consider whether you're more likely to wind up suggesting breakfast, lunch or dinner; then, with the listed items on hand, you'll always be ready to let go with that most popular of invitations: "Everyone back to my place!"

BREAKFAST

cereals

a variety of breads, including bagels and muffins

jams, jellies, preserves, butter, cream cheese

eggs and bacon

fruit such as berries, melon and oranges

milk, coffee and juice

LUNCH

tortillas, pita bread rounds, sandwich rolls

canned tuna, cooked sausages

assorted cheeses

lettuce, tomatoes

salsa, mustard, sour cream, roasted red peppers

chips

beer and sodas

cookies

DINNER

pasta, cooked chicken, potatoes

mixed greens

assorted dressings

good-quality tomato sauce

grated Parmesan cheese

bacon, red onion, olives, artichoke hearts, garbanzo beans, hard-boiled eggs

rolls and baguettes

wine and iced tea

ice cream and sorbets

GETTING TOGETHER

THE LAST SECTION OF THE BOOK IS DEVOTED to the typical weekend meals we all look forward to, the ones that find us sitting around a table talking, catching up, laughing and eating. For many families, the weekend is the only time it's a sure thing that everyone will be together, so you'll find menus here for a nutritious breakfast with the kids on Saturday morning, a lunch you can all pack up and take to wherever you're going (whether out of town or to the local soccer field), and a dinner that will make a Sunday night at home special. For all of us, the weekend is a time to reconnect with friends and relatives, something that's most easily done over a good meal, such as an elegant yet easy Saturday night dinner or a big potluck party that involves a gang of your nearest and dearest.

When it comes to organizing a weekend meal, be it with family or friends, the willingness to do so can vanish in the face of the anticipated time it will take, the amount it will cost, the cleaning it will require, and the effort it will demand. All of these obstacles are easily done away with (for tricks on finding and making the time to entertain, see the sidebar at right) when you give in to the urge to bring everyone together. Turn to the end of this book for recipes that can be made in minutes, with ingredients that won't break the bank. Then sweep the dust under the rug, use candlelight to camouflage any imperfections, ask a friend to bring dessert or pick it up at the local ice cream parlor, and relax in the company of those who mean the most to you.

Time on Your Side

For a lot of folks, finding the time to entertain can seem like one more thing to do in a weekend already packed with errands and activities. Sometimes this is the case (say, for instance, mid-kitchen remodel); but for the most part, when someone says, "I just don't have the time," it's more about attitude than it is about to-do lists. But once the attitude changes, it becomes a simple matter of finding a little time where there didn't seem to be any and then organizing those extra minutes most efficiently.

Say you decide on Monday that you'd like to have some friends over Saturday night, you pick up the phone and set the date. Now what? From that moment on, you can begin to look for ways to simplify things over the course of the week, such as:

ACCEPT ALL OFFERS OF HELP: When an invited friend asks to bring something, don't hesitate with the response: "Sure." Be ready with an easy suggestion or quick recipe.

MAKE A LIST: Write down everything you'll need, arranged by store; carry it around with you and by the end of the week, two or three of those stops will have been taken care of.

USE FOUND TIME: With that same list in hand, you can probably breeze through an entire store in that short stretch of time between the pickup of one child and the drop-off of another.

DON'T COOK THE NIGHT BEFORE: Give yourself Friday night off—from dinner, anyway. Order in pizza or Chinese food and use the extra time to clean up the house, set the table or just relax.

THINK THROUGH SATURDAY: Considering errands to run, cooking to do and house cleaning, break Saturday down into rough time slots and assignments, enlisting your kids and significant other, and giving yourself an extra hour to do nothing.

WHEN THE CALENDAR SHOWS A BIRTHDAY, ANNIVERSARY, wedding, graduation, moving day, or baby due soon, a weekend becomes a window of opportunity, a time when you can give a party that's worthy of the event. Occasions such as these are made that much more special when they are celebrated with friends and family and a wonderful meal, lovingly prepared and beautifully served.

Each of the ten menus in this first section of the book will frame a happy memory for years to come. And whatever the occasion, you'll want to celebrate it once you see how easy we've made the entire entertaining process, *A* to *Z*, invitations to cleanup. There are strategies that detail when to do what; there are photographs filled with information and ideas; and there are recipes made simple with concise instructions and do-ahead tips.

Since some occasions call out for an elegant event (a wedding, say) and others are more suited to something casual (like a child's birthday party), this festive mix of menus includes both, just as it includes both big and small parties. Flexibility is a key component of this section, as evidenced in each menu's "Options," which are dishes designed to help you tailor the meal to your specifications.

The next time the opportunity arises, go ahead and make an occasion of a significant event in someone's life: They'll remember the day—as will you—always.

OCCASIONS

Celebration Dinner

menu for eight or twelve

- SPICED PÂTÉ

- WARM SCALLOP SALAD WITH CUMIN IN
  CRISP CHEESE BASKETS

- RACK OF LAMB WITH
  PORT-CURRANT SAUCE

- SAUTÉED POTATOES WITH
  ROSEMARY AND GARLIC

- BROCCOLI WITH MUSTARD BUTTER

- MERLOT

- SABLÉS AND POACHED PEARS WITH
  POIRE WILLIAMS SABAYON AND
  CARAMEL SAUCE

menu options

- CROWN ROAST OF PORK WITH
  CORN BREAD STUFFING

- BRAIDED BUTTER BREAD

- WHITE CHOCOLATE MINT TERRINE WITH
  DARK CHOCOLATE SAUCE

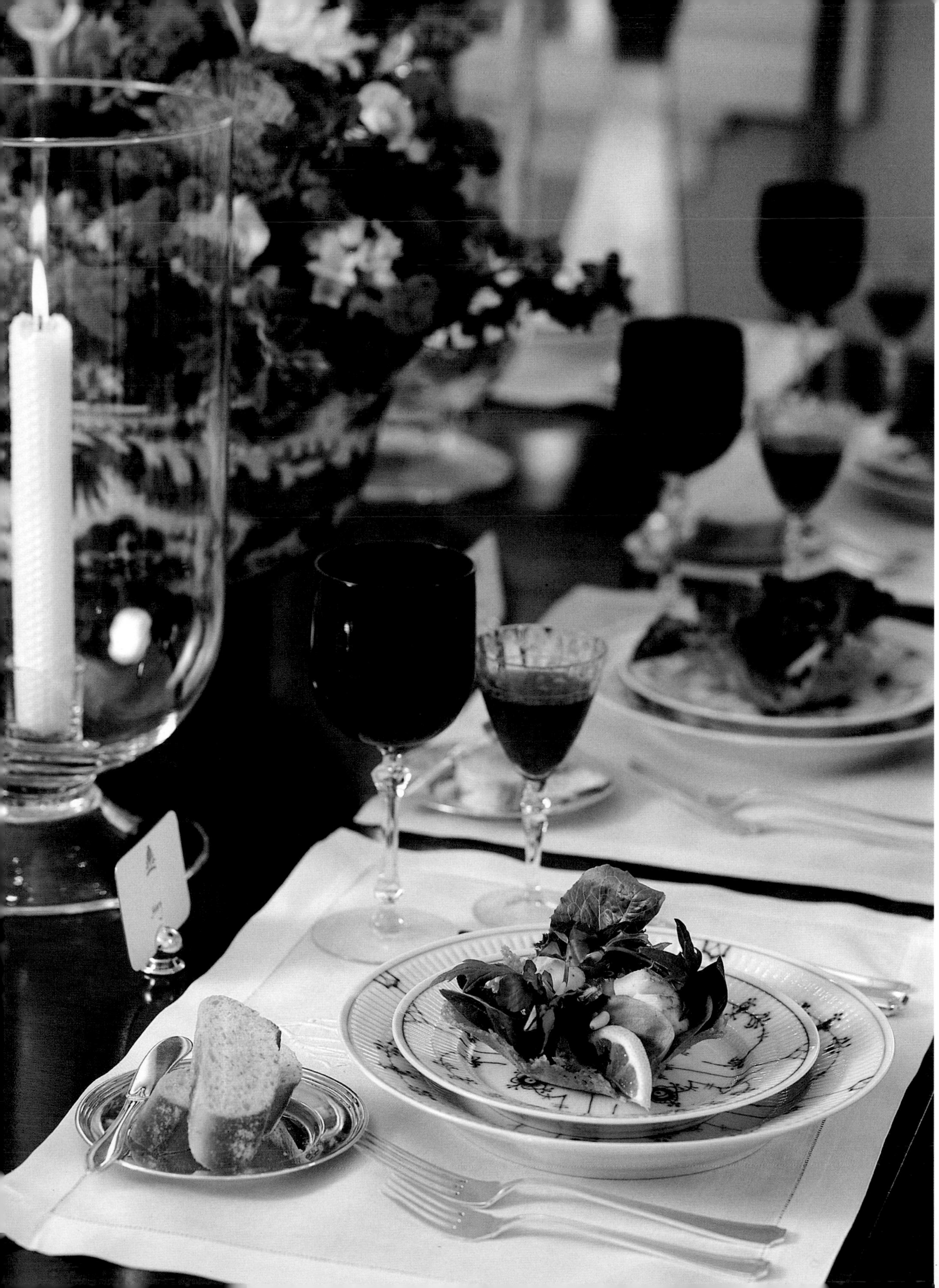

A reason to celebrate

IT'S GREAT TO HAVE A REASON TO CELEBRATE—MAYBE a new job, a promotion, an engagement, a homecoming or finally finishing that kitchen remodel. Whatever the occasion, use it as an excuse to dress up, light the candles, bring out those prized bottles of wine and cook up a menu as elegant and sophisticated as this one.

The dishes here are every bit as exciting as those you'll find at top restaurants across the country, but they've been designed to pass a reality check. The main course, for instance, is a regal rack of lamb that cooks to perfection in about 20 minutes. The rich Port sauce that accompanies the lamb can be prepared three days ahead and reheated just before you sit down to dinner. Side dishes are simple, too: an herbed potato sauté and steamed broccoli flavored with mustard butter (an idea you might want to keep in mind for sprucing up every-night vegetables). For an appetizer with drinks, there's a lovely

pâté that you make in the processor up to two days ahead (or feel free to purchase one).

But because it *is* a special occasion, there are two pull-out-all-the-stops dishes here, the kind of thing you'll enjoy making as much as eating. For a first course, sautéed scallops and a mix of baby greens fill crispy little cheese baskets; for dessert, poached pears, a pear brandy custard sauce, butter cookies called *sablés* and caramel sauce come together in a sweet that will stop conversation.

Knowing, however, that not every occasion worth celebrating necessarily comes with the time you'd like to give it, you'll find a simpler dessert alternative in the Options section (a luscious, minty, white chocolate terrine that no one needs to know took you less than 30 minutes to make); a simpler presentation for the scallop salad; and do-ahead tips throughout. Also offered among the Options is a

UP TO 3 WEEKS AHEAD:

- Invite guests.
- Make dough for *sablés*; freeze.

3 DAYS AHEAD:

- Make Port-currant sauce; chill.
- Make caramel sauce for sablés; chill.

2 DAYS AHEAD:

- Make pâté; chill.

1 DAY AHEAD:

- Make vinaigrette for scallop salad; keep at room temperature.
- Make mustard butter for broccoli; chill.
- Make sablés; store at room temperature.
- Poach pears; chill.

DAY OF:

- Prep greens for salad; chill.
- Make cheese baskets (up to 6 hours ahead); store at room temperature.
- Set up coffeemaker.

30 MINUTES BEFORE GUESTS ARRIVE:

- Roast lamb and potatoes.
- Reheat Port-currant sauce.
- Bring mustard butter to room temperature.

AFTER DINNER:

- Make sabayon.
- Rewarm caramel sauce.

big, beautiful crown roast of pork that will serve a larger crowd. Make it the main course for a party for 12, doubling the scallop salad and omitting the cheese baskets, doubling the broccoli and making the chocolate terrine for dessert.

This is one of those all-purpose, year-round menus that will suit a variety of occasions, lending itself to holiday celebrations (picture this meal as the focal point of your New Year's Eve festivities) and weekend dinners alike. If you belong to a gourmet group, consider this dinner not only for its sophistication but also for its cooking-together convenience: The do-ahead notes in the recipes mean that it won't take a lot of space for a number of cooks to complete dishes at the host's home. Those same do-ahead tips also mean that if you're staging this event on your own, you can complete the better part of it hours, even days, beforehand, leaving you free to enjoy the evening as much as your guests will.

SPICED PÂTÉ

Serve this easy starter with the classic accompaniments—slices of crusty French bread and small pickles called cornichons. MAKES 1⅓ CUPS

6 tablespoons (¾ stick) butter,
   room temperature
12 ounces chicken livers, trimmed
1 medium onion, chopped
2 large garlic cloves, chopped
1 tablespoon Dijon mustard
   Generous pinch of ground cloves
   Generous pinch of ground nutmeg

Melt 3 tablespoons butter in heavy medium skillet over medium-high heat. Add chicken livers and chopped onion and sauté until chicken livers are just cooked through, about 10 minutes. Transfer to processor. Add remaining 3 tablespoons butter, chopped garlic, Dijon mustard, cloves and nutmeg to processor. Using on/off turns, process chicken liver mixture until blended but not completely smooth. Season to taste with salt and pepper. Transfer pâté to small dish. Cover; refrigerate until chilled, about 30 minutes. *(Can be made 2 days ahead. Keep chilled.)*

WARM SCALLOP SALAD WITH CUMIN IN CRISP CHEESE BASKETS

In this sophisticated first course (opposite), sautéed scallops and baby greens fill fried Parmesan cheese baskets. (For a simpler presentation, serve the salad on its own.) 8 SERVINGS

3 tablespoons white wine vinegar
2 teaspoons dry mustard
1½ teaspoons sugar
¼ cup corn oil
3 tablespoons hazelnut oil or walnut oil

4 bacon slices, cut crosswise into ½-inch pieces
⅛ teaspoon ground cumin
16 large sea scallops, each cut
   horizontally in half
1 tablespoon fresh lemon juice

8 cups assorted baby greens
8 Crisp Cheese Baskets (see recipe opposite)
¼ cup pine nuts, toasted

Whisk vinegar, mustard and sugar in bowl. Gradually whisk in both oils. Season with salt and pepper. *(Can be made 1 day ahead; cover and let stand at room temperature.)*

Cook bacon in heavy large nonstick skillet over medium heat until crisp. Using slotted spoon, transfer bacon to paper towels; drain. Reserve drippings in skillet. Add cumin to skillet and cook over medium heat until aromatic, about 30 seconds. Add scallops in batches and cook until opaque in center, about 30 seconds per side. Return all scallops to skillet. Season to taste with salt and pepper. Drizzle with lemon juice. Remove from heat.

Place greens in large bowl. Toss with enough dressing to coat. Arrange 1 cheese basket on each plate. Fill with salad. Top with warm scallops. Sprinkle with pine nuts and bacon.

CRISP CHEESE BASKETS

Make these the morning of the party and store them at room temperature. MAKES 8

8 teaspoons unsalted butter
3 cups coarsely grated Parmesan cheese
   (about 9 ounces)

Invert one 1¼-cup custard cup on work surface. Cover with paper towel. Melt 1 teaspoon butter in large nonstick skillet over medium-low heat. Sprinkle generous ⅓ cup cheese into center of skillet, forming 6-inch round. Cook until cheese melts and bottom is golden, pressing on cheese with spatula to help flatten, about 4 minutes. Turn cheese over. Cook until second side is golden, about 3 minutes. Place cheese round atop paper towel-covered cup. Top with 2 folded paper towels and immediately press down on cheese to form cup shape, about 30 seconds. Remove paper towels. Turn cheese basket right side up; cool. Repeat with remaining cheese and butter, using clean paper towels for each basket. *(Can be made 6 hours ahead. Store airtight at room temperature.)*

RACK OF LAMB WITH PORT-CURRANT SAUCE

This impressive entrée is surprisingly simple to make. It would go especially well with a nice bottle of Merlot. 8 SERVINGS

SAUCE

1   cup plus 2 tablespoons ruby Port
⅔   cup fresh orange juice
½   cup red currant jelly
6   tablespoons fresh lemon juice
2   tablespoons matchstick-size strips orange peel
     (orange part only)
1½   tablespoons matchstick-size strips lemon peel
     (yellow part only)

LAMB

3   8-chop racks of lamb (about 1¾ pounds
     each), excess fat trimmed
2   tablespoons chopped fresh rosemary or
     2 teaspoons dried

Fresh rosemary sprigs

FOR SAUCE: Combine Port, orange juice, jelly, lemon juice and citrus peels in heavy medium saucepan. Bring to boil. Reduce heat; simmer until sauce thickens slightly, about 5 minutes. Set aside. *(Can be prepared up to 3 days ahead. Cover and keep refrigerated.)*

FOR LAMB: Preheat oven to 425°F. Place 1 rack on 1 baking sheet and remaining 2 racks on second baking sheet. Sprinkle lamb with salt, pepper and chopped rosemary. Roast until thermometer inserted into center registers 130°F for medium-rare, about 20 minutes.

Rewarm sauce over low heat, stirring occasionally. Cut lamb between bones into chops. Place 3 chops on each plate. Garnish with rosemary sprigs. Serve lamb, passing Port-currant sauce separately.

SAUTÉED POTATOES WITH ROSEMARY AND GARLIC

Divide the chunks of potato, rosemary and garlic between two large skillets to make sure the ingredients cook evenly. 8 SERVINGS

4   tablespoons extra-virgin olive oil
4   pounds russet potatoes, peeled,
    cut into ¾-inch pieces
2   tablespoons minced fresh rosemary or
    2 teaspoons dried
4   garlic cloves, minced

Divide oil between 2 heavy large skillets set over medium-high heat. Divide potatoes and rosemary between skillets. Cover; cook 15 minutes, stirring occasionally. Divide garlic between skillets; cook potatoes uncovered until brown and tender, stirring frequently, about 10 minutes. Season with salt and pepper.

BROCCOLI WITH MUSTARD BUTTER

A simple and delicious way to prepare a favorite vegetable. 8 SERVINGS

¼   cup (½ stick) butter, room temperature
2   tablespoons Dijon mustard

2½ pounds broccoli (about 2 large bunches),
    cut into florets

Mix butter and mustard in small bowl. *(Can be prepared 1 day ahead. Cover and chill. Bring mustard butter to room temperature before using.)*

Steam broccoli until crisp-tender. Transfer to large bowl. Add mustard butter and toss until melted. Season to taste with salt and pepper.

SABLÉS AND POACHED PEARS WITH POIRE WILLIAMS SABAYON AND CARAMEL SAUCE

This elegant dessert (below) is a layering of tender butter cookies—called sablés—*poached pears and a pear brandy custard sauce. Caramel sauce and raspberries add a final flourish.* 8 SERVINGS

SABLÉ COOKIES

15 tablespoons unsalted butter,
    room temperature
9   tablespoons sugar
2   large egg yolks
2¼ cups all purpose flour

PEARS

1   vanilla bean, split lengthwise
4   cups water
2   cups sugar
4   medium pears, peeled

Poire Williams Sabayon (see recipe opposite)
Powdered sugar
Caramel Sauce (see recipe opposite)
Fresh raspberries (optional)
8   fresh mint leaves (optional)

FOR COOKIES: Using electric mixer, beat butter and sugar in large bowl until light and fluffy. Beat in yolks. Add flour and mix just until blended. Gather dough into 2 balls. Flatten each into square. Wrap each in plastic; chill until cold, at least 5 hours. *(Dough can be prepared up to 3 weeks ahead and frozen.)*

Roll out 1 dough piece on floured surface to ¼-inch thickness. Cut out 3 x 2-inch rectangles; reserve scraps. Transfer cookies to ungreased baking sheet, spacing evenly. Repeat rolling and cutting with remaining dough piece to yield total of 24 cookies, rerolling scraps if necessary. Refrigerate cookies until cold, about 1 hour.

Preheat oven to 350°F. Bake cookies until golden brown on edges, about 8 minutes. Using spatula, transfer cookies to racks; cool.

FOR PEARS: Scrape seeds from vanilla bean into heavy large saucepan; add bean. Add 4 cups water and sugar; bring to boil, stirring to dissolve sugar. Boil 5 minutes. Add pears, reduce heat and simmer until tender when pierced with knife, about 15 minutes. Transfer pears to bowl. Pour poaching syrup over. *(Cookies and pears can be made 1 day ahead. Store cookies airtight at room temperature. Cover pears; chill.)*

Drain pears; reserve poaching syrup for another use. Quarter, core and thinly slice pears. Arrange 1 cookie on each of 8 plates. Top each with 1 sliced pear quarter. Spoon 2 tablespoons Poire Williams Sabayon over each. Repeat layering, using 8 more cookies, remaining sliced pears and 16 tablespoons sabayon. Top with 8 cookies. Dust with powdered sugar. Drizzle with Caramel Sauce. Top with berries and garnish with mint, if desired.

POIRE WILLIAMS SABAYON

MAKES ABOUT 2½ CUPS

½	cup water
6	tablespoons Poire Williams (clear pear brandy)
⅓	cup sugar
4	large egg yolks

Whisk all ingredients in large metal bowl. Set bowl over saucepan of simmering water (do not allow bottom of bowl to touch water). Using handheld electric mixer, beat sabayon mixture until candy thermometer registers 160°F, about 10 minutes. Remove bowl from over water. Serve sauce warm.

CARAMEL SAUCE

MAKES ABOUT 1⅓ CUPS

1	cup sugar
¼	cup water
1	cup whipping cream

Stir sugar and ¼ cup water in heavy medium saucepan over medium-low heat until sugar dissolves. Increase heat; boil without stirring until syrup turns deep amber, occasionally brushing down sides with wet pastry brush and swirling pan. Remove from heat. Slowly mix in cream (mixture will bubble vigorously). Stir over medium-low heat to dissolve hard bits. Cool slightly. *(Can be made 3 days ahead. Cover and refrigerate. Rewarm sauce over low heat before using.)*

CROWN ROAST OF PORK WITH CORN BREAD STUFFING

A crown roast makes such an impressive centerpiece that most folks think it must be loads of work. In fact, the butcher does the hard part; the home cook's job merely consists of putting it into the oven, taking it out at the right time and making a colorful stuffing as an accompaniment. This could substitute for the lamb and the potatoes, and feed a bigger crowd. (Double the scallop salad and the broccoli, and make the lovely chocolate terrine that follows for dessert.) 12 SERVINGS

STUFFING

6 tablespoons (¾ stick) unsalted butter
2 large red bell peppers, diced
2 celery stalks, minced
⅔ cup dried apricots, quartered
1 cup sliced green onions
12 cups Corn Bread Crumbs
   (see recipe at right)

PORK

1 crown roast of pork (about 10½ pounds)
1 cup dry white wine
1 cup canned low-salt chicken broth

1 egg, beaten to blend

FOR STUFFING: Butter 9 x 13 x 2-inch baking dish. Melt butter in heavy large skillet over medium-low heat. Add bell peppers and celery and cook until beginning to soften, stirring occasionally, about 7 minutes. Add apricots and green onions and continue cooking 3 minutes. Combine with Corn Bread Crumbs in large bowl. *(Can be prepared 1 day ahead. Cover and refrigerate.)*

FOR PORK: Preheat oven to 350°F. Set pork on rack in shallow roasting pan. Season with salt and pepper. Roast 1 hour. Remove from oven and pour off any drippings from pan. Pour wine and broth over roast. Cook pork roast 45 minutes, basting frequently.

Transfer roast to platter. Add juices and any browned bits from roasting pan to stuffing. Mix in egg. Season with salt and pepper. Return roast to pan and mound about 4 cups stuffing in center, packing slightly. Transfer remaining stuffing to prepared baking dish. Return roast and remaining stuffing to oven. Cook roast until thermometer inserted in thickest part registers 150°F, about 30 minutes. Bake stuffing until edges are crisp and brown, about 40 minutes. Transfer roast to cutting board, tent with foil and let rest 10 minutes. Carve roast by cutting between rib bones. Serve with stuffing.

CORN BREAD CRUMBS

MAKES ABOUT 12 CUPS

2 cups all purpose four
2 cups cornmeal
½ cup sugar
4 teaspoons baking powder
½ teaspoon salt
2 large eggs
3 cups buttermilk
½ cup (1 stick) unsalted butter, melted

Preheat oven to 400°F. Butter two 8-inch square baking pans. Combine first 5 ingredients in large bowl. Beat eggs, buttermilk and melted butter in medium bowl to combine. Gradually add to dry ingredients, stirring just until combined. Divide batter between prepared pans. Bake until tester inserted into center comes out clean, about 25 minutes. Cool completely on rack. Cover bread loosely and let stand at room temperature overnight. *(Can be prepared ahead. Store 2 days at room temperature or wrap in plastic and freeze up to 3 weeks.)* Crumble coarsely.

BRAIDED BUTTER BREAD

There's nothing like homemade bread to turn a meal into a celebration. MAKES 2 LOAVES

1 cup milk
½ cup (1 stick) unsalted butter, cut into pieces
½ cup sugar
½ teaspoon salt
1 envelope dry yeast
¼ cup warm water (105°F to 115°F)
1 large egg, beaten to blend, room temperature
4 cups (about) unbleached all purpose flour

1 large egg
2 tablespoons water

Bring milk to simmer in heavy medium saucepan. Add butter, sugar and salt. Let stand until butter melts. Pour mixture into large bowl. Cool to 105°F to 115°F. Sprinkle yeast over ¼ cup warm water in small bowl; stir to dissolve. Let stand 10 minutes.

Add yeast mixture and beaten egg to milk mixture. Stir in enough flour ½ cup at a time to form soft, slightly sticky dough. Lightly butter large bowl. Add dough, turning to coat. Cover with towel and let dough rise in warm draft-free area until doubled, 2 hours.

Butter 2 heavy large baking sheets. Turn dough out onto lightly floured work surface and knead until smooth, 2 minutes. Divide dough in half. Divide each half into 3 pieces. Roll each piece out between hands and floured surface to 18-inch-long rope.

Arrange 3 ropes side by side on 1 prepared sheet. Braid ropes. Pinch ends together and tuck under loaf. Repeat process with remaining 3 ropes on second baking sheet for second loaf. Cover each loaf with towel and let rise until almost doubled, about 1 hour.

Preheat oven to 350°F. Beat egg with 2 tablespoons water for glaze and brush over loaves. Bake until loaves are golden brown and sound hollow when tapped on bottom, about 25 minutes. Transfer to racks and cool. *(Can be prepared 1 week ahead and frozen.)*

WHITE CHOCOLATE MINT TERRINE WITH DARK CHOCOLATE SAUCE

The terrine and sauce can be made a week ahead. Freeze the terrine and chill the sauce. 12 SERVINGS

TERRINE

6 large egg yolks
¼ cup water
¼ cup light corn syrup
8 ounces good-quality white chocolate, chopped
1¼ teaspoons peppermint extract

2 cups chilled whipping cream

SAUCE

½ cup whipping cream
¼ cup dark corn syrup
¼ cup (½ stick) unsalted butter
8 ounces semisweet chocolate, chopped
½ ounce unsweetened chocolate, chopped
3 tablespoons water

FOR TERRINE: Line 9 x 5 x 2½-inch loaf pan with plastic wrap, allowing plastic to overhang edges by 3 inches. Place in freezer. Whisk first 3 ingredients in large metal bowl. Set bowl over saucepan of simmering water (do not allow bottom of bowl to touch water); whisk constantly until candy thermometer registers 160°F, about 4 minutes. Remove bowl from over water. Add white chocolate; whisk until melted and smooth. Mix in extract. Whisk until cool and thick, about 3 minutes.

Using electric mixer, beat cream in another large bowl until stiff peaks form. Fold cream into white chocolate mixture. Spoon into pan; smooth top. Cover; freeze overnight.

FOR SAUCE: Combine first 3 ingredients in heavy medium saucepan. Stir over medium heat until butter melts. Add both chocolates and whisk until smooth. Mix in 3 tablespoons water. Remove from heat; cool slightly.

Turn frozen terrine out onto platter. Peel off plastic. Cut terrine into ¾-inch-thick slices. Place 1 slice on each plate. Drizzle sauce over.

Elegant Shower

menu for twenty

- CRAB-FILLED PEPPER STRIPS

- CHICKEN, GREEN BEAN AND
  GOAT CHEESE SALAD

- HERB-BUTTERED FRENCH BREAD

- WHOLE BAKED SALMON WITH
  MUSTARD-DILL SAUCE

- WHITE WINE SPRITZERS AND ICED TEA

- STRAWBERRIES WITH CASSIS

- GINGER AND CHOCOLATE CHIP
  COOKIE HEARTS

menu options

- CITRUS VODKA PUNCH

- MINIATURE CHIVE MUFFIN AND
  SMOKED HAM SANDWICHES

- COCONUT CAKE WITH CANDIED VIOLETS

- BRANDIED CHOCOLATE TRUFFLES

Shower her with gifts

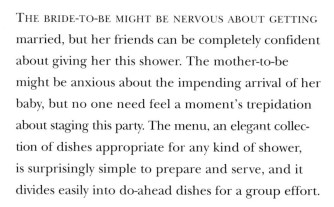

THE BRIDE-TO-BE MIGHT BE NERVOUS ABOUT GETTING married, but her friends can be completely confident about giving her this shower. The mother-to-be might be anxious about the impending arrival of her baby, but no one need feel a moment's trepidation about staging this party. The menu, an elegant collection of dishes appropriate for any kind of shower, is surprisingly simple to prepare and serve, and it divides easily into do-ahead dishes for a group effort.

The appealing recipes here are reminiscent of the kinds of dishes long served at occasions like this, but they've been updated and streamlined for how we eat now. Take the chicken salad: This shower staple takes on a whole new look and taste with the addition of crisp green beans, walnuts and goat cheese, a combination of flavors that will have everyone asking you for the recipe as they leave. Cold poached salmon, another familiar friend, arrives at the buffet

table in a covering of cucumber "scales" for a spectacular presentation, and gets served with a do-ahead mustard-dill sauce.

Dessert at a shower can be either a simple affair, like the heart-shaped chocolate chip cookies and fresh berries marinated in crème de cassis (a luscious berry liqueur), or something more extravagant, such as the coconut cake in the Options section, an ideal ending to a wedding shower. The berries can be any mix of what's in season, and they can be served in goblets, topped with whipped cream. The all-white cake lends itself to decoration with flowers.

The word *shower* comes from the old custom of showering the guest of honor with gifts. You might want to decorate with the present theme in mind: gift boxes to hold small pots of flowers as centerpieces; bows tied around vases; satin ribbons instead of nap-

- Arrange for rentals, if necessary.
- Buy shower favors and/or prizes for party games.

1 WEEK AHEAD:

- Shop for all nonperishables.
- Order fresh salmon.
- Make cookie hearts; freeze.

2 DAYS AHEAD:

- Make herb butter for French bread; chill.

1 DAY AHEAD:

- Prepare crab filling for pepper strips; chill.
- Prepare components for chicken and goat cheese salad; chill.
- Bake salmon and prepare mustard-dill sauce; chill.

MORNING OR DAY OF:

- Set up tables (set aside a gift table or area).
- Fill pepper strips with crab salad (up to 3 hours ahead); chill.
- Make strawberries with cassis (up to 3 hours ahead); chill.

AS GUESTS ARRIVE:

- Bring salad, butter and cookies to room temperature.
- Toast French bread slices.

kin rings, with gift tags attached rather than place cards. The actual gifts will likely be things the honoree needs for her new home or baby, but everyone needs souvenirs of good times. So ask each guest to bring a personal note for the bride or mom, take individual snapshots, and compile both in an album, along with copies of the recipes served, for a keepsake that will long be treasured.

As easy as this big party is, it's even easier when the recipes are halved and the menu is brought out on the occasion of Mother's Day, Easter, or any sunny spring Sunday when brunch or lunch is planned. To serve ten, make the entire crab appetizer, halve the chicken salad and substitute the ham and chive muffin sandwiches in the Options section for the salmon and French bread. The berries are easily halved, too. Go ahead and make all of the cookies, since the leftovers keep well—if there are any.

CRAB-FILLED PEPPER STRIPS

Use bell peppers of different colors for an attractive presentation (below). If you cannot find chervil, use 1½ teaspoons each fresh parsley and tarragon, plus enough extra for a garnish. 20 SERVINGS

8 ounces flaked crabmeat (about 2 cups lightly packed), well drained
⅓ cup mayonnaise
2 green onions, finely chopped
½ plum tomato, seeded, minced
1 tablespoon chopped fresh chervil or ¾ teaspoon dried
2 teaspoons fresh lemon juice
½ teaspoon grated lemon peel
   Generous pinch of cayenne pepper

2 large yellow, red or green bell peppers, cut into 1 x 2-inch strips
   Fresh chervil sprigs (optional)

Place crab in medium bowl. Mix in mayonnaise, green onions, tomato, chopped chervil, lemon juice, lemon peel and cayenne. *(Can be prepared 1 day ahead. Cover crab filling; chill.)*

Spoon 1 or 2 teaspoons of crab filling onto each bell pepper strip. Garnish each with small sprig of chervil, if desired; arrange on platter. *(Can be prepared up to 3 hours ahead. Cover tightly with plastic wrap and refrigerate.)*

CHICKEN, GREEN BEAN AND GOAT CHEESE SALAD

Components of this salad can be prepared one day ahead, then tossed together at the last minute. Offer white wine spritzers and iced tea with the meal. Colorful ornamental kale, used here to line the platter, can be found at some supermarkets and specialty foods stores. 20 SERVINGS

18 large chicken breast halves (about 9 pounds)
6   tablespoons plus 1 cup olive oil
¼   cup plus 2 tablespoons soy sauce

3   pounds green beans, trimmed, halved crosswise

3   tablespoons Dijon mustard
3   tablespoons balsamic vinegar
3   tablespoons minced shallots
2   tablespoons minced fresh thyme

3   cups coarsely chopped walnuts (about 12 ounces)
    Ornamental kale or red leaf lettuce
6   ounces soft fresh goat cheese (such as Montrachet), crumbled
    Additional minced fresh thyme

Preheat oven to 450°F. Arrange chicken breasts on rimmed baking sheets or in baking pans. Brush both sides with 6 tablespoons olive oil and soy sauce. Sprinkle both sides with pepper. Arrange chicken skin side up. Roast until cooked through, 20 minutes. Cool slightly. Skin and bone chicken; reserve drippings in pans. Cut chicken into ½-inch-wide strips. Return to pans and turn to coat with drippings. Cool. Transfer chicken and drippings to large bowl.

Cook beans in large pot of boiling salted water until crisp-tender, about 5 minutes. Drain. Rinse with cold water; drain well.

Combine mustard and vinegar in medium bowl. Gradually whisk in remaining oil. Add shallots and 2 tablespoons thyme. *(Can be made 1 day ahead. Cover chicken and beans separately; chill. Store dressing at room temperature.)*

Add beans, dressing and walnuts to chicken and toss to coat. Season with salt and pepper. Line platter with kale. Top with salad. Sprinkle with cheese and additional thyme.

HERB-BUTTERED FRENCH BREAD

A nice accompaniment to the chicken salad and the baked salmon. 20 SERVINGS

1½   cups fresh basil leaves
¾   cup (1½ sticks) butter, room temperature
2   tablespoons drained capers
¾   teaspoon salt

3   French-bread baguettes, halved lengthwise

Chop basil in processor. Add butter, capers, salt and generous amount of pepper and process until well combined. *(Can be prepared 2 days ahead. Cover and refrigerate. Bring butter mixture to room temperature before using.)*

Preheat oven to 500°F. Arrange bread cut side up on baking sheets. Bake until golden brown, about 5 minutes. Spread cut surfaces with basil butter. Cut crosswise and serve.

WHOLE BAKED SALMON WITH MUSTARD-DILL SAUCE

Here's an easy, do-ahead technique for cooking whole salmon. Bake the fish a day ahead, then garnish with cucumber "scales" just before serving. White wine spritzers and iced tea are the ideal beverages. 20 SERVINGS

1½   cups mayonnaise
1½   cups sour cream
½   cup Dijon mustard
⅔   cup chopped fresh dill

2   4-pound whole salmon, heads and tails removed, scaled
12   green onions, chopped
10   tablespoons fresh lemon juice
¼   cup olive oil
⅔   cup dry white wine
20   whole black peppercorns

Paper-thin cucumber slices
Lemon wedges
Fresh dill sprigs

Whisk first 4 ingredients in medium bowl to blend. Season with salt and pepper. Cover and refrigerate at least 4 hours.

Preheat oven to 325°F. Stack 2 heavy-duty foil sheets on each of 2 large baking sheets. Place 1 fish on each prepared baking sheet. Sprinkle ¼ of green onions and 2½ tablespoons lemon juice inside each fish. Drizzle remaining 5 tablespoons lemon juice over fish. Drizzle oil over. Pour wine over; sprinkle with peppercorns. Sprinkle remaining green onions around fish. Bring up foil around fish, sealing tightly but leaving airspace between fish and foil. Bake fish 1 hour. Remove from oven. Open foil and let fish cool 1 hour. Reseal foil and refrigerate until cold, about 4 hours. *(Sauce and fish can be prepared 1 day ahead. Keep refrigerated.)*

Open foil. Carefully remove skin from fish. Scrape off any grayish flesh. Transfer fish to platters. Garnish top of each fish with cucumber slices. Surround with lemon wedges and dill sprigs. Serve with sauce.

STRAWBERRIES WITH CASSIS

If available, substitute other seasonal berries for some of the strawberries (below). A mix of fresh raspberries, blueberries and strawberries is very pretty. 20 SERVINGS

6 12-ounce baskets strawberries, hulled, halved or quartered (depending on size of berries)
1¼ cups crème de cassis or other berry liqueur
⅓ cup sugar
2 tablespoons fresh lemon juice

3 cups chilled whipping cream
3 tablespoons powdered sugar

Combine first 4 ingredients in large bowl. Let stand at room temperature 1 hour, stirring occasionally. *(Can be made 3 hours ahead. Cover and refrigerate.)*

Whip cream and powdered sugar in large bowl until stiff peaks form. Spoon ⅔ cup fresh berries and some of juices into each of 20 balloon glasses. Top each with spoonful of whipped cream and serve.

GINGER AND CHOCOLATE CHIP COOKIE HEARTS

Easy, do-ahead heart-shaped cookies (below) to go with the strawberries. MAKES ABOUT 4 DOZEN

3 cups all purpose flour
1 cup sugar
7½ tablespoons cornstarch
⅜ teaspoon salt
1½ cups (3 sticks) chilled unsalted butter, cut into ½-inch pieces
2¼ teaspoons vanilla extract
1½ cups pecans (about 6 ounces)
1 cup miniature semisweet chocolate chips
9 tablespoons finely chopped crystallized ginger

Additional sugar

Preheat oven to 350°F. Combine first 4 ingredients in processor and blend. Add butter and vanilla and process until mixture resembles fine meal, using on/off turns. Add pecans and process until finely chopped. Mix in chocolate chips and ginger.

Transfer mixture to bowl and gather together. Divide dough into thirds. Roll 1 piece out between sheets of waxed paper to ¼-inch thickness. Using 3-inch heart-shaped cutter, cut out cookies. Transfer to baking sheets. Gather scraps. Repeat rolling and cutting with remaining dough. Reroll scraps and cut more cookies. Sprinkle cookies with sugar. Bake until just beginning to brown, 20 minutes. Cool on sheets on rack 5 minutes. Transfer cookies to rack and cool. *(Cookies can be prepared ahead. Store in airtight container up to 3 days at room temperature or freeze up to 1 week.)*

Options

These recipes expand or change the menu to suit your individual needs.

CITRUS VODKA PUNCH

If you don't have a punch bowl, combine the ingredients in a large mixing bowl and serve in tall glasses filled with ice. MAKES ABOUT 13 CUPS

7 cups orange juice
3 cups vodka
1½ cups grapefruit juice
¾ cup fresh lime juice
¾ cup fresh lemon juice
⅓ cup sugar
50 ice cubes
1 orange, sliced
1 lemon, sliced
2 6-ounce baskets strawberries
Additional ice cubes

Combine first 6 ingredients in punch bowl. Stir until sugar dissolves. Add 50 ice cubes, orange slices, lemon slices and berries and stir gently to combine. Fill glasses with additional ice. Ladle punch into glasses and serve.

MINIATURE CHIVE MUFFIN AND SMOKED HAM SANDWICHES

These sandwiches, which would work in place of either the chicken salad or the salmon, look nice arranged in a shallow basket. Make the muffins three weeks ahead and freeze them. MAKES 36

CHIVE MUFFINS

2 cups all purpose flour
1 tablespoon baking powder
1 tablespoon sugar
1 tablespoon golden brown sugar
¾ teaspoon salt
1 cup milk (do not use low-fat or nonfat)
¼ cup (½ stick) butter, melted
1 large egg
½ cup chopped fresh chives

SANDWICHES

6 tablespoons (¾ stick) unsalted butter, room temperature
½ pound smoked ham, sliced ⅛ inch thick
Coarsely ground pepper
Fresh chives, cut into 2-inch pieces

FOR MUFFINS: Preheat oven to 400°F. Lightly butter 36 miniature muffin cups. Sift first 5 ingredients into medium bowl. Whisk milk, butter and egg in small bowl; stir in chives. Make well in center of flour mixture. Slowly add milk mixture; stir until just blended.

Spoon batter into prepared muffin cups, filling each ¾ full. Bake until light brown on top, about 18 minutes. Remove muffins from cups and cool on rack. *(Can be made ahead. Seal in plastic bags; chill 2 days or freeze up to 3 weeks. Bring to room temperature before continuing.)*

FOR SANDWICHES: Slice muffins in half crosswise. Spread with butter. Place 2 to 3 small pieces ham on bottom half of each muffin, draping excess ham over sides. Grind pepper over ham. Place 1 or 2 chive pieces on each. Replace muffin tops. Arrange sandwiches on platter. *(Can be prepared 3 hours ahead. Cover tightly with plastic wrap. Refrigerate.)* Serve sandwiches at room temperature.

COCONUT CAKE
WITH CANDIED VIOLETS

If it's a bridal shower, this cake would be an ideal dessert. (You'll need to make two, most likely.) Candied violets from a specialty foods store are a lovely garnish; fresh pansies or violets would be nice, too. 12 SERVINGS

CAKE

3	cups cake flour
1	tablespoon baking powder
¾	teaspoon salt
¾	cup (1½ sticks) unsalted butter, room temperature
1¾	cups sugar
4	large eggs, separated
1	teaspoon vanilla extract
1	teaspoon coconut extract
1	14-ounce can unsweetened coconut milk*
¼	teaspoon cream of tartar

FROSTING

6	ounces cream cheese, room temperature
¼	cup (½ stick) unsalted butter, room temperature
1	16-ounce box powdered sugar, sifted
¼	cup (about) unsweetened coconut milk (reserved from cake)
1	7-ounce package sweetened shredded coconut Candied violets

FOR CAKE: Preheat oven to 350°F. Line bottoms of two 9-inch-diameter cake pans with 2-inch-high sides with waxed paper. Sift flour, baking powder and salt into large bowl. Using electric mixer, beat butter in large bowl until smooth. Gradually add sugar and beat until light and fluffy. Add yolks 1 at a time, beating well after each addition. Mix in vanilla and coconut extracts. Reserve ¼ cup coconut milk for frosting. Add dry ingredients to butter mixture alternately with remaining coconut milk, beginning and ending with dry ingredients and beating just until combined. Using clean beaters, beat egg whites and cream of tartar in another large bowl until medium-firm peaks form. Fold ⅓ of egg whites into cake batter to lighten, then fold in remaining egg whites.

Divide batter evenly between prepared pans; smooth tops. Bake until tester inserted into center comes out clean, about 30 minutes. Transfer cakes to racks. Cool in pans 15 minutes. Run small sharp knife around pan sides to loosen cakes. Turn out cakes onto racks; peel off waxed paper. Cool completely. (*Can be made 1 day ahead. Wrap tightly in plastic and store at room temperature.*)

FOR FROSTING: Using electric mixer, beat cream cheese and butter in large bowl until smooth. Gradually sift powdered sugar over, mixing until well combined. Gradually add enough of reserved ¼ cup coconut milk by tablespoons to make frosting spreadable.

Place 1 cake layer on platter. Tuck waxed paper strips under cake to protect platter. Spread ¾ cup frosting over top. Sprinkle ½ cup coconut over. Top with second cake layer. Spread remaining frosting over top and sides of cake. Lightly press remaining coconut over top and sides of cake, covering completely. Remove waxed paper. (*Can be made 1 day ahead. Cover with cake dome and chill. Let stand at room temperature 2 hours before continuing.*) Decorate cake with candied violets.

*Available at Indian, Southeast Asian or Latin American markets and many supermarkets.

BRANDIED CHOCOLATE TRUFFLES

A little something chocolate to have with coffee after the presents have been opened. MAKES ABOUT 26

¾ cup whipping cream
3   tablespoons unsalted butter
½   pound plus ¾ pound bittersweet
    (not unsweetened) or semisweet
    chocolate, chopped
2   tablespoons Cognac or other brandy

Bring whipping cream and unsalted butter to simmer in heavy medium saucepan. Reduce heat to low. Add ½ pound bittersweet chocolate and stir until melted. Mix in 2 tablespoons Cognac. Let truffle mixture stand at room temperature until firm enough to mound on spoon, about 3½ hours.

Line baking sheet with foil. Spoon truffle mixture by rounded tablespoonfuls onto prepared baking sheet, spacing apart. Refrigerate until firm, about 1 hour.

Roll 1 truffle between palms of hands into ball. Place on same sheet. Repeat with remaining truffles; refrigerate. Melt remaining ¾ pound chocolate in top of double boiler over simmering water, stirring frequently until smooth. Remove from over water. Grasp 1 truffle between thumb and index finger. Dip into chocolate, coating completely. Shake gently to remove excess chocolate. Place on same sheet. Repeat dipping with remaining truffles. Refrigerate until firm, about 30 minutes. Remove truffles from foil. *(Can be prepared 1 week ahead. Refrigerate in airtight container.)* Serve truffles cold.

The Buffet Table

Set an elegant buffet table like a stage, taking these different design elements into consideration.

To create different levels, use pedestals, tiered platters and cake stands. For added visual interest, cover a box with a beautiful cloth or scarf and place a bowl of flowers or fruit on top, with ivy and ribbons trailing down the sides. Candles of different heights and shapes will also add to the effect.

For a mix of textures, experiment with different fabrics depending on the season. In summer, combine delicate sheers and voiles with crisp linen, or mix heirloom lace and cotton piqué. Velvet looks lavish in winter, especially in colors like aubergine and moss green. Top it with a tapestry or damask runner; tie napkins with velvet ribbons of contrasting color.

For a centerpiece with impact (since you're not limited to something your guests can "see" over), fill a larger-than-usual container, such as a garden urn, an antique pitcher or a galvanized flower pail with everything from wild grasses and garden flowers to exotic fruits and colorful vegetables.

Bring a spark of creativity to the table with improvised "holders" for the flatware and napkins. Keep the cutlery in an old wooden tool box; pile napkins, pulled through unique napkin rings, in a flat wicker basket; use three tall sturdy glasses for forks, spoons and knives; stand rolled napkins in terra-cotta pots.

Romantic Dinner

menu for two

- Black and Gold Caviar Pizzas

- Champagne

- Grilled Lemon-Tarragon Lobster

- Tomato and Green-Onion Rice

- Fennel-Radicchio Salad

- Sauvignon Blanc

- Dark Chocolate-Orange Soufflé with White Chocolate Chunk Whipped Cream

menu options

- Oysters on the Half Shell with Oriental Mignonette

- Fettuccine with Shiitake Mushroom Sauce

- Strawberry-Lemon Cream Tart

Just the two of you

IF YOUR IDEA OF A ROMANTIC EVENING INCLUDES staying at home, lighting a fire, opening a nice bottle of wine and cooking up something wonderfully decadent—together—then this menu will appeal to both of you. And while you don't really need an excuse to indulge in a meal like this, consider any of the following reasons and occasions to celebrate: the anniversary of your first dinner date; the night *all* the children are away on sleepovers; the purchase of new china, even a new stockpot; because you can't remember the last time.

When it's just the two of you, caviar and lobster—the stars of this uptown show—are affordable and doable. The Black and Gold Caviar Pizzas here are actually toasted baguette slices spread with crème fraîche and topped with two types of caviar: The

"gold" is luxe but not pricey whitefish caviar, and the "black" can be anything from imported sturgeon caviar to a variety made from other fish. Pressed caviar is a good compromise; it has the flavor but not the contours of the sturgeon roe from which it's made. Another choice is red salmon caviar, a bright accent that's especially nice when you want to multiply this recipe for a bigger group.

Lobster, too, is easy when it's just the two of you, and almost affordable. Head out on Saturday afternoon to do the shopping together, if you can. At the fishmonger's (if there is still such a thing in your neighborhood; Asian markets are another good source for live seafood), look for lobsters that are lively, and select females if you like the delicate roe. If you're not one for knowing your food

UP TO 1 WEEK AHEAD:

- Buy nonperishables.

2 DAYS AHEAD:

- Buy all perishables (except lobsters).

1 DAY AHEAD:

- Chill Champagne and wine.

DAY OF:

- Buy lobsters and prepare to point of grilling (up to 8 hours ahead); chill.
- Make sauce for lobsters (up to 8 hours ahead); store at room temperature.
- Make dressing and prep vegetables for salad (up to 4 hours ahead); chill.
- Prepare chocolate chunk whipped cream (up to 4 hours ahead); chill.
- Make soufflé mixture (up to 2 hours ahead); let stand at room temperature.
- Set up coffeemaker.

THAT EVENING:

- Prepare soufflé 1 hour before baking.
- Prepare barbecue; cook lobsters.
- Broil bread for caviar pizzas.
- Start rice.

personally before eating it, choose swordfish steaks or sea scallops, and baste and serve them with the same lemony butter sauce.

If events collide, as they will, and the evening you've planned together is looking less and less possible, there are alternatives and solutions here. You can't get out to buy the lobster, or it's pouring/snowing/ blowing and outdoor barbecuing is not in the cards: Try the opulent pasta with shiitake mushroom sauce in the Options section. Your soul mate gets stuck with a last-minute business trip, and won't be back until after 9:00 P.M.: Never mind the main course, go straight to dessert, popping the soufflés into the oven as he or she walks in the door. Or, opt for the oysters here and a bottle of Champagne, a homecoming if ever there was one.

BLACK AND GOLD CAVIAR PIZZAS

Well, not really pizzas, but toasted French bread crowned with golden and black caviar. Let your budget determine what type of black caviar you choose—and what kind of Champagne you pour with this appetizer. 2 SERVINGS

8   ⅓-inch-thick slices French-bread baguette
    Butter, room temperature

½   cup crème fraîche or sour cream
1   bunch fresh chives, minced
2   ounces golden caviar
2   ounces black caviar

Preheat broiler. Broil bread until toasted, about 1 minute. Spread second side with butter; sprinkle with freshly ground pepper. Broil bread until golden brown, about 2 minutes.

Spread crème fraîche over bread slices. Sprinkle chives in diagonal line across center of each. Spoon golden caviar on one side of chives, black on other side, and serve.

GRILLED LEMON-TARRAGON LOBSTER

Cooking live lobster together (and cornering the loose ones) has been romantic since Annie Hall. *But if it's more convenient, thaw two frozen uncooked lobster tails (skip the parboiling). A Sauvignon Blanc would go well.* 2 SERVINGS

¼   cup (½ stick) butter
2   tablespoons fresh lemon juice
1½   teaspoons grated lemon peel
2   tablespoons chopped chives
1   tablespoon chopped fresh tarragon or
     1 teaspoon dried

2   live lobsters, each about 1½ pounds

Prepare barbecue (medium-high heat). Stir butter, lemon juice and lemon peel in heavy small saucepan over low heat until butter melts. Mix in chives and tarragon; season

with salt and pepper. Keep sauce warm. *(Can be prepared 8 hours ahead. Cover and keep at room temperature. Remelt butter sauce before using.)*

Meanwhile, bring large pot of water to boil. Drop lobsters headfirst into water. Cover pot; boil lobsters 2 minutes. Transfer lobsters to work surface. Using heavy large knife or cleaver, split lobsters in half lengthwise. Scoop out and discard gray intestinal tract, gills and sand sac from head. Leave any red roe or green tomalley intact, if desired. Crack claws. *(Can be prepared 8 hours ahead. Wrap lobsters in foil and refrigerate.)* Brush cut side of lobsters with 1 tablespoon butter sauce.

Grill lobsters, cut side down, 4 minutes. Turn and grill 4 minutes. Turn again so that cut side is down and grill until lobster meat is just opaque but still juicy, about 2 minutes. Transfer to plates. Brush lightly with sauce. Serve, passing remaining sauce separately.

TOMATO AND GREEN-ONION RICE

Chopped tomato and green onions lend freshness and color to this simple dish. 2 SERVINGS

2   teaspoons olive oil
½   cup long-grain rice
1   cup canned low-salt chicken broth
1   large plum tomato, seeded, chopped
    (about ½ cup)
2   green onions, chopped

Heat olive oil in heavy small saucepan over medium-high heat. Add rice and stir until rice is coated with oil and slightly translucent, about 2 minutes. Add chicken broth and bring to simmer. Reduce heat to low; cover saucepan and cook until broth is absorbed and rice is tender, about 20 minutes. Stir in tomato and green onions. Season with salt and pepper and serve.

FENNEL-RADICCHIO SALAD

Sliced fennel, olives and radicchio make an attractive, interesting salad. 2 SERVINGS

3 tablespoons olive oil
1 tablespoon fresh lemon juice
1 shallot, minced

1 small fresh fennel bulb, trimmed,
  cut vertically into thin slices
1½ cups bite-size pieces radicchio
3 tablespoons sliced pitted black olives

Whisk olive oil, lemon juice and minced shallot to blend in small bowl. Season dressing to taste with salt and pepper. *(Can be prepared up to 4 hours ahead. Cover and refrigerate. Bring to room temperature before using.)*

Toss fennel and radicchio with dressing in medium bowl. Divide salad between 2 plates. Garnish with sliced olives and serve.

DARK CHOCOLATE-ORANGE SOUFFLÉ WITH WHITE CHOCOLATE CHUNK WHIPPED CREAM

Make this soufflé an hour before dinner, then slip into the kitchen after you've finished the lobster and pop it into the oven. In just 20 to 30 minutes, it's ready to eat. 2 SERVINGS

¼ cup whipping cream
4 ounces bittersweet (not unsweetened) or
  semisweet chocolate, coarsely chopped
2 large egg yolks
1 tablespoon Cointreau or other
  orange liqueur
1 teaspoon grated orange peel

  Sugar
3 large egg whites, room temperature
  Pinch of cream of tartar
2 tablespoons sugar
  Powdered sugar
  White Chocolate Chunk Whipped Cream
  (see recipe at right)

Cook cream and chocolate in heavy small saucepan over low heat, stirring until chocolate melts and mixture is smooth. Remove from heat and beat in yolks 1 at a time. Mix in Cointreau and orange peel. Cool to lukewarm. *(Can be made 2 hours ahead. Cover and let stand at room temperature. Stir over low heat until lukewarm before continuing.)*

Preheat oven to 375°F. Butter one 4-cup or two 1¾-cup soufflé dishes; dust with sugar. Beat whites and cream of tartar in medium bowl until soft peaks form. Beat in 2 tablespoons sugar. Fold ¼ of whites into chocolate. Gently fold in remaining whites. Spoon into prepared dishes. *(Can be prepared 1 hour ahead. Cover; let stand in draft-free area at room temperature.)* Bake until soufflé rises but still moves in center when touched, about 20 minutes for individuals and 30 minutes for one large. Dust tops with powdered sugar. Serve immediately, passing whipped cream separately.

WHITE CHOCOLATE CHUNK WHIPPED CREAM

Perfect with the chocolate-orange soufflé, this is also delicious over berries. MAKES 1¼ CUPS

1 ounce good-quality white chocolate
  (such as Lindt or Baker's)
½ cup chilled whipping cream
1 tablespoon sugar
½ teaspoon grated orange peel
1 tablespoon Cointreau or other
  orange liqueur

Cut chocolate into ¼-inch pieces. Combine cream, sugar and orange peel in medium bowl and beat until stiff peaks form. Mix in Cointreau. Fold in chocolate. *(Can be prepared 4 hours ahead. Cover and refrigerate.)*

Options

OYSTERS ON THE HALF SHELL WITH ORIENTAL MIGNONETTE

Though definitely romantic, oysters aren't for everyone. But if you and yours do like them, here's a great substitute for the pizzas. (The sauce would also work well with steamed clams.) 2 SERVINGS

¼ cup rice vinegar
1½ teaspoons minced peeled fresh ginger
1 green onion (green part only), thinly sliced
½ teaspoon grated lemon peel

12 fresh oysters

Combine first 4 ingredients in small bowl. Let sauce stand for 15 minutes.

To open oysters: Using towel, hold oyster flat on work surface, flat shell up. Insert tip of oyster knife into hinge and twist to open shell. Slide knife along inside of upper shell to free oyster from shell; discard upper shell. Slide knife under oyster to free from lower shell; leave in shell. Repeat with remaining oysters. Arrange oysters on edge of 2 plates. Divide sauce between 2 small bowls. Place 1 bowl in the center of each plate and serve.

FETTUCCINE WITH SHIITAKE MUSHROOM SAUCE

This pasta works with either appetizer, the salad and either dessert. Pour a Merlot. 2 SERVINGS

1 1-ounce package dried shiitake mushrooms
1½ cups hot water

1 tablespoon olive oil
6 bacon slices, minced
3 shallots, minced
4 ounces fresh shiitake mushrooms or button mushrooms, sliced
½ teaspoon dried rosemary
1 cup canned beef broth
1¼ cups half and half

8 ounces fettuccine

⅔ cup freshly grated Parmesan cheese
    Minced fresh Italian parsley
    Additional freshly grated Parmesan cheese

Place dried mushrooms in bowl. Add 1½ cups hot water; soak until softened, 30 minutes. Remove from water, squeezing excess water back into bowl. Strain and reserve soaking liquid. Slice mushrooms, discarding stems.

Heat oil in heavy large skillet over medium heat. Add bacon and cook 3 minutes. Pour off half of fat. Add shallots to bacon in skillet and sauté 1 minute. Add dried and fresh mushrooms and rosemary and sauté 3 minutes. Add broth and reserved soaking liquid. Boil until reduced to glaze, 10 minutes. Add half and half and simmer until beginning to thicken, 5 minutes. Remove from heat. *(Can be prepared 3 days ahead. Cover and chill.)*

Cook pasta in large pot of boiling salted water until just tender but still firm to bite.

Meanwhile, rewarm mushroom sauce.

Drain pasta. Add to sauce and stir until coated. Mix in ⅔ cup Parmesan. Season with salt and pepper. Transfer to plates. Sprinkle with parsley. Pass Parmesan separately.

STRAWBERRY-LEMON CREAM TART

If the object of your desire doesn't like chocolate, here's a pretty alternative. And prepared puff pastry makes it easy. 2 TO 4 SERVINGS

½ cup chilled whipping cream
⅓ cup purchased lemon curd

1 frozen puff pastry sheet (half of 17¼-ounce package), thawed
1 large egg
1 tablespoon water
   Sugar

1 12- ounce basket strawberries, hulled, halved lengthwise

Whip cream to stiff peaks. Place lemon curd in medium bowl. Stir in half of whipped cream. Fold in remaining cream. *(Can be prepared 1 day ahead. Cover and refrigerate.)*

Preheat oven to 350°F. Roll pastry out on lightly floured surface to 14 x 11-inch rectangle. Cut four 1-inch-wide strips off short side and four 1-inch strips off long side. Transfer pastry rectangle to baking sheet. Pierce with fork. Beat egg and 1 tablespoon water in small bowl. Brush pastry with some of egg glaze. Arrange 1 pastry strip on each edge of rectangle so outside edges meet, trimming as neccesary, to form tart edges. Brush top of strips with glaze. Repeat with remaining pastry strips. Brush top of strips with glaze; sprinkle with sugar. Bake tart 5 minutes. Pierce with fork if puffed. Continue baking until golden brown, about 20 minutes. Cool.

Spread cream mixture in tart. Arrange strawberries atop lemon cream in rows, cut side down. *(Can be prepared 2 hours ahead. Cover loosely and keep at cool room temperature.)*

A Movable Feast

A romantic getaway, without leaving home, can be as simple as a change of setting. Stage your dinner à deux somewhere completely different, such as:

BY THE FIRE. Spread a blanket in front of the hearth and add lots of cushions. Set the coffee table for dinner, dim the lights and keep the music low.

UNDER THE STARS. On a beautiful evening, carry everything out on the lawn. Bring blankets, pillows and candles (the insect-repellent kind would be a wise choice), and dinner on trays or in a wide basket.

ON THE ROOF. Dine elegantly outdoors, at a small table (a folding card table would work well) beautifully set. Add lighting in the form of votive candles and torches.

IN THE BEDROOM. Pile pillows on the bed, light candles, turn on some music and cozy up to dinner served from trays lined with place mats and set with your best china and crystal. Treat yourselves like company.

AT AN UNEXPECTED TIME. Break with routine and dine in the late afternoon. Even if it's your everyday dining room or patio, it will look different in the light of an unaccustomed mealtime. And for busy people, the hours stolen in the daytime can be the most romantic of all.

Kid's Birthday Party

menu for ten

- Super Nachos

- Basil-Buttermilk Fried Chicken

- Apple and Raisin Slaw

- Orzo Salad with Fresh Vegetables

- Lemonade, Sodas and Milk

- Old-fashioned Sour Cream
  Fudge Birthday Cake

menu options

- Turkey Cheeseburgers

- Frozen Strawberry-Banana Cake
  with Strawberry Sauce

It comes just once a year

NO COMPLIMENT REACHES DEEPER THAN A CHILD'S birthday request for "the same thing we had last year." It's what gets you pulling out the cake pans even if you rarely bake, and flipping through recipe clippings late into the night for those treasured dishes of memory.

This menu anticipates a "same thing" tradition (and its inclusion in these pages will make the dishes much easier to find year after year). You can serve it to toddlers and their mothers, and then, before you know it, to teens and their steady "others." Its irresistible highlights are crispy fried chicken, made juicy and tender with buttermilk, and an old-fashioned chocolate birthday cake, complete with fudge icing. To take the edge off appetites, there are nachos, a favorite across all ages, and to go with the chicken, there are a couple

of kid-friendly salads, one made with the rice-shaped pasta called orzo (available at supermarkets everywhere), the other, a slightly sweet cabbage, apple, carrot and raisin slaw.

A homemade birthday cake is a labor of love, though the three-layered beauty here is actually quite simple to make. Prepare it the day before if you like, leaving plenty of time the morning of the party to decorate it (a project the birthday boy or girl may want to direct). Hobby and fabric shops, along with party and candy stores, have all kinds of things you can use, from little plastic characters to silk flowers, ribbons to gumdrops and jelly rings. For those whose favorite flavor *isn't* chocolate, the no-bake frozen strawberry-banana cake in the Options section is a delicious alternative (and great for a mid-summer birthday).

UP TO 3 WEEKS AHEAD:

- Send out invitations.
- Shop for nonperishable food items and paper goods (including paper plates, napkins, plastic forks, knives and spoons), decorations and candles.
- Plan party games and favors; shop accordingly.

2 WEEKS AHEAD:

- Bake and freeze cake layers for fudge birthday cake.

2 DAYS AHEAD:

- Prepare bean and tomato mixtures for nachos; chill.
- Make dressing for coleslaw; chill.

1 DAY AHEAD:

- Thaw and frost birthday cake; store at room temperature.
- Marinate chicken in buttermilk mixture; chill.
- Shred cabbage and grate carrots for coleslaw; chill.
- Make orzo salad.

DAY OF:

- Make apple and raisin slaw (up to 3 hours ahead); chill.
- Fry chicken (up to 2 hours ahead); serve at room temperature.
- Pick up balloons and decorate party room or back yard.

Nothing in this menu needs to be rushed to the table; it can all spend a little time on the buffet while everyone has a turn at the piñata or a last chance at pin the tail on the donkey. And everything can be made ahead, leaving you free to control the chaos, even chat with other parents. This menu also packs up easily, which means you can take your party to the park if more room is required, or even inside and onto the family room floor if it turns out to be a rainy day.

In fact, you may find yourself returning to this menu for its picnic potential, making a batch of fried chicken for that Saturday hike in the hills or Sunday day at the beach. Then again, it may be that this birthday meal stays just that—a special feast reserved for the special day that comes just once a year.

SUPER NACHOS

What child doesn't like nachos (or what parent, for that matter)? Adjust the spiciness of this recipe with the jalapeños. MAKES 36

1 tablespoon vegetable oil
½ onion, chopped
1 teaspoon minced garlic
1 cup canned black beans, rinsed, drained
2 teaspoons chili powder

4 plum tomatoes, seeded, diced (about 1 cup)
1 to 3 jalapeño chilies, seeded, minced
2 green onions, chopped
36 tortilla chips
1 cup (packed) grated sharp cheddar cheese (about 4 ounces)
1 cup (packed) grated Monterey Jack cheese (about 4 ounces)

1 small avocado, peeled, pitted, chopped
¼ cup minced fresh cilantro

Preheat oven to 475°F. Heat oil in heavy medium skillet over medium heat. Add onion and garlic and sauté until onion is translucent, about 4 minutes. Reduce heat to low. Add beans and chili powder and sauté until flavors are combined, about 5 minutes. Season to taste with salt and pepper.

Mix tomatoes, jalapeños and green onions in small bowl. *(Bean mixture and tomato mixture can be prepared 2 days ahead. Cover separately and refrigerate.)* Arrange tortilla chips on 2 large baking sheets. Top each chip with generous teaspoon of bean mixture and scant teaspoon of tomato mixture. Combine cheddar and Monterey Jack cheeses in medium bowl. Sprinkle evenly over chips.

Bake nachos until cheese melts, about 5 minutes. Using spatula, transfer nachos to platter. Garnish with chopped avocado and cilantro.

BASIL-BUTTERMILK FRIED CHICKEN

Dried basil infuses the chicken (opposite) with its subtle flavor; garnish the platter with small sprigs of fresh basil. Serve ice-cold lemonade and a variety of sodas to drink. 10 SERVINGS

2 cups buttermilk
5 tablespoons dried basil
2 teaspoons hot pepper sauce
2 3- to 3½-pound chickens, each cut into 8 pieces

2 cups all purpose flour
2 teaspoons salt
2 teaspoons pepper

Vegetable oil (for deep frying)
Fresh basil

Combine buttermilk, 2 tablespoons dried basil and hot pepper sauce in large bowl. Add chicken; turn to coat with buttermilk mixture. Let stand at room temperature 2 hours, turning occasionally. *(Can be prepared 1 day ahead. Cover and refrigerate.)*

Place rack atop large baking sheet. Combine flour, salt, pepper and remaining 3 tablespoons dried basil in large shallow dish. Drain chicken. Working in batches, toss chicken pieces in flour mixture turning to coat; shake off excess. Transfer chicken to prepared rack. Refrigerate 30 minutes.

Pour oil into heavy large pot to depth of ¾ inch. Heat oil over medium-high heat to 375°F. Working in batches, fry chicken thighs and drumsticks in hot oil until golden and cooked through, about 10 minutes per side. Using tongs, transfer chicken to paper towels; drain. Fry chicken breasts and wings until golden and cooked through, about 6 minutes per side. Transfer to paper towels. Place on platter and garnish with basil. Serve warm or let stand up to 2 hours at room temperature.

APPLE AND RAISIN SLAW

An interesting and slightly sweet salad (below) that's great with the fried chicken. (Its kid-friendly ingredients include apples, raisins, carrots and sunflower seeds.) 10 SERVINGS

1½ cups plain nonfat yogurt
½ cup chopped fresh dill or 3 tablespoons dried dillweed
2 tablespoons vegetable oil
2 tablespoons apple cider vinegar

5 cups coarsely chopped red cabbage (about ½ medium head)
5 cups coarsely chopped green cabbage (about ½ medium head)
1 cup coarsely grated carrots (about 2 medium)
1 large tart green apple (such as Granny Smith), cored, coarsely chopped
½ cup raisins
½ cup raw unsalted sunflower seeds, toasted

Whisk yogurt, dill, vegetable oil and vinegar in medium bowl to blend. *(Can be prepared 2 days ahead. Cover and refrigerate.)*

Combine cabbages, carrots, apple, raisins and sunflower seeds in very large bowl.

Add dressing to cabbage mixture and toss to coat. Season to taste with salt and pepper. *(Can be prepared 3 hours ahead. Cover and refrigerate.)*

ORZO SALAD WITH FRESH VEGETABLES

Sugar snap peas, cucumber, tomatoes, green onions, parsley and mint combine with orzo in this make-ahead salad (below). 10 SERVINGS

SALAD

6 ounces sugar snap peas, trimmed, cut into ¾-inch pieces
2⅔ cups orzo (rice-shaped pasta)

1¼ cups chopped seeded tomatoes
¾ cup chopped seeded peeled cucumber
½ cup chopped green onions
¼ cup chopped fresh parsley
¼ cup chopped fresh mint
2 teaspoons finely chopped lemon peel

DRESSING

¼ cup fresh lemon juice
2 teaspoons finely chopped lemon peel
1 teaspoon minced garlic
¾ cup olive oil

1 head Boston lettuce

FOR SALAD: Bring large pot of salted water to boil. Add sugar snap peas; cook 1 minute. Using slotted spoon, transfer peas to strainer. Rinse with cold water and drain. Add orzo to same pot. Boil until tender but still firm to bite, about 8 minutes. Drain and cool.

Place orzo in large bowl. Mix in sugar snap peas, tomatoes, cucumber, onions, parsley, mint and peel. Season with salt and pepper.

FOR DRESSING: Combine lemon juice, lemon peel and garlic in medium bowl. Gradually whisk in oil. Season with salt and pepper.

Pour half of dressing over salad; toss to coat. *(Can be made 1 day ahead. Cover salad and remaining dressing separately and chill. Bring to room temperature before continuing.)* Toss salad with enough remaining dressing to coat generously. Season with salt and pepper. Line shallow serving bowl with lettuce. Mound salad in bowl and serve.

OLD-FASHIONED SOUR CREAM FUDGE BIRTHDAY CAKE

Small kids and teenagers (and more than a few adults) will be thrilled with this all-American chocolate cake (below). Decorate the cake with candles, of course, and surround with ribbons, streamers or confetti for more fun. 10 SERVINGS

CAKE

2   cups cake flour
2   teaspoons baking powder
1   teaspoon baking soda
¼   teaspoon salt
3   ounces unsweetened chocolate, chopped
½   cup warm water
¾   cup (1½ sticks) unsalted butter, room temperature
1¾ cups sugar
3   large eggs
1   cup sour cream

FROSTING

¾   cup (1½ sticks) unsalted butter
4½ ounces unsweetened chocolate, chopped
3   cups powdered sugar
3   tablespoons unsweetened cocoa powder
¾   cup (about) sour cream

FOR CAKE: Preheat oven to 350°F. Butter and flour three 8-inch-diameter cake pans with 1½-inch-high sides. Combine first 4 ingredients in medium bowl. Combine chocolate and ½ cup warm water in heavy small saucepan. Bring to boil, stirring constantly until melted. Cool to lukewarm. Using electric mixer, beat butter and sugar in large bowl until fluffy. Add eggs 1 at a time, beating well after each addition. Mix in sour cream, then melted chocolate, beating just until smooth. Add dry ingredients and mix just until blended.

Divide batter among prepared pans; smooth tops. Bake until cakes shrink away from sides of pans and tester inserted into center comes out clean, about 35 minutes. Transfer to racks and cool in pans 15 minutes. Turn out cakes onto racks and cool completely. *(Cakes can be prepared up to 2 weeks ahead. Wrap tightly in plastic and freeze. Thaw cakes before continuing.)*

FOR FROSTING: Melt butter and chocolate in heavy small saucepan over low heat, stirring until smooth. Transfer to large bowl. Whisk in 1 cup powdered sugar, cocoa powder and half of sour cream. Whisk in remaining 2 cups powdered sugar. Gradually whisk in enough of remaining sour cream to form spreadable frosting.

Place 1 cake layer on platter. Tuck waxed paper strips under cake to protect platter. Spread ½ cup frosting evenly over cake. Top with second cake layer. Spread ½ cup frosting over. Top with remaining cake layer. Spread remaining frosting over sides and top of cake, swirling frosting decoratively. Remove waxed paper strips. *(Can be prepared 1 day ahead. Cover with cake dome and let stand at room temperature.)*

Options

TURKEY CHEESEBURGERS

That all-time kid favorite—cheeseburgers—updated with ground turkey. Have these in place of the chicken, if you like. 10 SERVINGS

3⅓ cups fresh sourdough breadcrumbs
    (from about 5 large slices)
 10 tablespoons minced shallots
6½ tablespoons olive oil
  3 tablespoons minced fresh tarragon or
    3 teaspoons dried
  1 teaspoon (generous) salt
3⅓ pounds ground turkey

    Nonstick vegetable oil spray
    Swiss or Monterey Jack cheese slices
    Hamburger buns, toasted
    Red onion slices (optional)

Mix first 5 ingredients in medium bowl. Add ground turkey and generous amount of pepper. Form mixture into ten ½-inch-thick patties. *(Can be prepared 1 day ahead. Wrap tightly in plastic and refrigerate.)*

Prepare barbecue (medium heat). Spray burgers with nonstick spray. Grill until cooked through, about 5 minutes per side. Top each patty with cheese. Cover and cook until just melted. Transfer to buns. Top with onion slices, if desired, and serve.

FROZEN STRAWBERRY-BANANA CAKE WITH STRAWBERRY SAUCE

Purchased sorbet, frozen yogurt and pound cake make this a surprisingly easy birthday cake. Prepare it a week before the party to really get a jump on things. 10 SERVINGS

  1 12-ounce purchased pound cake
  1 cup strawberry preserves
  ¼ cup orange juice
  2 pints strawberry sorbet, softened

  2 pints banana-strawberry
    frozen yogurt, softened

  1 10-ounce package frozen sliced strawberries
    in syrup, thawed

  3 large ripe bananas, peeled, cut diagonally
    into ¼-inch-thick slices
    Sliced fresh strawberries

Cut cake into ¼-inch-thick slices. Arrange enough slices in bottom of 9-inch-diameter springform pan with 2¾-inch-high sides to just cover bottom, fitting tightly. Cook preserves and juice in heavy small saucepan over medium heat until reduced to ⅔ cup, stirring frequently, about 14 minutes. Spread half of preserves mixture over cake in pan. Freeze 10 minutes. Spoon sorbet over cake in pan; smooth top. Arrange more cake slices over to just cover sorbet. Spread remaining preserves over cake. Freeze 10 minutes.

Spoon frozen yogurt over cake; smooth top. Cover and freeze overnight. *(Can be prepared up to 1 week ahead.)*

Puree thawed berries in processor. Cover; chill until cold. *(Can be made 2 days ahead.)*

Release pan sides from cake. Place banana slices around cake edge. Mound berries in center. Serve cake with sauce.

Afternoon Tea

menu for eight

- SMOKED TURKEY FINGER SANDWICHES ON ORANGE DATE BREAD

- CRANBERRY-BUTTERMILK SCONES

- LEMON CURD

- CLOTTED CREAM

- HONEY-SPICE LOAF CAKE

- NUT AND RAISIN CARAMEL TARTLETS

- HOT TEA AND SHERRY

menu options

- OLD-FASHIONED STRAWBERRY PRESERVES

- GINGER BEARS

- TEA PUNCH

A civilized interlude

IT'S AN IRRESISTIBLE INVITATION: A COUPLE OF HOURS of calm in the middle of an active weekend; some civilized gossip among friends; an excuse to wear a dress; dainty sandwiches, decadent scones, tarts and cakes and a cup of tea. It is, of course, afternoon tea, an easy, carefree and versatile interlude, as right for a baby shower as it would be for a young girl's dream of a birthday party.

The appeal of afternoon tea, like a good movie or riveting theater, is in how it can transport you, from a weekend filled with errands and obligations to a place in time when hats were entirely appropriate and conversation was considered entertainment. Keep this in mind when planning a tea, giving in to the urge to decorate with antique linens, flowery china, weighty silver and an abundance of flowers. Think old lace, tulle, yards of ribbon and lengths of ivy and you're on your way to a stage set for tea.

The menu for afternoon tea is a familiar one—sandwiches, scones and sweets—but there is room for improvisation within the expected fare. Take those sandwiches: Here, they're made with a delicious home-baked orange-flavored bread studded with chopped dates. Add slices of gingerbread-like spice cake to the selection, plus scones, clotted cream and lemon curd, and tea becomes a real treat. For a sweet finish to the afternoon, there are nut- and raisin-filled caramel tartlets, which, like the sandwiches, the cake and the scones, can be made ahead. (Another dessert idea is the Ginger Bears in the Options section, which can be frosted in pink or blue if it's a baby shower, or set out as a decorating project for girls attending a birthday tea.)

A teatime group can always be increased, especially when you consider that these recipes require almost no last-minute attention, that you don't need table

- Invite guests.
- Plan party games.
- Buy shower favors and/or prizes for party games.
- Bake honey-spice loaf cake; freeze.

1 WEEK AHEAD:

- Bake orange date bread; freeze.

3 DAYS AHEAD:

- Make lemon curd; chill.

1 DAY AHEAD:

- Bake scones; store at room temperature.
- Bake tartlets; chill.

DAY OF:

- Set up and decorate.
- Thaw honey-spice loaf cake and orange date bread.
- Make smoked turkey sandwiches (up to 4 hours ahead); chill (bring to room temperature before serving).
- Bring tartlets to room temperature.

AS GUESTS ARRIVE:

- Reheat scones, if desired.
- Make tea.

settings to serve the food and that unmatched teacups only make things more interesting. To expand this menu for 16, make two loaves of the orange bread and twice the number of sandwiches, bake one spice cake and the full recipe of scones (or purchase 16 scones from your favorite bakery) and have cookies for dessert.

Tea itself is the only rule at afternoon tea, although you can certainly offer coffee as well. Brew a pot of black tea, using one teaspoon per cup and making sure the water is boiling-hot. Steep five minutes, then serve with a choice of milk (not cream) or lemon and sugar. You might make a pot of herb tea, too. And if it's a warm afternoon, pour the tea into a pitcher, cool to room temperature and serve over ice cubes made from the same tea. Or make a batch of fruity Tea Punch from the Options section and enjoy every icy-cold sip.

SMOKED TURKEY FINGER SANDWICHES ON ORANGE DATE BREAD

What's afternoon tea without at least one dainty sandwich? Here, you make your own sandwich spread with smoked turkey (up to four hours ahead). Purchased firm sandwich bread, white or whole wheat, can be substituted for the Orange Date Bread, if desired. Offer your guests a few different types of hot tea and small glasses of Sherry for sipping. 8 SERVINGS

½ pound skinless smoked turkey breast, cut into 1-inch pieces
¾ cup (1½ sticks) unsalted butter, room temperature
3 teaspoons Dijon mustard
2 teaspoons Worcestershire sauce
2 teaspoons fresh lemon juice
⅔ cup minced fresh parsley
3 tablespoons chopped fresh chives or green onions

16 thin slices Orange Date Bread (see recipe at right) or other firm bread, crusts trimmed

Finely chop turkey in processor. Add ½ cup butter, mustard, Worcestershire sauce and lemon juice and process until smooth, scraping down sides of work bowl occasionally. Transfer mixture to medium bowl. Stir in ¼ cup minced fresh parsley and chives. Season to taste with salt and pepper.

Spread 8 bread slices with turkey mixture, dividing equally. Top with remaining 8 bread slices. Press lightly to compact. Using serrated knife, cut each sandwich crosswise into thirds. *(Sandwiches can be prepared 4 hours ahead. Cover tightly and refrigerate. Let stand 1 hour at room temperature before continuing.)*

Place remaining parsley on plate. Spread long edges of sandwiches with remaining ¼ cup butter. Dip buttered edges into parsley. Arrange sandwiches on platter and serve.

ORANGE DATE BREAD

For easiest slicing, bake this a day before. Any leftover bread can be toasted and served with a favorite jam or marmalade. MAKES 1 LOAF

1 cup orange juice
¼ cup plus 1 tablespoon water
3 tablespoons unsalted butter
3 tablespoons minced orange peel
2 tablespoons honey
2 teaspoons salt

2 teaspoons dry yeast
3½ cups (about) unbleached all purpose flour

1 tablespoon vegetable oil

¾ cup chopped pitted dates

1 large egg

Combine orange juice, ¼ cup water, butter, orange peel, honey and salt in heavy small saucepan. Stir over low heat until butter melts. Transfer to large bowl of heavy-duty mixer and let cool to warm (105°F to 115°F).

Stir yeast into orange juice mixture and let stand until foamy, about 5 minutes. Using dough hook, beat in enough flour, ½ cup at a time, to form sticky dough. Transfer to generously floured surface. Knead until smooth and elastic, adding more flour by tablespoonfuls if dough is sticky, about 10 minutes.

Pour 1 tablespoon oil into large bowl. Transfer dough to bowl; turn dough until coated completely. Cover with plastic wrap, then kitchen towel. Let rise in warm draft-free area until doubled in volume, 1½ hours.

Punch down dough. Knead on floured surface 3 minutes. Return dough to same large bowl, cover with plastic wrap and towel and let rise in warm draft-free area until doubled in volume, about 1 hour.

Butter 9 x 5 x 3-inch loaf pan. Punch down dough. Turn out onto lightly floured work surface and flatten slightly. Scatter dates evenly over dough. Gather dough into ball and knead briefly to distribute dates evenly throughout bread dough.

Form dough into loaf shape and transfer to prepared pan. Cover pan with plastic wrap and kitchen towel. Let rise in warm draft-free area until dough rises to top edge of pan, approximately 40 minutes.

Position rack in center of oven and preheat to 400°F. Whisk egg and remaining 1 tablespoon water in small bowl to blend. Brush some of egg mixture over dough. Bake bread 20 minutes. Reduce oven temperature to 350°F. Bake until bread is golden and sounds hollow when tapped on top, about 25 minutes. Transfer to rack; cool. *(Can be made ahead. Wrap tightly in foil; store 1 day at room temperature or wrap tightly in plastic wrap and freeze up to 1 week; thaw 4 hours at room temperature.)*

CRANBERRY-BUTTERMILK SCONES

Dried cranberries add extra flavor to these treats. Serve them with butter, Lemon Curd (see recipe at right) or, in the true high-tea tradition, with Devon cream, also known as clotted cream (the thick semi-spreadable cream that rises to the surface when fresh milk is heated). It's available at some cheese shops and specialty foods stores. MAKES 16

3   cups unbleached all purpose flour
¼   cup plus 2 teaspoons sugar
1¾ teaspoons baking powder
¼   teaspoon salt
10 tablespoons (1¼ sticks) chilled unsalted
    butter, cut into small pieces
¾   cup dried cranberries
½   cup buttermilk
3   large eggs

1   teaspoon water

Position rack in center of oven and preheat to 375°F. Butter two 9-inch-diameter cake pans. Combine flour, ¼ cup sugar, baking powder and salt in large bowl. Add butter; rub in with fingertips until mixture resembles coarse meal. Add cranberries. Whisk buttermilk and 2 eggs in small bowl. Stir into dry ingredients. Turn out onto floured surface. Knead gently just until soft dough forms.

Divide dough into 2 pieces. Form each piece into ball. Transfer each ball to 1 prepared pan; press out dough into 8-inch-diameter rounds. Using sharp knife, score top of each round into 8 wedges. Whisk remaining egg with 1 teaspoon water in small bowl. Brush egg glaze over scones. Sprinkle with remaining 2 teaspoons sugar.

Bake scones until golden, about 30 minutes. Cool 5 minutes. Invert scones onto platters. Turn right side up. Cut along score marks. *(Can be prepared 1 day ahead. Cool completely. Wrap in foil; store at room temperature.)* Serve scones warm or at room temperature.

LEMON CURD

A simple recipe for an English classic. If time is running short, substitute the purchased kind, which is available at most markets. 8 SERVINGS

2   large eggs
2   large egg yolks
¾   cup sugar
⅓   cup fresh lemon juice
2   teaspoons grated lemon peel
3   tablespoons butter, cut into small pieces

Whisk eggs, yolks and sugar in heavy medium saucepan until well blended and slightly thickened. Whisk in lemon juice and peel. Add butter. Stir over medium-low heat until curd thickens and just comes to boil, about 5 minutes. Immediately transfer mixture to bowl. Refrigerate until well chilled, about 8 hours. *(Can be made up to 3 days ahead.)*

HONEY-SPICE LOAF CAKE

This gingerbread-like spice cake is a simple and tasty addition to the teatime selection. It is nice on its own or paired with the Lemon Curd (see recipe on page 55). MAKES 1 LOAF

½ cup (1 stick) unsalted butter, room temperature
½ cup (packed) golden brown sugar
1 large egg
½ cup honey
½ cup mild-flavored (light) molasses
1¾ cups all purpose flour
1 tablespoon ground ginger
1 teaspoon ground pepper
1 teaspoon baking soda
¼ teaspoon ground cinnamon
¼ teaspoon ground allspice
¼ teaspoon ground cloves
¼ teaspoon salt
½ cup hot water

Position rack in center of oven and preheat to 350°F. Butter and flour 9 x 5 x 3-inch loaf pan. Beat butter and sugar in large bowl until well blended. Add egg and beat to blend. Mix in honey and molasses. Combine flour, ginger, pepper, baking soda, cinnamon, allspice, cloves and salt in large bowl. Gradually add to honey mixture, beating just until combined. Stir in ½ cup hot water.

Pour batter into prepared pan. Bake until tester inserted into center of cake comes out clean (cake will be very dark in color), about 1 hour. Transfer to rack; cool 10 minutes. Invert cake onto rack. Cool completely. *(Can be made ahead. Wrap tightly in plastic; store 1 day at room temperature or freeze up to 2 weeks. Thaw 4 hours at room temperature.)*

NUT AND RAISIN CARAMEL TARTLETS

Pine nuts and walnuts star in these individual tartlets. Make them a day ahead. MAKES 8

CRUST

1 cup powdered sugar
¾ cup (1½ sticks) unsalted butter, room temperature
¼ cup water
2 large egg yolks
½ teaspoon salt
2½ cups all purpose flour

FILLING

2½ cups sugar
⅔ cup water
2 tablespoons fresh lemon juice
⅔ cup whipping cream
6 tablespoons unsalted butter
⅔ cup toasted pine nuts
⅔ cup toasted walnuts
⅔ cup raisins

FOR CRUST: Mix powdered sugar, butter, ¼ cup water, egg yolks and salt in medium bowl. Add flour and stir until smooth. Cover and refrigerate for 30 minutes.

Roll dough out to thickness of ⅛ inch. Cut out eight 6-inch rounds using small plate as guide. Line eight 4-inch-diameter tart pans with dough, trimming excess. Pierce bottoms with fork. Cover and chill crusts 30 minutes.

Preheat oven to 375°F. Bake crusts until golden, about 20 minutes. Cool.

FOR FILLING: Heat sugar, ⅔ cup water and lemon juice in heavy large saucepan over medium heat, stirring until sugar dissolves. Boil until syrup turns deep amber, swirling pan occasionally (do not stir), about 12 minutes. Remove from heat. Carefully mix in cream and butter (mixture will bubble vigorously). When bubbling subsides, stir in all toasted nuts and raisins.

Immediately divide filling among crusts. Cool tarts. *(Can be made 1 day ahead. Cover; chill.)*

OLD-FASHIONED STRAWBERRY PRESERVES

Homemade preserves to have instead of, or in addition to, the Lemon Curd. MAKES 3 CUPS

3   12-ounce baskets fresh strawberries, hulled
2   cups sugar

Place hulled strawberries in heavy large saucepan and mash coarsely. Cook strawberries over medium heat until beginning to thicken, stirring frequently, about 6 minutes. Reduce heat to low. Add 2 cups sugar and stir until dissolved. Increase heat to medium and boil gently until mixture thickens and mounds on spoon, stirring frequently, about 20 minutes. Remove saucepan from heat. Cool. *(Can be made 1 week ahead; chill.)*

GINGER BEARS

If it's a baby you're welcoming with this tea, make these cookies for dessert. Using a standard powdered sugar icing tinted pink, blue or yellow, decorate them however you like. MAKES ABOUT 18

1   cup all purpose flour
⅓   cup (packed) dark brown sugar
2½   tablespoons cornstarch
¾   teaspoon ground ginger
½   teaspoon ground allspice
¼   teaspoon ground nutmeg
⅛   teaspoon ground cloves
⅛   teaspoon salt
½   cup (1 stick) chilled unsalted butter, cut into ½-inch pieces
½   cup walnuts (about 2½ ounces)

Preheat oven to 375°F. Blend first 8 ingredients in processor. Add butter and process until mixture resembles fine meal, using on/off turns. Add walnuts and chop finely using on/off turns.

Turn dough out onto sheet of waxed paper. Knead until dough holds together. Top with another sheet of waxed paper and roll out to thickness of ¼ inch. Cut out cookies using 3-inch bear-shaped cutter. Transfer to baking sheet. Gather scraps, reroll and cut additional cookies. Bake cookies until just firm to touch, about 18 minutes. Cool in pan on rack 5 minutes. Transfer cookies to rack and cool. *(Can be made ahead. Store in airtight container 2 days at room temperature or freeze up to 2 weeks.)*

TEA PUNCH

This would be nice at a summertime tea, when it's too hot to pour the brewed kind. 8 SERVINGS

8   cups water
1   family-size tea bag or 4 standard-size tea bags
1   cinnamon stick
¾   cup sugar
½   cup frozen orange juice concentrate, thawed
½   cup frozen lemonade concentrate, thawed

Ice cubes
8   lemon slices
8   fresh mint sprigs

Bring 4 cups water to boil in medium saucepan. Remove from heat. Add tea bag and cinnamon stick to water; let stand 5 minutes. Remove tea bag. Add sugar and stir to dissolve. Stir in orange juice and lemonade concentrates. Pour tea mixture into pitcher. Add remaining 4 cups water and stir well. Chill until cold, about 4 hours or overnight. Discard cinnamon stick.

Fill 8 glasses with ice. Pour tea punch over. Garnish each glass with 1 lemon slice and 1 mint sprig and serve.

Celebrating a Birthday Milestone

menu for six

- Baked Radicchio and Herbed Goat Cheese

- Champagne

- Jumbo Shrimp with Chive Butter Sauce

- Sauté of Zucchini and Bell Peppers

- Risotto with Parmesan

- Chardonnay

- Hazelnut and Espresso Birthday Dacquoise

menu options

- Three-Onion Tart

- Veal Chops with Tomato-Orange-Basil Sauce

- Double-Chocolate Cheesecake with Chocolate Leaves

Share the day

EVERYONE LIKES A SURPRISE BIRTHDAY PARTY: THE conspiring host, the secret-keeping guests and the stunned, aging honoree. But even if the birthday person knows of it, the party can surprise with wonderful food, a remarkable cake and, perhaps, an unexpected old friend, a longed-for gift, or even a memorable bottle of wine. And there's no reason not to throw a birthday bash for yourself. After all, whether you've made it to 30 or 60, you'd probably like to share the day with some people you've known along the way.

A surprise dinner for someone you live with requires a lot of kitchen flexibility. It's easier to keep things clandestine if you can arrange to do some of the preparations, store food and decorations and maybe even hold the party at a friend's or neighbor's house. Otherwise, you'll probably have to enlist someone else to get the

honoree out of the house for several hours before party time (a game of golf? an afternoon of shopping?). Either way, the cooking has to go quickly—and the dishes here do.

The radicchio and goat cheese appetizer can be popped into the oven right after the big shout of "Surprise!" and be ready in 15 minutes. The shrimp sauté and zucchini and bell peppers side dish require little prep work and even less stove time. The textures are complemented by a classic, creamy risotto, which does need tending but not the kind that doesn't allow friends to talk while they help. And as birthday requests go, chances are risotto is right up there at the top of the most-wanted list.

For a heartier main course, consider the veal chops in the Options section, a dish just as surprise-ready as the shrimp because the fragrant tomato-orange

UP TO 2 WEEKS AHEAD:

- Invite guests.
- Order flowers and/or choose centerpiece.
- Buy all nonperishables.
- Bake and freeze meringues for birthday *dacquoise*.

2 DAYS AHEAD:

- Buy all perishables (except shrimp).
- Thaw meringues; finish making and frosting birthday dacquoise; chill.

1 DAY AHEAD:

- Chill white wine and Champagne.
- Buy shrimp.

DAY OF:

- Pick up flowers.
- Set table.
- Prepare zucchini and bell peppers for sauté (up to 6 hours ahead); keep on ice.
- Make chive butter (up to 4 hours ahead); keep at room temperature.
- Assemble radicchio and goat cheese appetizer (up to 3 hours ahead); keep at room temperature.
- Cut bread for goat cheese appetizer (up to 1 hour ahead); keep at room temperature.
- Set up coffeemaker.

sauce that tops the veal can be made ahead. So can the crust for the onion tart, a delicious "sit-down" first course to have instead of—or in addition to, if you're going all out—the goat cheese spread.

At any birthday celebration, but especially at a "big" birthday, the cake's the thing, and there are two very grown-up versions to choose from here. In the main menu, layers of nut meringue and espresso buttercream make for a sophisticated combination of textures and flavors in a *dacquoise* that can be prepared two days ahead. For cheesecake lovers, there's a white and dark chocolate version in the Options section, decorated not with candles but with chocolate leaves (which are surprisingly simple to make), Grand Marnier whipped cream and orange peel threads. Either cake could star in a smaller celebration, too, with Champagne and coffee at an after-dinner hour.

BAKED RADICCHIO AND
HERBED GOAT CHEESE

*Serve this baked appetizer with crusty bread and
Champagne.* 6 SERVINGS

2 medium heads radicchio,
   cut into ¼-inch-thick strips
4 ounces soft fresh goat cheese
   (such as Montrachet), cut into ½-inch pieces
¼ cup olive oil
1 garlic clove, coarsely chopped
1 teaspoon dried basil
1 teaspoon dried marjoram
½ teaspoon dried rosemary
   Sliced Italian bread

Preheat oven to 400°F. Place radicchio in
large shallow baking dish. Arrange goat
cheese over. Heat oil in heavy small saucepan
over medium heat. Add garlic and sauté until
golden, about 1 minute. Discard garlic.
Add basil, marjoram and rosemary to oil.
Season with pepper. Drizzle over goat cheese
and radicchio. *(Can be prepared 3 hours ahead.
Cover with plastic wrap and keep at room temperature.)* Bake until cheese begins to melt, about
15 minutes. Serve with bread slices.

JUMBO SHRIMP WITH
CHIVE BUTTER SAUCE

*Made in minutes and very elegant. Pour a chilled
Chardonnay with this entrée (opposite).* 6 SERVINGS

1 cup (2 sticks) butter
¼ cup Dijon mustard
¼ cup fresh lemon juice
6 tablespoons chopped fresh chives

36 uncooked jumbo shrimp, peeled,
   deveined and butterflied
   Whole chives

Preheat broiler. Melt butter in heavy small
saucepan over low heat. Place mustard in
bowl. Whisk in lemon juice. Gradually whisk
in butter. Add chopped chives. Season with
pepper. *(Chive butter can be prepared 4 hours
ahead. Cover and keep at room temperature.
Remelt over low heat before using.)*

Arrange shrimp cut side up on broiler pan.
Brush with some of butter mixture. Broil
until just cooked through, about 4 minutes.
Arrange on plates; garnish with whole chives.
Serve, passing remaining butter separately.

SAUTÉ OF ZUCCHINI AND BELL PEPPERS

This side dish (opposite and below) takes only 10 minutes, start to finish. 6 SERVINGS

¼   cup (½ stick) unsalted butter or olive oil
1   large garlic clove, minced
1   large green bell pepper,
    cut into matchstick-size strips
1   large yellow bell pepper,
    cut into matchstick-size strips
1   pound zucchini, cut into matchstick-size strips
1   tablespoon fresh lemon juice

Melt butter or heat olive oil in heavy large skillet over medium-high heat. Add garlic, then bell peppers and sauté until peppers begin to soften, about 5 minutes. Add zucchini and sauté until crisp-tender, about 4 minutes. Add lemon juice. Season with salt and pepper and serve.

RISOTTO WITH PARMESAN

Made in the traditional manner, this luscious risotto (opposite and below) requires slow cooking and frequent stirring—an easy job to offer a helpful guest. 6 SERVINGS

5   cups (about) canned low-salt chicken broth

4   tablespoons (½ stick) butter
1½ cups finely chopped onion
1½ cups arborio rice or
    medium-grain white rice
1   cup grated Parmesan cheese
2   tablespoons chopped fresh Italian parsley
    Shaved Parmesan cheese

Bring broth to boil in medium saucepan. Reduce heat to low; cover saucepan.

Melt 2 tablespoons butter in heavy medium saucepan over medium-low heat. Add onion; sauté until very tender but not brown, about 15 minutes. Increase heat to medium. Add rice and stir 1 minute. Add 1½ cups warm broth. Boil gently until broth is absorbed, stirring frequently. Add another 1 cup broth; stir until broth is absorbed. Add remaining 2½ cups broth, ½ cup at a time, allowing broth to be absorbed before adding more and stirring frequently until rice is tender and mixture is creamy, about 25 minutes. Stir in remaining 2 tablespoons butter and 1 cup grated cheese. Season with salt and pepper. Transfer to bowl. Sprinkle with parsley and shaved Parmesan.

HAZELNUT AND ESPRESSO BIRTHDAY DACQUOISE

This layered meringue treat is a sophisticated—and delicious—way to conclude a birthday dinner. Plan to bake and assemble it at least a day or two before the big day. 12 SERVINGS

MERINGUES

1   cup hazelnuts (about 5 ounces), toasted, husked
1¼ cups sugar
3   tablespoons cornstarch
6   large egg whites, room temperature
1   teaspoon cream of tartar
¼   teaspoon salt
1   teaspoon vanilla extract

BUTTERCREAM

6   large egg yolks
1½ cups sugar
1   cup whipping cream
2   tablespoons instant espresso or instant coffee powder
⅛   teaspoon salt

1½ cups (3 sticks) unsalted butter, cut into pieces, room temperature

½   cup hazelnuts, toasted, husked, finely chopped
24 whole hazelnuts, toasted
     Birthday candles or short votive candles (optional)

FOR MERINGUES: Preheat oven to 225°F. Line 2 large lightweight baking sheets with parchment. Draw two 12 x 4-inch rectangles on 1 parchment sheet. Draw one 12 x 4-inch rectangle on second sheet. Turn parchment over.

Finely grind hazelnuts, ¼ cup sugar and cornstarch in processor. Using electric mixer, beat egg whites, cream of tartar and salt in large bowl until thick and foamy. Gradually add remaining 1 cup sugar, beating until whites are very thick and glossy peaks form when beaters are lifted. Fold hazelnut mixture and vanilla into meringue. Spread 1½ cups meringue mixture evenly inside each traced rectangle.

Bake meringues until firm and beginning to color but not hard, about 1 hour 10 minutes. Turn oven off and let meringues dry in oven with door closed overnight. Carefully peel parchment off meringues. *(Can be made ahead. Wrap tightly and store at room temperature 1 day or freeze in airtight container up to 2 weeks.)*

FOR BUTTERCREAM: Using electric mixer, beat yolks and ½ cup sugar in large bowl until thick and light. Combine 1 cup sugar, cream, instant espresso and salt in heavy medium saucepan. Whisk over medium heat until mixture boils. Gradually whisk cream mixture into yolk mixture. Return mixture to same saucepan and stir over medium heat until custard is thick and candy thermometer registers 160°F, about 7 minutes.

Transfer custard to large bowl. Beat at low speed until cooled to lukewarm. Add butter in 3 batches, beating until very thick and smooth after each addition. Cover and refrigerate until well chilled, about 6 hours.

Place 1 meringue layer on platter. Spread 1 cup buttercream over. Top with second meringue layer. Spread 1 cup buttercream over. Top with third meringue layer, bottom side up. Press lightly to adhere. Frost top and sides of dacquoise with remaining buttercream. Press chopped nuts onto sides of cake. Place whole hazelnuts along top edge. Chill until buttercream sets, about 1 hour. Cover; chill overnight. *(Can be made 2 days ahead. Keep chilled.)* Arrange birthday candles atop cake or votive candles around cake, if desired.

These recipes expand or change the menu to suit your individual needs.

THREE-ONION TART

This could stand in for the baked radicchio as a "sit-down" appetizer. 6 SERVINGS

CRUST

2¾ cups all purpose flour
¼ teaspoon salt
1 large egg, beaten to blend
1½ tablespoons olive oil
6 tablespoons (¾ stick) unsalted butter, melted, cooled
⅓ cup cold milk (do not use low-fat or nonfat)

TOPPING

3½ cups thinly sliced leeks (white and pale green parts only; about 2 medium)
3 tablespoons extra-virgin olive oil
1 large red onion, thinly sliced
1 cup sliced green onions
1 large egg, beaten to blend
8 ounces Brie, rind removed, chopped
2 tablespoons grated Parmesan cheese

FOR CRUST: Mix flour and salt in large bowl. Make well in center of flour mixture. Add egg and oil to well. Pour melted butter and milk into well. Mix ingredients in well, gradually incorporating flour until dough forms. Turn dough out onto floured surface and knead until smooth, about 10 minutes. Form into ball. Wrap in kitchen towel; let stand at room temperature 2 hours. *(Can be made 2 weeks ahead. Wrap in plastic and freeze.)*

FOR TOPPING: Combine leeks and oil in large nonstick skillet. Cover and cook over medium-low heat until leeks are tender but not brown, stirring frequently, about 15 minutes. Stir in red onion and green onions. Sauté uncovered until all onions are very tender, about 25 minutes longer. Season with salt and pepper. Cool. Mix in egg, then Brie.

Prcheat oven to 375°F. Roll out dough on floured surface, forming 13-inch round. Transfer to large rimless baking sheet. Fold outer 1 inch of dough over, forming double-thick rim. Spread topping evenly over crust. Bake tart 10 minutes. Sprinkle Parmesan over. Bake until crust is golden brown, about 15 minutes longer. Cut into wedges.

VEAL CHOPS WITH TOMATO-ORANGE-BASIL SAUCE

For something a little heartier than the shrimp, try these chops. Substitute a Pinot Noir for the Chardonnay. 6 SERVINGS

1 cup plus 2 tablespoons fresh orange juice
¾ cup dry white wine
6 tablespoons minced shallots
3 tablespoons minced orange peel
6 tablespoons whipping cream

7½ tablespoons butter
6 6-ounce veal loin chops

1½ cups chopped seeded peeled tomato
6 tablespoons thinly sliced fresh basil or 1 tablespoon dried
Fresh basil springs (optional)

Combine first 3 ingredients and 1½ tablespoons orange peel in heavy small saucepan. Boil until mixture is reduced to generous ¼ cup, about 15 minutes. Add cream and boil 1 minute. Set sauce aside. *(Can be prepared 1 day ahead. Cover and refrigerate.)*

Melt 1½ tablespoons butter in heavy large skillet over medium heat. Season veal with salt and pepper. Working in batches, sauté veal until just cooked through, about 4 minutes per side. Transfer to plates; keep warm.

Reheat sauce over low heat. Whisk in remaining 6 tablespoons butter. Stir in tomato, sliced basil and remaining 1½ tablespoons orange peel. Season to taste with salt and pepper. Ladle sauce over veal. Garnish with basil sprigs, if desired, and serve.

Options

DOUBLE-CHOCOLATE CHEESECAKE WITH CHOCOLATE LEAVES

This decadent dessert combines white and dark chocolate with an elegant touch of orange. It's topped with white and dark chocolate leaves, which are simple to do but make a very impressive presentation. (Begin preparations at least one and up to two days ahead.) 12 SERVINGS

CRUST

18 chocolate wafer cookies
    (about 4 ounces), broken
 1 cup pecans (about 4 ounces)
¼ cup sugar
 2 ounces semisweet chocolate,
    coarsely chopped
¼ cup (½ stick) chilled unsalted butter,
    cut into pieces

FILLING

4½ ounces unsweetened chocolate, chopped

28 ounces cream cheese, softened
½ cup sugar
 5 large eggs, room temperature
 1 cup plus 2 tablespoons (packed)
    golden brown sugar
 1 tablespoon light corn syrup

¼ cup whipping cream
 1 tablespoon plus 1 teaspoon
    grated orange peel
 1 teaspoon grated lemon peel
 6 ounces good-quality white chocolate
    (such as Lindt or Baker's), finely chopped
¼ cup Grand Marnier or other orange liqueur

DARK AND WHITE CHOCOLATE LEAVES

 3 ounces semisweet chocolate, chopped
 1 teaspoon solid vegetable shortening
12 medium camellia or lemon leaves,
    wiped clean

 3 ounces good-quality white chocolate
    (such as Lindt or Baker's), chopped

ORANGE THREADS

 1 orange

WHIPPED CREAM TOPPING

⅔ cup chilled whipping cream
 1 tablespoon powdered sugar
2½ teaspoons Grand Marnier or
    other orange liqueur

FOR CRUST: Position rack in center of oven and preheat to 350°F. Place cookies, pecans, sugar and chocolate in processor. Process until finely chopped. Add butter and process until moist crumbs form. Transfer crumb mixture to 10-inch-diameter springform pan with 2¾-inch-high sides. Press crumb mixture onto bottom and 2 inches up sides of pan. Set on baking sheet and bake 10 minutes. Transfer to rack and cool.

FOR FILLING: Preheat oven to 350°F. Melt unsweetened chocolate in top of small double boiler over barely simmering water, stirring occasionally, until smooth. Remove from over water. Cool slightly.

Using electric mixer, beat cream cheese with ½ cup sugar in large bowl until fluffy. Add eggs 1 at a time, beating until just incorporated and stopping occasionally to scrape down bottom and sides of bowl. Transfer 2½ cups batter to medium bowl; set aside. Add brown sugar to remaining batter in large bowl and beat until combined. Mix corn syrup, then melted chocolate into batter in large bowl. Pour ⅔ cup chocolate batter into small bowl and set aside. Pour remaining chocolate batter into prepared crust. Set on baking sheet and bake until filling is barely set, about 15 minutes. Transfer to rack and cool 5 minutes. Maintain oven temperature.

Meanwhile, combine cream, orange peel and lemon peel in heavy small saucepan. Bring to simmer. Remove from heat. Add white chocolate and stir until melted and smooth. Cool mixture slightly. Add white chocolate mixture to reserved 2½ cups batter and stir to combine. Mix in Grand Marincr.

Starting at outside edge, carefully spoon white chocolate batter over chocolate layer in pan. Set on baking sheet and bake until cake sides are puffed and center moves only slightly when pan is shaken, 35 to 40 minutes. Transfer cake to rack and cool 5 minutes. Maintain oven temperature.

Spoon reserved ⅔ cup chocolate batter by tablespoons onto center of white chocolate layer. Using back of spoon, spread chocolate in smooth even circle to within ½ inch of cake edge. Set on baking sheet; bake 10 minutes. Transfer to rack. Using small sharp knife, cut around cake pan sides to loosen. Cool cheesecake completely in pan. Cover; chill overnight. *(Can be made 2 days ahead.)*

FOR DARK AND WHITE CHOCOLATE LEAVES: Line 2 baking sheets with foil. Place semisweet chocolate and ½ teaspoon shortening in small bowl. Set bowl over saucepan of barely simmering water. Cook until melted and smooth, stirring occasionally. Remove from over water. Using small metal spatula or spoon, spread thin layer of chocolate over veined underside of 6 leaves, being careful

not to drip over edges. Place on 1 prepared baking sheet. Chill until set, about 5 minutes. Spread second thin layer of chocolate on each leaf, remelting chocolate over barely simmering water if necessary. Refrigerate leaves until chocolate sets, about 30 minutes.

Place white chocolate and ½ teaspoon shortening in small bowl. Set bowl over saucepan of barely simmering water. Cook until melted and smooth, stirring occasionally. Remove from over water. Spread thin layer of white chocolate on veined underside of 6 leaves, being careful not to drip over edges. Place on second prepared baking sheet. Chill until set, about 5 minutes. Spread second thin layer of white chocolate on each leaf, remelting chocolate over barely simmering water if necessary. Refrigerate leaves until chocolate is completely set, about 30 minutes.

Starting at stem end, gently peel leaves off dark and white chocolate. *(Can be prepared 1 day ahead. Refrigerate dark and white chocolate leaves in single layers in airtight containers.)*

FOR ORANGE THREADS: Using vegetable peeler, remove orange peel in large strips. Cut into matchstick-size strips. Blanch orange strips in saucepan of boiling water 30 seconds. Drain well. Dry thoroughly on paper towels. *(Can be prepared 1 day ahead. Cover and refrigerate.)*

FOR WHIPPED CREAM TOPPING: Beat cream and sugar in medium bowl to soft peaks. Add Grand Marnier; beat until stiff peaks form.

TO ASSEMBLE: Release pan sides from cheesecake. Spoon whipped cream into pastry bag fitted with large star tip. Pipe decorative border of whipped cream around edge of cake. Set alternating white and dark chocolate leaves at slight angle atop whipped cream border. Arrange orange threads on cake. Cut cheesecake into wedges and serve.

Cookout for a Crowd

menu for twelve

- Lime Daiquiris

- White Bean Dip with Chips and Sticks

- Steak Sandwiches on Garlic Baguettes with Arugula and Tomatoes

- Corn, Tomato and Basil Salad

- Tricolor Roasted Peppers

- Beer and Iced Tea

- Mississippi Mud Cake

menu options

- Curried Marmalade-Mustard Chicken

- Apple-Peach Crumble

Light up the grill

WHEN THE WEATHER WARMS UP AND THE DAYS STAY light longer, almost everyone with a back yard and a barbecue gets the itch to light up the grill and cook a feast for friends. It's some kind of instinctive behavior. It's also an ideal way to celebrate any of the many occasions that crop up come summer, graduations chief among them.

Whether you're marking the step up from elementary to middle school or honoring a high school diploma, the completion of a college degree or a newly earned doctorate, a graduation is an accomplishment deserving of a celebration. This one comes with terrific food, all of it summery, simple and even better when made ahead, which, of course, leaves you free to enjoy the weather, the crowd of well-wishers and the glow of a child's (young or grown) significant accomplishment.

A cookout not carefully considered can mean you're tied to the grill for what may seem like hours, taking orders and flipping burgers. Not this one: Here, the strip steaks for the sandwiches can be grilled ahead, sliced and arranged on a platter along with the other make-your-own accompaniments, including baguettes, arugula and tomatoes. The colorful corn salad that gets served with the sandwiches needs to chill for at least three hours (and up to eight) before serving to allow the flavors to meld. The same is true of the roasted peppers in the menu. In the Options section, there's a great barbecued chicken recipe that you might want to make instead of, or in addition to, the steak sandwiches.

There are frosty lime daiquiris here to toast the grown-up graduate; you'll likely want to offer beer, iced tea and sodas, too. Fill a couple of picnic coolers

- Invite guests.

2 DAYS AHEAD:

- Buy all perishables (except bread).
- Make bean dip; chill.

1 DAY AHEAD:

- Make cake; chill.
- Chill beer.
- Make roasted peppers; chill.
- Make iced tea; chill.
- Clean barbecue.
- Grill steaks for sandwiches; chill.

DAY OF:

- Buy French bread baguettes.
- Prepare vegetables for dip
  (up to 8 hours ahead); chill.
- Prepare corn, tomato and basil salad
  (up to 8 hours ahead); chill.
- Prepare steak sandwiches
  (up to 2 hours ahead).
- Bring roasted peppers to room temperature.
- Bring cake to room temperature.
- Make daiquiris as guests arrive.

with ice to keep the drinks chilled outside. Make coffee and tea ahead and refrigerate them in pitchers, ready to pour over ice to serve with dessert. Then, after everyone has sworn they couldn't eat another bite, prove them wrong by bringing out the irresistible Mississippi Mud Cake. It has everything—rich chocolate underscored by brown sugar, melted marshmallows and crunchy pecans.

Though this menu invites patio lounging, it's also a convenient one to transport to the park, the beach or an outdoor concert, since the sandwiches can be assembled, wrapped in foil and kept at room temperature for two hours. Pack the corn salad in a plastic container and tuck a cold pack next to it in the picnic basket to keep it at the right temperature. Substitute brownies or cookies for dessert.

LIME DAIQUIRIS

These will quench a cookout thirst. 12 SERVINGS

6 cups (generous) ice cubes
2 cups frozen limeade concentrate
1½ cups fresh lime juice
1½ cups amber Barbados rum

Additional ice cubes
12 lime wedges

Working in batches, combine 1½ cups ice, ½ cup limeade concentrate, 6 tablespoons lime juice and 6 tablespoons rum in blender. Blend until ice is crushed and mixture is blended.

Place additional ice cubes in 3 glasses. Pour daiquiri mixture over ice. Repeat 3 more times. Garnish with lime wedges.

WHITE BEAN DIP WITH CHIPS AND STICKS

A new and delicious twist on the usual bean dip, made with cannellini *and served with tortilla chips and vegetable "sticks."* 12 SERVINGS

3 garlic cloves
3 15-ounce cans cannellini (white kidney beans), rinsed, drained
¼ cup fresh lemon juice
½ cup olive oil
2¼ teaspoons ground cumin
1½ teaspoons chili powder
3 tablespoons chopped fresh cilantro
Additional chopped fresh cilantro
Fresh vegetables (such as carrot sticks, celery sticks and cauliflower)
Tortilla chips

Finely chop garlic in processor. Add beans and lemon juice and puree. Mix in oil, cumin and chili powder. Season with salt and pepper. Add 3 tablespoons cilantro and mix in using on/off turns. Transfer to large bowl. *(Can be prepared 2 days ahead. Cover and refrigerate.)* Sprinkle dip with additional cilantro. Serve with vegetables and chips.

STEAK SANDWICHES ON GARLIC BAGUETTES WITH ARUGULA AND TOMATOES

The easy thing about making steak sandwiches for a crowd this large is that the steak doesn't have to be served straight off the grill; in fact, it's better to let it cool. Pass bottles of beer and pour lemony iced tea to drink. 12 SERVINGS

1 tablespoon plus ½ cup olive oil
1 tablespoon herbes de Provence*
4 1-pound New York strip steaks (each about ¾ to 1 inch thick), trimmed

12 5- to 6-inch-long French-bread baguette pieces, halved lengthwise
4 large garlic cloves, halved

7 cups arugula (about 4 ounces)
4 large plum tomatoes, thinly sliced

Prepare barbecue (medium-high heat). Mix 1 tablespoon oil and herbes de Provence in small bowl to blend. Rub oil mixture over both sides of steaks. Sprinkle with salt and pepper. Grill steaks to desired doneness, about 8 minutes per side for medium-rare. Cool. *(Can be made 1 day ahead. Wrap steaks tightly with plastic. Refrigerate. Bring to room termperature before serving.)*

Preheat broiler. Working in batches, place bread, cut side up, on baking sheet. Lightly brush cut sides of bread with remaining ½ cup oil. Broil until bread is golden, about 1 minute. Rub garlic clove halves over toasted sides of bread halves.

Cut steaks into ⅛-inch-thick slices. Place arugula over bottoms of bread. Top with meat, then tomatoes. Season with salt and pepper. Cover with bread tops. Cut sandwiches in half. *(Can be prepared ahead. Wrap in foil; store at room temperature up to 2 hours.)*

*A dried herb mixture available at specialty foods stores and some supermarkets. Or use dried thyme, basil, savory and fennel seeds instead.

CORN, TOMATO AND BASIL SALAD

Fresh, colorful and simple, this salad (below) goes especially well with the sandwiches. 12 SERVINGS

12	large ears white corn, husked
10	tablespoons olive oil
2	tablespoons finely chopped garlic
1	cup (packed) thinly sliced fresh basil
10	plum tomatoes, seeded, chopped
6	tablespoons balsamic vinegar

Using large knife, cut corn kernels from cob. Heat 2 tablespoons oil in each of 2 heavy large skillets over medium-high heat. Add half of garlic to each skillet; sauté 1 minute. Add half of corn to each skillet; sauté until just cooked through, 5 minutes. Remove from heat. Add half of basil to skillets.

Transfer corn mixture to 2 large bowls. Cool slightly, stirring occasionally. Stir in tomatoes, vinegar, 6 tablespoons oil and remaining basil, dividing equally. Season with salt and pepper. Cover; chill 3 hours or up to 8 hours.

TRICOLOR ROASTED PEPPERS

Do-ahead roasted peppers to have as a side dish— or add them to the sandwiches. 12 SERVINGS

3	red bell peppers
3	yellow bell peppers
3	green bell peppers
3	poblano chilies*
¾	cup olive oil
6	tablespoons balsamic vinegar
4½	tablespoons chopped fresh basil
3	tablespoons fresh lemon juice
1	tablespoon minced garlic

Char all peppers and chilies over gas flame or in broiler until blackened all over. Enclose in paper bag. Let stand 10 minutes. Peel and seed peppers and chilies. Cut peppers and chilies into large triangles.

Mix all remaining ingredients in large bowl. Add roasted peppers and chilies and toss. Season to taste with salt and pepper. Cover; chill at least 3 hours or overnight. Bring to room temperature.

*Fresh green chilies, often called pasillas; *available at Latin American markets and some supermarkets.*

MISSISSIPPI MUD CAKE

*This classic chocolate cake gets its unlikely moniker
from its color—the same as the deep, rich soil that
lines Old Man River. It's usually made in a single-
layer rectangular baking pan, but this one is fash-
ioned into a layer cake.* 12 SERVINGS

CAKE

1½   cups (3 sticks) unsalted butter,
       room temperature
1½   cups (packed) dark brown sugar
 1   cup sugar
 3   ounces unsweetened chocolate,
       chopped, melted
 ¼   cup whipping cream
 2   teaspoons vanilla extract
 6   large eggs, room temperature
2¼   cups all purpose flour
 ½   cup unsweetened cocoa powder
 ½   teaspoon baking soda
 ¼   teaspoon salt

 3   cups mini marshmallows
 2   cups coarsely chopped toasted pecans
       (about 7 ounces)

FROSTING

 1   cup (packed) dark brown sugar
 1   cup whipping cream
 ½   cup (1 stick) unsalted butter, cut into pieces
 5   ounces unsweetened chocolate, chopped
 2   ounces bittersweet (not unsweetened) or
       semisweet chocolate, chopped
 2   tablespoons dark corn syrup
 1   teaspoon vanilla extract

FOR CAKE: Preheat oven to 350°F. Line two
9-inch-square cake pans with 2-inch-high sides
with foil, extending foil over sides. Butter and
flour foil. Using electric mixer, beat butter
and both sugars in large bowl until fluffy.
Beat in melted chocolate, cream and vanilla.
Add eggs 1 at a time, beating well after each
addition. Sift flour, cocoa, baking soda and
salt into medium bowl. Stir dry ingredients
into batter, which will be very thick. Divide
batter between prepared pans; spread evenly.
Bake until tester inserted into centers comes
out clean, about 20 minutes. Remove cakes
from oven. Maintain oven temperature.

Sprinkle 1½ cups marshmallows and 1 cup
pecans over each cake. Bake just until marshmallows begin to melt, about 6 minutes.
Transfer to racks. Cool cakes in pans.

FOR FROSTING: Combine sugar and cream in
heavy medium saucepan. Stir over medium
heat until sugar dissolves. Cook without stirring until candy thermometer registers 220°F,
about 8 minutes. Remove from heat and
whisk in remaining ingredients. Whisk until
all chocolate melts and frosting is smooth.
Refrigerate frosting until thick and spreadable, about 1 hour 15 minutes.

Using foil as aid, lift cakes from pans. Remove
foil. Place 1 cake layer on plate, marshmallow
side up. Spread 1½ cups frosting over. Top
with second cake layer, marshmallow side up.
Spread remaining frosting in waves on sides
(not top) of cake. *(Can be prepared 1 day ahead.
Cover with cake dome and refrigerate. Bring to
room temperature before serving.)*

These recipes expand or change the menu to suit your individual needs.

CURRIED MARMALADE-MUSTARD CHICKEN

An alternative to the steak sandwiches. Sweet glazes like the one used here can burn quickly if special steps are not taken when barbecuing. Remove the chicken skin (less fat to drip and cause flare-ups) and place an aluminum foil pan filled with wood chips atop coals under chicken to deflect direct heat. (Cook the chicken in two batches if your grill is small.) 12 SERVINGS

2   cups orange marmalade
2   cups Dijon mustard
½   cup honey
2   tablespoons curry powder
2   tablespoons fresh lemon juice

12 chicken breast halves with ribs, skin removed
1   teaspoon salt

Simmer first 5 ingredients in heavy medium saucepan over low heat 5 minutes, stirring constantly. Cool. *(Glaze can be prepared 3 days ahead. Cover tightly and refrigerate. Bring glaze to room temperature before using.)*

Brush chicken breasts on all sides with half of glaze. Let stand 1 hour at room temperature. Sprinkle chicken breasts with salt.

Prepare barbecue (medium heat). Place breasts meaty side down on grill. Cover with grill lid or heavy-duty foil and cook 10 minutes. Brush chicken breasts with glaze. Continue cooking chicken until brown and cooked through, turning breasts occasionally, about 10 minutes. Arrange chicken on serving platter. Brush with remaining glaze and serve.

APPLE-PEACH CRUMBLE

A simpler alternative to the chocolate cake, this summery fruit dessert can be readied ahead and baked just before serving. 12 SERVINGS

TOPPING

1   cup all purpose flour
1   cup (packed) golden brown sugar
⅔   cup old-fashioned oats
1   teaspoon ground cinnamon
½   cup (1 stick) unsalted butter, room temperature
⅔   cup slivered almonds

FRUIT

1½   cups sugar
3   tablespoons cornstarch
2¾   pounds Granny Smith apples, peeled, cored, cut into ½-inch-thick slices (about 9 cups)
2½   1-pound bags frozen sliced peeled peaches (about 9 cups)
1   tablespoon fresh lemon juice
2   teaspoons grated lemon peel
1¼   teaspoons almond extract

Vanilla ice cream

FOR TOPPING: Mix first 4 ingredients in medium bowl. Add butter; rub in with fingertips until mixture resembles coarse meal. Mix in almonds. *(Can be prepared 1 day ahead; chill.)*

FOR FRUIT: Preheat oven to 400°F. Butter 13 x 9 x 2-inch glass baking dish. Mix sugar and cornstarch in large bowl. Add apples, peaches, lemon juice, lemon peel and extract; toss to combine. Transfer to prepared dish. Place on baking sheet. Bake until juices bubble, 1 hour 10 minutes. *(Can be made 4 hours ahead. Let stand at room temperature.)*

Preheat oven to 400°F. Sprinkle topping over fruit. Bake until topping is brown, about 25 minutes. Serve warm with ice cream.

Big Anniversary with Family and Friends

menu for ten

- Broccoli, Spinach and Leek Soup

- Beef Tenderloin with Mushroom, Onion and Red Wine Sauce

- Garlic-layered Potatoes

- Green Beans with Shallots, Rosemary and Hazelnuts

- Cabernet Sauvignon

- Chocolate Anniversary Cake

menu options

- Gorgonzola and Camembert Fondue with Vegetables

- Veal with Prosciutto and Sage

- Heart-shaped Genoise with Champagne-Raspberry Mousse

It seems like yesterday

IN THEIR HEART OF HEARTS, NO HAPPILY MARRIED couple can ever believe it's been 10, 25 or 50 years since they were wed. No matter how long the two of them have been together, it seems like yesterday that they walked down the aisle together, hand and hand, into the future. To celebrate that journey and all that it has encompassed, this menu pulls out all the stops, making a wonderfully special occasion to mark a significant accomplishment.

Get things started with a lovely soup, a puree of broccoli, spinach and leeks topped with strips of roasted red pepper and chives. To follow, there is beef tenderloin in a rich red wine-mushroom sauce. Side dishes include a creamy gratin of potatoes layered with roasted garlic, and green beans sautéed with shallots and rosemary and tossed with hazelnuts. And for the couple who never got around to a slice of their wedding cake (or don't remember it

with much fondness), there's a dessert here to make up for it: a heart-shaped flourless chocolate cake with white chocolate sauce.

Not unlike a good marriage, these dishes celebrate romance in a practical way: Every recipe can be prepared at least partially ahead. If the party is a group effort, perhaps among siblings to honor parents, the preparations can be divided up, and the dishes completed at one location. And it's easy to make this party a surprise, since nothing depends on tricky timing. If the event you're planning is a less-formal, outdoor affair, be sure to take a look at the dishes in the Options section, which are lighter, if every bit as delicious.

Set the party mood with music of the same vintage as the marriage, whether Beatles or big band, disco or bebop. Bring mementos to the center of the

UP TO 3 WEEKS AHEAD:

• Invite guests.

1 WEEK AHEAD:

• Buy all nonperishables.
• Order beef tenderloin.

3 DAYS AHEAD:

• Make wine and Port reduction
  for beef; chill.
• Toast, husk and chop hazelnuts for green
  beans; keep at room temperature.
• Make sauce and syrup
  for chocolate cake; chill.

2 DAYS AHEAD:

• Make soup; chill.
• Make place cards.

1 DAY AHEAD:

• Pick up beef tenderloin.
• Make mushroom sauce for beef; chill.
• Prepare and bake layered potatoes; chill.
• Boil green beans; chill.
• Bake chocolate cake; store
  at room temperature.
• Chill Champagne.

DAY OF:

• Set table.
• Set up coffeemaker.
• Begin roasting tenderloin (1 hour ahead).
• Begin reheating potatoes (1 hour ahead).

table with old photos in frames arranged around a
floral centerpiece. Copies of old snapshots could
decorate the place cards. And if you'd like to note
the anniversary's symbolic material, tie napkins with
silver ribbons for the twenty-fifth, pearl-white for
the thirtieth, ruby-red for the fortieth and gold for
the fiftieth. For ten years of marriage, the traditional gift is something tin; diamond jewelry is the mod-
ern interpretation. Crystal signifies 15 years and
china stands for 20; either could suggest a centerpiece bowl or vase to send home with the couple.

To bridge the years, ask friends and relatives, present or not, to write down a recollection of the
wedding or some event in the couple's marriage.
Compile them in an album, along with the recipes
from the party, then read them aloud after dinner,
and toast the stories told with a memorable bottle
of Cabernet Sauvignon.

BROCCOLI, SPINACH AND LEEK SOUP

*Garnished with roasted red bell pepper and chives,
this delicious soup makes a pretty first course.
(Prepare it two days ahead and rewarm before
serving.)* 10 SERVINGS

¼ cup (½ stick) butter
4 large leeks (white and pale green parts only),
   chopped (about 6 cups)
1½ pounds broccoli, florets separated from
   stems, stems peeled and cut into pieces
1 pound russet potatoes, peeled,
   cut into 2-inch pieces
5 14½-ounce cans low-salt chicken broth

1 10-ounce package frozen chopped spinach,
   thawed, undrained

1 large red bell pepper

   Fresh chives or green onion tops

Melt butter in heavy large pot over medium-
high heat. Add leeks and sauté until tender
but not brown, about 15 minutes. Add
broccoli stems and florets and potatoes and
stir 3 minutes. Add broth and bring to boil.
Reduce heat, cover and simmer until
vegetables are very tender, about 25 minutes.
Cool soup 15 minutes.

Add spinach to soup. Puree soup in batches
in blender until smooth. Return soup to pot.

Char red pepper over gas flame or in broiler
until blackened on all sides. Wrap in paper
bag and let stand 10 minutes. Peel and seed.
Cut pepper into pieces. *(Soup and pepper can
be made 2 days ahead. Cover separately; chill.)*

Rewarm soup over medium heat. Season with
salt and pepper. Ladle into bowls. Top with
bell pepper and chives.

BEEF TENDERLOIN WITH MUSHROOM, ONION AND RED WINE SAUCE

*Here's a rich, intensely flavored main course
(below) that is a perfect special-occasion dish.
Uncork a favorite Cabernet Sauvignon to go
with it.* 10 SERVINGS

2 750-ml bottles dry red wine
   (such as Cabernet Sauvignon)
1 750-ml bottle tawny Port
4 cups canned beef broth

6 tablespoons (¾ stick) butter
1½ pounds onions, chopped
2 tablespoons chopped fresh thyme or
   2 teaspoons dried
2 pounds assorted mushrooms (such as
   stemmed shiitake and crimini), thickly sliced
2 tablespoons all purpose flour

2 2- to 2¼-pound well-trimmed beef
   tenderloins (from center or thick end)
2 tablespoons olive oil

Boil wine, Port and broth in heavy large pot
until reduced to 6 cups, about 40 minutes.
(Can be made 3 days ahead. Cover; chill.)

Meanwhile, melt 4 tablespoons butter in heavy large skillet over medium-high heat. Add onions and sauté until tender, about 15 minutes. Mix in thyme and sauté until onions are deep brown, about 10 minutes longer. Transfer onions to bowl. Melt 2 tablespoons butter in same skillet. Add mushrooms and sauté until tender, about 15 minutes. Return onions to skillet. Add flour and stir 3 minutes. Stir mushroom mixture into wine mixture. Simmer sauce over medium heat until thickened and reduced to 6 cups, stirring occasionally, about 1 hour. Season to taste with salt and pepper. *(Can be prepared 1 day ahead. Cover sauce and refrigerate.)*

Preheat oven to 400°F. Rub tenderloins with olive oil. Season with salt and pepper. Place in roasting pan. Roast until thermometer inserted into thickest part of meat registers 125°F, about 40 minutes for rare. Remove from oven and let stand 10 minutes.

Rewarm sauce over low heat; mix in any juices from roasting pan. Slice tenderloins crosswise into ½-inch-thick slices. Overlap beef slices on platter. Spoon some sauce over. Serve, passing remaining sauce separately.

GARLIC-LAYERED POTATOES

A lovely partner for the beef. Use a processor fitted with a four-millimeter slicing disk to make cutting the potatoes into thin rounds easy. 10 SERVINGS

1   large head garlic, separated
     into cloves, unpeeled
2   tablespoons olive oil

4   pounds russet potatoes (about 6 large),
     peeled, thinly sliced
1   tablespoon chopped fresh thyme or
     1 teaspoon dried
¼   teaspoon ground nutmeg
2½   cups canned low-salt chicken broth
1½   cups whipping cream

Additional chopped fresh thyme

Preheat oven to 375°F. Place garlic in small baking dish; drizzle oil over. Bake until garlic is tender and brown in spots, about 45 minutes. Cool briefly. Transfer garlic to work surface; reserve oil in dish. Peel garlic; chop coarsely. Increase oven temperature to 400°F.

Brush 13 x 9 x 2-inch glass baking dish generously with reserved garlic oil. Layer potatoes in prepared dish, sprinkling each layer with chopped garlic, thyme, nutmeg, salt and pepper. Overlap slices for top layer in decorative pattern, if desired. Bring broth and cream to boil in heavy medium saucepan. Pour broth mixture over potatoes. Cover dish with foil.

Bake potatoes 45 minutes. *(Can be made 1 day ahead. Cool potatoes. Cover with plastic wrap and refrigerate.)* Uncover and bake until potatoes are tender and brown on top and liquids thicken, about 45 minutes longer. Let stand 10 minutes. Sprinkle additional thyme over potatoes and serve.

GREEN BEANS WITH SHALLOTS, ROSEMARY AND HAZELNUTS

Toast the hazelnuts up to three days ahead and store in an airtight container. Cook the beans (below) briefly ahead of time (up to the day before), then sauté just before serving. 10 SERVINGS

2 pounds green beans, trimmed

¼ cup (½ stick) butter
⅔ cup chopped shallots (about 3 large)
1 teaspoon chopped fresh rosemary or
 1 teaspoon dried
½ cup hazelnuts, toasted, husked, chopped

Cook green beans in large pot of boiling salted water until crisp-tender, about 5 minutes. Drain. Rinse green beans with cold water; drain well. Pat dry with paper towels. *(Can be prepared 1 day ahead. Cover and refrigerate.)*

Melt butter in heavy large skillet over medium-high heat. Add shallots and rosemary and sauté until shallots are tender, about 5 minutes. Add green beans and toss until heated through, about 5 minutes. Season to taste with salt and pepper. Add chopped hazelnuts and toss. Transfer green beans to bowl; serve.

CHOCOLATE ANNIVERSARY CAKE

Baked in a heart-shaped pan, this dense, flourless chocolate cake (opposite)—enhanced with a white chocolate sauce and a red wine syrup—is perfect for a big anniversary party. The cake looks romantic when it is dusted with powdered sugar over leaf stencils to create a pretty design. Or you can decorate with small rosebuds. 10 SERVINGS

SAUCE

½ cup whipping cream
2 tablespoons water
8 ounces good-quality white chocolate
 (such as Lindt or Baker's), chopped

SYRUP

⅔ cup dry red wine
⅔ cup sugar

CAKE

1 10-inch cardboard round

8 ounces semisweet chocolate, chopped
½ cup (1 stick) unsalted butter,
 room temperature
½ cup sugar
5 large eggs, separated
⅓ cup finely ground walnuts
2 tablespoons dry red wine
¼ teaspoon cream of tartar

Powdered sugar

FOR SAUCE: Combine cream and 2 tablespoons water in small saucepan and bring to simmer. Remove from heat. Add chopped white chocolate and stir until melted and smooth.

FOR SYRUP: Stir wine and sugar in heavy medium saucepan over low heat until sugar dissolves. Increase heat and boil until liquid is syrupy and reduced to ⅔ cup, about 4 minutes. *(Sauce and syrup can be made 3 days ahead. Cover and chill separately. Rewarm sauce over very low heat before serving.)*

FOR CAKE: Preheat oven to 325°F. Cut cardboard into heart shape slightly smaller than 8-inch bottomless heart-shaped pan with 2-inch-high sides.* Set cardboard heart aside. Place sheet of heavy-duty foil on heavy baking sheet. Set heart-shaped pan on foil. Wrap foil around outside of pan, pressing so that foil adheres to sides. Butter foil base and insides of pan. (If heart-shaped pan is unavailable, use 8-inch-diameter springform pan. Line bottom of pan with aluminum foil; butter foil and sides of pan.)

Stir 8 ounces chocolate in top of double boiler set over simmering water until melted. Cool chocolate until lukewarm, stirring occasionally. Using electric mixer, beat unsalted butter and ¼ cup sugar in large bowl until light and fluffy. Add egg yolks 1 at a time, beating well after each addition. Add ground walnuts and red wine. Mix in melted chocolate. Using clean beaters, beat egg whites and cream of tartar in another large bowl until foamy. Gradually add ¼ cup sugar and beat until thick and glossy. Fold ⅓ of whites into chocolate mixture to lighten, then fold in remaining whites. Pour into prepared pan (batter will reach top of pan). Smooth top.

Bake cake until top is puffed and cracked and tester inserted into center comes out with a few moist crumbs still attached, about 40 minutes. Transfer baking sheet with cake to rack and cool in pan 40 minutes (cake may fall in center). Press down cake edge to even top. Cool cake completely.

Using small sharp knife, cut around pan sides. Fold down foil on sides of pan. Lift pan from cake. Place cardboard heart atop cake. Invert cake onto cardboard; peel off foil.

Place cake on platter. Sift powdered sugar over cake. *(Can be made 1 day ahead. Cover with plastic wrap. Let stand at room temperature.)*

To serve, place cake slice on each plate. Spoon 2 tablespoons white chocolate sauce alongside. Drizzle syrup over sauce; serve.

Available at most cookware stores.

These recipes expand or change the menu to suit your individual needs.

GORGONZOLA AND CAMEMBERT FONDUE WITH VEGETABLES

Not just fondue, this rich and creamy version is made with two different cheeses and served with steamed vegetables and chunks of bread. Have it instead of the soup, if you like. 10 SERVINGS

18	small red-skinned potatoes, rinsed, halved
3	large carrots, peeled, cut lengthwise into quarters, then into 1½-inch pieces
18	small brussels sprouts
1	small cauliflower, separated into florets
2	tablespoons all purpose flour
1	pound chilled Camembert cheese
12	ounces chilled Gorgonzola cheese
1¾	cups dry white wine
2	garlic cloves, minced
1	1½-pound crusty bread loaf, cubed

Steam vegetables until tender, about 12 minutes for potatoes, 10 minutes for carrots and brussels sprouts and 8 minutes for cauliflower. Arrange vegetables on platter. Tent with foil to keep warm.

Meanwhile, place flour in large bowl. Cut rind from Camembert cheese. Cut cheese into cubes; drop into flour. Toss to coat. Crumble Gorgonzola cheese into same bowl; toss to coat. Combine wine and garlic in heavy medium saucepan. Simmer over medium heat 2 minutes. Reduce heat to medium-low. Add cheese by handfuls, stirring until melted after each addition. Stir until smooth. Season with salt and pepper. Transfer to fondue pot. Set pot over candle or canned heat.

Pile bread into basket. Serve fondue with bread and steamed vegetables.

VEAL WITH PROSCIUTTO AND SAGE

For a special-occasion dish that's better suited to warm weather than the hearty tenderloin, try this flavorful veal sauté. Be sure to have the butcher bone the veal chops for you. 10 SERVINGS

2	tablespoons butter
½	cup chopped shallots
24	fresh sage leaves or 2 teaspoons dried
4	teaspoons chopped fresh thyme or 2 teaspoons dried
2	bay leaves
2	cups dry white wine
2	cups beef stock or canned broth
2	cups chicken stock or canned low-salt broth
1	cup whipping cream
20	4-ounce boneless veal rib chops All purpose flour
2	tablespoons (or more) olive oil
20	paper-thin prosciutto slices

Melt butter in heavy large saucepan over medium heat. Add shallots, sage, thyme and bay leaves and sauté 3 minutes. Add wine and both stocks and boil until reduced to 1¼ cups, about 30 minutes. Add cream; boil until reduced to sauce consistency, about 10 minutes. Season with salt and pepper. *(Can be prepared 4 hours ahead. Cover and refrigerate.)*

Pound each veal chop between sheets of waxed paper to ½-inch thickness. Sprinkle veal with salt and pepper. Dredge veal in flour; shake off excess. Heat 2 tablespoons olive oil in heavy large nonstick skillet over medium-high heat. Working in batches and adding more oil as necessary for each batch, add veal to skillet and sauté until cooked through, about 3 minutes per side.

Wrap 1 prosciutto slice around each piece of veal. Arrange 2 veal pieces on each plate. Strain sauce, if desired. Bring sauce to simmer. Pour around veal and serve immediately.

HEART-SHAPED GENOISE WITH CHAMPAGNE-RASPBERRY MOUSSE

In keeping with the anniversary theme here, both this cake and the chocolate one in the main menu are heart-shaped. But where the chocolate one is dense and quite sinful, this one is light and lovely. To each his own. 10 SERVINGS

GENOISE

1   cup cake flour
¼   teaspoon salt
6   tablespoons (¾ stick) unsalted butter, melted, lukewarm
1½ teaspoons vanilla extract

6   large eggs
¾   cup sugar

SOAKING SYRUP

½   cup sugar
½   cup water
2   tablespoons fresh lemon juice

CHAMPAGNE-RASPBERRY MOUSSE

1   6-ounce basket raspberries
1   cup dry Champagne
2   teaspoons unflavored gelatin

8   tablespoons sugar
3   large egg yolks
1   teaspoon fresh lemon juice
2   ounces good-quality white chocolate (such as Lindt or Baker's), chopped

1   cup chilled whipping cream

ASSEMBLY

½   cup raspberry jam

2   6-ounce baskets raspberries
1¼ cups chilled whipping cream
2   tablespoons sugar

FOR GENOISE: Preheat oven to 350°F. Wrap outside of 9½-inch-wide by 3-inch-high heart-shaped springform pan* with foil. Butter and flour pan. Mix flour and salt in bowl. Stir butter and vanilla in a glass measuring cup.

Whisk eggs and sugar in large stainless steel bowl to blend. Set bowl over saucepan of simmering water (do not allow bowl to touch water). Whisk constantly until mixture is very warm to touch, about 3 minutes. Remove from over water. Using electric mixer, beat mixture at high speed until it triples in volume and is thick enough to fall in heavy ribbon when beaters are lifted, about 10 minutes. Sift flour over batter in 4 additions, gently folding just to combine after each addition. Drizzle butter mixture over while gently folding to combine (do not overfold or batter will deflate). Transfer batter to prepared pan.

Bake genoise until golden and tester inserted into center comes out clean, about 25 minutes. Cool in pan on rack; cake will fall slightly. *(Can be made 1 day ahead. Cover tightly; store at room temperature.)*

FOR SOAKING SYRUP: Stir sugar and water in heavy small saucepan over low heat until sugar dissolves. Increase heat and bring to a boil. Remove from heat; mix in lemon juice. Cool. *(Can be prepared 1 day ahead. Cover and let stand at room temperature.)*

FOR MOUSSE: Using rubber spatula, push ½ cup raspberries through sieve into small bowl. Set berry puree aside; discard seeds. Pour ¼ cup Champagne into another small bowl. Sprinkle gelatin over Champagne; let stand until gelatin softens, about 10 minutes.

Whisk 6 tablespoons sugar, yolks, lemon juice and ¼ cup Champagne in medium-size stainless steel bowl to blend. Set bowl over saucepan of simmering water (do not allow bowl to touch water). Whisk constantly until mixture is thick and fluffy and candy thermometer registers 160°F, about 2 minutes. Remove bowl from over water. Add chocolate and gelatin mixture. Set bowl over simmering water again; whisk gently until chocolate melts and gelatin dissolves. Remove bowl from over water. Using rubber spatula, gradually fold in ½ cup Champagne. Chill mousse base until cold and beginning to thicken but not set, about 20 minutes.

Beat cream with 2 tablespoons sugar in medium bowl to stiff peaks. Fold in raspberry puree. Fold raspberry cream into mousse base. Fold in remaining berries. Let stand at room temperature while beginning cake assembly or up to 30 minutes.

TO ASSEMBLE: Cut around pan sides to loosen cake. Release pan sides. Using large metal spatula, loosen cake from pan bottom. Transfer cake to work surface. Clean pan.

Cut cake in half crosswise, making 2 equal layers. Return bottom layer, cut side up, to cake pan bottom. Brush layer with 5 tablespoons soaking syrup; then spread with ¼ cup jam. Reattach sides of pan. Spoon mousse in

even layer over jam. Place second cake layer, cut side down, on mousse. Brush top of cake with 5 tablespoons syrup; then spread with ¼ cup jam. Cover pan; chill until mousse sets, about 4 hours or up to 1 day.

Using sharp knife, cut around pan sides to loosen cake. Release pan sides. Run icing spatula around cake to remove excess mousse (mousse should be flush with sides of cake). Slide large metal spatula under cake on all sides to loosen from pan bottom. Using tart pan bottom as aid, transfer cake to platter.

Arrange raspberries on top of cake, leaving ¾-inch border at edge. Beat cream with sugar in large bowl until stiff peaks form. Spread about ⅔ of cream around sides of cake. Transfer remaining cream to pastry bag fitted with medium star tip. Pipe border around edge of cake. Cover cake with cake dome; refrigerate up to 8 hours.

Available at most cookware stores.

1

The warm egg mixture needs to be beaten on
high speed until it triples in volume and falls off the
beaters in a thick, heavy ribbon.

2

For the mousse, chill the white chocolate mixture
until it is thickened but not set, then fold in the
raspberry-whipped cream mixture.

3

A long, thin serrated or plain-edged knife
can be used to cut the cake horizontally in half;
a gentle sawing motion will make a clean cut.

4

To hold the components in place, the dessert is assembled
in the cake pan. Brush the bottom cake layer with syrup
and spread with jam; then spoon the mousse over the jam
(the mousse should be at room temperature).

5

After the cake is chilled for a few hours to set the mousse,
the dessert can be removed from the pan. Use a large
icing spatula to scrape away any excess mousse so that the
filling is even with the sides of the cake.

6

The top of the cake is decorated with fresh raspberries,
and the sides are frosted with whipped cream. Use a pastry
bag fitted with a star tip to pipe a simple whipped cream
border around the top edge.

Potluck Housewarming Party

menu for eight

- Anchovy-Bell Pepper Spread
- Marinated Mushrooms
- Three-Cheese Lasagna with Italian Sausage
- Mixed Greens Salad with Creamy Parmesan-Garlic Dressing
- Carrot Salad with Green Onions
- Garlic Bread
- Red Wine, Beer, Bottled Water
- Mocha Ice Cream Torte

menu options

- Clam Dip Loaf
- Baked Ziti with Four Cheeses
- Old-fashioned Lime Pie
- Apricot Bar Cookies

Make the house a home

WHEN THE DOORBELL ECHOES IN A HALF-FURNISHED new home, it's hard to say just which is more welcome—the sound of friendly voices or the smell of home-cooked food. There's nothing like a table spread with a selection of great-looking dishes, and a crowd of happy friends around it, to make a house seem much more of a home.

Potluck food, by definition, needs to be do-ahead, portable, hearty and, of course, delicious. The menu itself should be flexible, easily accommodating an extra "specialty" or two. But for everyone on the guest list who "knows just what to bring," there are three others who would happily welcome a suggestion from you—something easy, something quick to cook, something familiar but tasty. That's where this menu comes in, a tried-and-true mix of dishes that everyone at the party will love and no one (not even the novice) will find too hard to make.

There are two appetizers to serve with drinks here, a savory bell pepper and anchovy spread to have with sliced French bread and cucumber rounds, and garlicky marinated mushrooms. Both dishes can be prepared ahead, making them ideal to parcel out to a couple of guests. The same is true of both salads, one a simple mix of greens, the other a grated carrot salad that gets served in cabbage leaves. Assign these recipes, too, as well as the garlic bread, leaving only the lasagna and the dessert for you to make.

The three-cheese, beef and sausage lasagna is the star of this menu, a big, beautiful main course that you make the day before, then simply bake before serving. Even easier: Substitute the baked ziti in the Options section, a child-pleasing variation on macaroni and cheese that you can prepare two weeks ahead and freeze. You can also pull dessert out of your freezer, a coffee ice cream torte.

UP TO 3 WEEKS AHEAD:

• Invite guests and make assignments.

2 TO 3 DAYS AHEAD:

• Make ice cream torte; freeze.
• Prepare salad dressing; chill.
• Make marinated mushrooms; chill.

1 DAY AHEAD:

• Chill beer and bottled water.
• Make anchovy-bell pepper spread; chill.
• Assemble lasagna; chill.

DAY OF:

• Set up buffet.
• Set up coffeemaker.
• Prepare carrot salad (up to 8 hours ahead); chill.
• Prepare garlic bread (up to 6 hours ahead); keep at room temperature.
• Put lasagna in oven 1½ hours before guests arrive.
• Slice baguette and cucumber for anchovy-bell pepper spread (up to 1 hour ahead).

A potluck is a wonderful way to gather friends together when you don't have the time or energy to cook for a crowd yourself. And while it's ideal for "warming up" a new house, a potluck is also just the thing for a get-together of team families at the end of a sports season; a group of school volunteers looking to eat and meet at the same time; colleagues hoping to finish an important project together, after hours and over dinner.

And once you've become good at organizing potlucks, consider doing just that for a friend or a family member who recently moved. It could be the best gift they get: A group of smiling faces at their door, all carrying fragrant dishes of good things to eat. Just don't forget to bring the serving bowls and implements yourself, so that no one has to unpack a moving box before everyone can sit down and eat.

ANCHOVY-BELL PEPPER SPREAD

This is a good recipe (below) to "assign" to a party guest since it can be prepared quickly, easily and ahead of time. MAKES ABOUT 1⅔ CUPS

2   red bell peppers

1   2-ounce can anchovies with oil
½   cup coarsely chopped onion
2   tablespoons fresh parsley leaves
2   tablespoons red wine vinegar

Baguette slices
Cucumber rounds

Char peppers over gas flame or in broiler until blackened on all sides. Wrap in paper bag; let stand 10 minutes. Peel and seed peppers.

Coarsely chop roasted peppers and anchovies with oil in processor. Add onion, parsley and vinegar and process until onion is finely chopped. Transfer mixture to bowl. Season to taste with salt and pepper. Cover and refrigerate at least 2 hours to allow flavors to blend. *(Spread can be made 1 day ahead. Keep chilled.)*

Serve with baguette slices and cucumber.

MARINATED MUSHROOMS

Another good recipe (below) to parcel out to a volunteer cook. It can be prepared up to two days ahead and refrigerated. 8 SERVINGS

½   cup olive oil
4   large garlic cloves, halved lengthwise
2   pounds small mushrooms, stems trimmed
½   cup chopped fresh Italian parsley
1½   cups dry white wine
¼   cup fresh lemon juice
2   tablespoons plus 2 teaspoons
    red wine vinegar
6   whole cloves
2   bay leaves

Heat oil in heavy large skillet over medium-low heat. Add garlic; sauté until golden, about 6 minutes. Discard garlic. Increase heat to medium-high. Add mushrooms and parsley; sauté until mushrooms are golden, about 8 minutes. Reduce heat to medium-low. Stir in remaining ingredients. Cover and simmer 5 minutes. Season with salt and pepper. Cool. Transfer to container; cover and chill until cold. *(Can be made 2 days ahead. Keep chilled.)* Drain mushrooms before serving.

THREE-CHEESE LASAGNA WITH ITALIAN SAUSAGE

Ricotta, Parmesan and mozzarella flavor this rich and tasty lasagna, which can be made the day before the party. Offer a choice of red wine, beer and bottled water to drink. 8 SERVINGS

SAUCE

1 tablespoon olive oil
1 cup chopped onion
¾ cup finely chopped peeled carrots
2 tablespoons minced garlic
8 ounces lean ground beef
6 ounces spicy Italian sausages,
 casings removed
1 28-ounce can crushed tomatoes with
 added puree
¼ cup tomato paste
¼ cup chopped fresh basil
1 tablespoon golden brown sugar
1 tablespoon dried oregano
1 bay leaf
½ teaspoon dried crushed red pepper

LASAGNA

15 lasagna noodles (about 12 ounces)

2 15-ounce containers part-skim ricotta cheese
1 cup grated Parmesan cheese
 (about 3 ounces)
1 10-ounce package frozen chopped spinach,
 thawed, drained, squeezed dry
2 large eggs

4¾ cups grated mozzarella cheese
 (about 1¼ pounds)

FOR SAUCE: Heat oil in heavy large saucepan over medium heat. Add onion, carrots and garlic; sauté until tender, about 12 minutes. Add beef and sausages to pan; sauté until cooked through, breaking up meat with back of spoon, about 5 minutes. Add next 7 ingredients. Cover; simmer until flavors blend and sauce measures 5 cups, stirring occasionally, about 15 minutes. Discard bay leaf. Cool.

FOR LASAGNA: Preheat oven to 350°F. Cook noodles in large pot of boiling salted water until almost tender but still firm to bite, 7 minutes. Drain; cover with cold water.

Combine ricotta and ¾ cup Parmesan cheese in medium bowl. Mix in spinach. Season to taste with salt and pepper. Mix in eggs.

Drain pasta and pat dry. Spread ½ cup sauce over bottom of 13 x 9-inch glass baking dish. Place 5 noodles over sauce, overlapping to fit. Spread half of ricotta-spinach mixture evenly over noodles. Sprinkle 2 cups grated mozzarella evenly over ricotta-spinach mixture. Spoon 1½ cups sauce over mozzarella, spreading with spatula to cover (sauce will be thick). Repeat layering with 5 noodles, remaining ricotta-spinach mixture, 2 cups mozzarella and 1½ cups sauce. Arrange remaining 5 noodles over sauce. Spread remaining sauce over noodles. Sprinkle remaining ¾ cup mozzarella and ¼ cup Parmesan evenly over lasagna. *(Can be prepared up to 1 day ahead. Cover tightly with plastic wrap; chill.)* Cover baking dish with aluminum foil. Bake lasagna 40 minutes; uncover and continue baking until hot and bubbly, about 40 minutes. Let lasagna stand 15 minutes before serving.

MIXED GREENS SALAD WITH CREAMY PARMESAN-GARLIC DRESSING

This refreshing salad mixes four kinds of greens. Serve the dressing on the side to keep the salad at its best throughout the evening. 8 SERVINGS

2 heads romaine lettuce,
   torn into bite-size pieces
2 heads Boston or Bibb lettuce,
   torn into bite-size pieces
1 large bunch arugula
1 large bunch watercress
1 medium-size red onion, sliced into rings
   Creamy Parmesan-Garlic Dressing
   (see recipe below)
   Freshly grated Parmesan cheese

Combine romaine, Boston lettuce, arugula and watercress in large bowl. Top with onion rings. Serve with Creamy Parmesan-Garlic Dressing and Parmesan.

CREAMY PARMESAN-GARLIC DRESSING

MAKES ABOUT 2½ CUPS

⅓ cup fresh lemon juice, strained
¼ cup freshly grated Parmesan cheese
1 cup mayonnaise
4 anchovy fillets, chopped
1 tablespoon Worcestershire sauce
1 medium garlic clove
1 teaspoon pepper
½ teaspoon salt
1 cup olive oil

Combine first 8 ingredients in processor and blend until smooth, about 1 minute. With machine running, add oil through feed tube in slow steady stream and blend until thick. Season to taste with salt and pepper. *(Can be prepared 3 days ahead. Cover; chill. Let dressing stand 30 minutes before using.)*

CARROT SALAD WITH GREEN ONIONS

Another salad (opposite) to round out the selection. Make the grated carrot mixture ahead of time and spoon it into cabbage leaves. 8 SERVINGS

2 pounds carrots, peeled,
   coarsely grated (about 7 cups)
6 green onions, chopped
3 tablespoons minced fresh parsley

3 tablespoons white wine vinegar
1 tablespoon grated lemon peel
2 teaspoons Dijon mustard
½ cup olive oil

8 whole red cabbage leaves

Mix carrots, green onions and parsley in large bowl to blend.

Whisk vinegar, lemon peel and mustard in small bowl to blend. Gradually whisk in oil. Season to taste with salt and pepper. Pour dressing over carrot mixture. Toss to coat evenly. Cover and refrigerate at least 2 hours. *(Can be prepared 8 hours ahead. Keep chilled. Let stand 1 hour at room temperature before serving.)*

Spoon carrot salad into cabbage leaves; arrange on platter and serve.

GARLIC BREAD

A classic companion to lasagna, and an easy recipe for a friend to make. 8 SERVINGS

1 cup (2 sticks) butter, melted
8 garlic cloves, minced
2 1-pound unsliced French-bread baguettes, halved lengthwise
½ cup grated Parmesan cheese
Paprika

Preheat broiler. Combine butter and garlic. Place bread on 2 baking sheets. Brush bread halves with butter mixture. Sprinkle each bread half with 2 tablespoons Parmesan. Season with paprika and pepper. *(Can be prepared 6 hours ahead. Wrap in plastic and keep at room temperature.)* Broil until golden brown. Cut into 1-inch-wide slices and serve.

MOCHA ICE CREAM TORTE

A simple but sumptuous dessert. 8 SERVINGS

CRUST

1½ cups chocolate cookie crumbs (about 6½ ounces)
6 tablespoons (¾ stick) unsalted butter, melted
3 tablespoons sugar
2 tablespoons coffee-flavored liqueur (such as Kahlúa)

FILLING

1 quart coffee ice cream, slightly softened
4 tablespoons Irish whiskey

½ cup chilled whipping cream
1 teaspoon instant coffee powder or espresso powder
1 tablespoon powdered sugar
Chocolate shavings

FOR CRUST: Preheat oven to 350°F. Mix all ingredients in medium bowl. Press crust mixture onto bottom (not sides) of 9-inch-diameter springform pan with 2¾-inch-high sides. Bake crust until firm to touch, 8 minutes. Transfer pan to rack; cool crust completely.

FOR FILLING: Mix ice cream and 2 tablespoons whiskey in large bowl to blend. Spoon over crust; smooth top. Freeze until firm, 1 hour.

Mix cream and coffee powder in medium bowl until coffee powder dissolves. Add sugar and 2 tablespoons whiskey; beat until stiff peaks form. Spoon into pastry bag fitted with medium star tip. Pipe rosettes around edge of torte. Sprinkle torte with chocolate shavings. Freeze until firm, about 4 hours. *(Can be prepared 3 days ahead. Cover and keep frozen.)*

Using small knife, cut around sides of pan to loosen torte. Remove pan sides. Let torte stand at room temperature 5 minutes. Cut into wedges and serve.

These recipes expand or change the menu to suit your individual needs.

CLAM DIP LOAF

In place of the bell pepper spread, serve this appealing appetizer with cut-up fresh vegetables and breadsticks. 8 SERVINGS

1   1½-pound unsliced round
     sheepherder's bread
2   8-ounce packages cream cheese,
     room temperature
1   cup mayonnaise
1   tablespoon prepared white horseradish
3   6½-ounce cans minced clams, drained
4   large green onions, chopped

Preheat oven to 350°F. Slice top 2 inches off bread and reserve for lid. Cut out insides of bread, leaving 1-inch-thick shell. (Reserve cut-out bread for another use.) Using electric mixer, beat cream cheese, mayonnaise and horseradish in large bowl until blended. Mix in clams and green onions. Season with salt and pepper. (*Bread and filling can be prepared 8 hours ahead. Wrap bread in foil and store at room temperature. Cover filling and refrigerate.*) Spoon filling into bread. Place lid on bread. Wrap bread in 2 layers of heavy-duty foil; place on heavy large baking sheet.

Bake until filling is very hot and bread is crusty, about 1½ hours. Unwrap bread. Place loaf on large platter. Remove lid; lean lid against bread at angle.

BAKED ZITI WITH FOUR CHEESES

A simpler, meatless alternative to the lasagna. Kids, especially, like this dish. 8 SERVINGS

4   cups half and half
1   teaspoon dried basil
½   teaspoon dried crushed red pepper
     (optional)

2½   cups grated provolone cheese
2½   cups grated mozzarella cheese
2½   cups grated Swiss cheese
¼   cup grated Parmesan cheese
4   large egg yolks, beaten to blend
1   pound ziti or other tubular pasta,
      freshly cooked

Preheat oven to 375°F. Butter two 2-quart ovenproof casseroles. Bring half and half, basil and crushed red pepper to simmer in heavy large saucepan over medium-high heat. Add cheeses 1 handful at a time, stirring after each addition until cheeses are melted and smooth. Remove from heat and stir in egg yolks. Season with salt and pepper. Add ziti and mix gently. Spoon into prepared dishes. Bake in oven until heated through, about 10 minutes. Sprinkle with additional pepper. (*Can be prepared ahead. Cover with foil and keep at room temperature 4 hours or freeze up to 2 weeks. Reheat covered in 350°F oven 20 minutes, or if frozen, thaw overnight in refrigerator; reheat covered in 350°F oven 40 minutes.*)

OLD-FASHIONED LIME PIE

Attractive and refreshing, this simple pie bakes in about half an hour and can be prepared the day before. 8 SERVINGS

36   vanilla wafer cookies (about 4¾ ounces)
¼   cup (½ stick) unsalted butter, melted
½   teaspoon plus 1 tablespoon grated lime peel

1   14-ounce can sweetened condensed milk
¾   cup fresh lime juice
2   large eggs

Lime slices

Preheat oven to 350°F. Finely grind vanilla wafers in processor. Add melted butter and ½ teaspoon grated lime peel; process until moist crumbs form. Transfer to 9-inch-diameter glass pie dish. Using plastic wrap as aid, press crumbs onto bottom and up sides of dish (crust will be thin). Bake just until crust turns golden on edges, 10 minutes. Remove from oven. Maintain oven temperature.

Meanwhile, whisk condensed milk, lime juice and 1 tablespoon lime peel in medium bowl to blend. Whisk in eggs.

Pour filling into warm crust. Bake until filling is set, about 20 minutes. Cool. Refrigerate until chilled, about 3 hours. *(Can be prepared 1 day ahead. Cover and keep refrigerated.)* Garnish with lime slices. Cut into wedges; serve.

APRICOT BAR COOKIES

A shortbread crust, apricot filling and a nut topping add up to a terrific cookie. MAKES 24

1	cup hazelnuts, toasted, husked
1½	cups powdered sugar
¼	teaspoon ground cinnamon
1	cup all purpose flour
½	cup (1 stick) unsalted butter, room temperature
2	large eggs, separated
1	teaspoon vanilla extract
¼	teaspoon salt
¾	cup apricot preserves

Preheat oven to 350°F. Butter 13 x 9 x 2-inch baking pan. Blend nuts, 1 cup sugar and cinnamon in processor until nuts are finely ground.

Combine ½ cup sugar, flour, butter, egg yolks, vanilla and salt in processor; blend just until combined. Spread dough over bottom of prepared pan. Bake until golden, about 15 minutes. Cool 10 minutes. Maintain oven temperature.

Spread preserves over crust. Beat whites in medium bowl until stiff but not dry. Fold in nut mixture. Spread nut meringue over preserves layer. Bake until meringue is firm to touch, about 25 minutes. Cool completely. Cut into squares. *(Can be prepared 1 day ahead. Cover and keep at room temperature.)*

Taking the Luck out of Potluck

There's no need to worry about too many cooks spoiling anyone's broth if you coordinate your party's menu and the preparations. Here are some tips.

Prepare the main course yourself, and ask guests to bring complementary dishes.

When the guests call to R.S.V.P., ask if they'd like to bring a particular kind of dish: an appetizer, a salad, a dessert? Then try to determine whether they have a recipe that would work within the menu or they would like you to provide one.

Send out simple, quick-cooking recipes, unless someone is ambitious and requests a showstopping dessert.

Talk to each guest about what serving dishes and utensils they will need you to provide, and any finishing ingredients—butter, cream, Parmesan cheese, lemon wedges, herbs or spices—they would like you to have on hand.

Set the party time roughly an hour or so earlier than usual to allow for all of the pre-dinner preparations.

Have plenty of "munchies" on hand—nuts, olives, chips, salsa and dips, cheese and crackers for cooks to nibble while they finish up in the kitchen.

Set the table in advance, and as elegantly as you wish. Beautiful flowers, good wine and candlelight will let everyone know you cherish their friendship and help.

To take the predictability out of a potluck, add a surprise element: a special dish no one else knew you were making; an unforgettable bottle of wine; a game with prizes for the winners.

Gala Buffet

menu for fifty

- CARAWAY CHEESE STRAWS

- SMOKED CHICKEN AND GORGONZOLA SALAD
  IN ENDIVE SPEARS

- CHAMPAGNE

- ICED SPICED LEMONADE

- MEDITERRANEAN FRITTATAS

- LEG OF LAMB WITH MINT PESTO

- CORN SALAD WITH
  CILANTRO-JALAPEÑO DRESSING

- GREEN VEGETABLE SALAD WITH
  ORANGE-HAZELNUT DRESSING

- ZINFANDEL AND SAUVIGNON BLANC

- CHEESECAKES WITH FRESH BERRY TOPPING

- TOASTED COCONUT BARS

- CHOCOLATE-RASPBERRY BARS

menu options

- SUN-DRIED TOMATO AND
  HERB-CHEESE STRUDELS

- GRILLED CHICKEN WITH OLIVE PUREE

- DOUBLE-LEMON WEDDING CAKE

You *can* do it

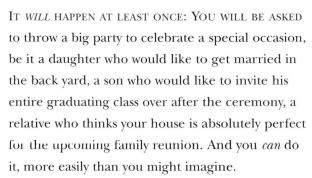

IT *WILL* HAPPEN AT LEAST ONCE: YOU WILL BE ASKED to throw a big party to celebrate a special occasion, be it a daughter who would like to get married in the back yard, a son who would like to invite his entire graduating class over after the ceremony, a relative who thinks your house is absolutely perfect for the upcoming family reunion. And you *can* do it, more easily than you might imagine.

There are three keys to cooking for a big buffet: scheduling over a comfortable period of time, simple recipes, and foods that hold well at room temperature. This menu meets these conditions with quick marriages of convenience: the cheese straws are made from purchased puff pastry; the chicken salad in endive spears uses deli smoked chicken; the frittatas taste best at room temperature; the beautiful leg of lamb is served with a bright green and blender-quick mint pesto. The

gorgeous colors of the corn salad and the green vegetable salad (with sugar snap peas, green beans, broccoli and asparagus giving the recipe its name) belie the sturdiness of these dishes, which will keep overnight. The lemon cheesecakes are crustless; and both the coconut bars and the chocolate raspberry bars can be made ahead.

This food is easily dressed up for a wedding, perhaps in the garden, complete with lace-covered tables, flowers, silver and china. For such an occasion, there is a showstopper of a wedding cake here, as flavorful as it is beautiful, along with step-by-step photographs to help guarantee you success with the end result.

But this menu can also go casual, for a back-yard gathering, a graduation, an open house. Change the setting, adding Mediterranean-inspired fabrics, chunky pottery, even paper plates and napkins. If

1 TO 2 MONTHS AHEAD:

- Send out invitations.
- Arrange for party rentals.

3 WEEKS AHEAD:

- Bake cheesecakes; freeze.

2 WEEKS AHEAD:

- Bake brownie for raspberry bars; freeze.

2 DAYS AHEAD:

- Make dressing for corn salad; chill.
- Thaw lemon cheesecakes in refrigerator.
- Make coconut bars.
- Chill Champagne and white wine.

1 DAY AHEAD:

- Make lemonade; chill.
- Make cheese straws; store at room temperature.
- Prepare chicken salad; chill.
- Roast lamb and prepare pesto; chill.
- Prepare corn salad; chill.
- Make green vegetable salad and dressing; chill.
- Make berry topping for cheesecakes; chill.
- Make topping for raspberry bars; chill.

DAY OF:

- Prepare vegetables and cheeses for frittatas (up to 8 hours ahead); chill.
- Toss chicken salad (up to 8 hours ahead); chill. Assemble in endive spears (up to 1 hour ahead).
- Cook frittatas (up to 2 hours ahead); serve at room temperature.
- Bring lamb and pesto to room temperature.
- Bring green salad to room temperature.

it's likely that your guests will be standing up to eat, eliminate the need for knives by tucking slices of the lamb into pita pockets or thin shepherd-bread wraps. And don't hesitate to substitute purchased items, such as store-bought breadsticks, a deli pasta salad or lentil salad, or bakery sweets, for any of the dishes here. If you'd rather serve chicken than lamb, in the Options section there are chicken breasts spread with olive paste, which are grilled and served either hot or at room temperature.

Depending on the formality of the occasion, you may or may not want to rent china, glasses, silver, linens and tables. In either case, do consider bringing in some extra hands, possibly a bartender to help with drinks and someone in the kitchen to help with the serving and cleaning up. And don't forget parking, especially if there aren't many spaces on your street. Maybe friendly neighbors would donate their driveways.

CARAWAY CHEESE STRAWS

Purchased puff pastry makes these hors d'oeuvres quick and easy to prepare. For added flair, twist the dough strips before baking. MAKES 80

2   17¼-ounce packages frozen puff pastry
    (4 sheets), thawed
2   eggs, beaten to blend (glaze)
1   cup (generous) freshly grated
    Parmesan cheese (about 4 ounces)
4   teaspoons caraway seeds
2   teaspoons pepper

Preheat oven to 400°F. Roll out each pastry sheet on lightly floured surface to 10-inch square. Brush each sheet with egg glaze. Sprinkle each with ¼ of cheese, caraway seeds and pepper. Cut each sheet into twenty ½-inch-wide strips. Transfer strips to heavy large cookie sheets, spacing strips evenly. Bake pastries until puffed and golden brown, about 15 minutes. Cool pastries on sheets on racks. *(Can be prepared 1 day ahead. Store in airtight container at room temperature.)*

SMOKED CHICKEN AND GORGONZOLA SALAD IN ENDIVE SPEARS

Elegant and easy "finger food" to serve with the lemonade and Champagne. MAKES ABOUT 50

2   ounces green beans (preferably
    haricots verts)
8   ounces smoked chicken or smoked turkey,
    cut into ¼-inch pieces
½   red bell pepper, cut into ¼-inch pieces
⅓   cup watercress leaves, chopped
1   large shallot or green onion, minced
1   tablespoon chopped fresh tarragon or
    1 teaspoon dried

¼   cup walnut oil or olive oil
2   tablespoons white wine vinegar
¾   cup crumbled Gorgonzola or other
    blue cheese (about 3 ounces)
3   tablespoons chopped toasted walnuts

4   Belgian endive heads, separated into spears
    Watercress leaves

Bring small saucepan of water to boil. Add green beans. Cook until just tender, about 4 minutes. Drain. Refresh with cold water and drain again. Thinly slice crosswise. Combine with chicken, red bell pepper, chopped watercress, shallot and tarragon in medium bowl. *(Can be made 1 day ahead. Cover; chill.)*

Place oil and vinegar in heavy small saucepan. Bring mixture just to simmer, swirling pan occasionally. Stir in Gorgonzola. Pour over salad mixture. Toss to coat. Stir in toasted walnuts. Season with salt and pepper. Cover; chill at least 30 minutes or up to 8 hours.

Form 2 teaspoons salad into ball. Press onto bottom portion of endive spear. Repeat with remaining salad and endive spears. Garnish each endive spear with watercress.

ICED SPICED LEMONADE

Honey and spices update a classic lemonade. Also have Champagne on hand. MAKES 64 CUPS

16 lemons
64 cups water (16 quarts)
80 whole cloves
 2 tablespoons cardamom pods
 4 cups honey

Ice cubes
Lemon slices

Cut lemons in half and juice; reserve shells. Bring water to boil in 2 large pots. Remove from heat. Add lemon juice and lemon shells, cloves and cardamom to water, dividing equally. Cover and let stand 20 minutes. Add honey to lemonade and stir to dissolve. Strain lemonade through sieve into pitchers. Chill until very cold, at least 3 hours. *(Can be prepared 1 day ahead; keep refrigerated.)*

Fill tall glasses with ice cubes. Pour spiced lemonade over. Garnish with lemon slices.

MEDITERRANEAN FRITTATAS

This recipe makes four frittatas, which are much like crustless quiches (below). They can be made ahead and served at room temperature. Offer your guests Zinfandel or Sauvignon Blanc. 50 SERVINGS

36 large eggs
16 ounces feta cheese, crumbled
1½ cups freshly grated Parmesan cheese
    (about 6 ounces)
1½ cups thinly sliced fresh basil leaves
 2 teaspoons salt
 1 teaspoon pepper

 1 cup olive oil
 2 small onions, finely chopped
 2 small eggplants, peeled, cut into ½-inch cubes
 2 red bell peppers, finely chopped
 2 yellow bell peppers, finely chopped
⅔ cup Kalamata olives,* pitted, chopped

Preheat oven to 400°F. Whisk eggs in 2 large bowls to blend. Mix in cheeses, basil, salt and pepper, dividing equally.

Heat ¼ cup oil in each of 2 heavy 10-inch nonstick ovenproof skillets over medium heat. Add ¼ of onion and ¼ of eggplant to each skillet and sauté until vegetables are soft and golden brown, about 15 minutes. Add ¼ of red and yellow bell peppers to each and cook until soft, stirring occasionally, about 5 minutes. Mix ¼ of olives into each skillet. Increase heat to high. Add ¼ of egg mixture to each skillet and cook until curds form but eggs are still very wet, stirring frequently, about 3 minutes. Place in oven. Cook until eggs are completely set, about 8 minutes. Run rubber spatula around skillet sides to loosen frittatas. Invert onto plates. Repeat with remaining oil, onion, eggplant, bell peppers, olives and eggs to make 2 more frittatas. Serve frittatas warm or at room temperature. *(Can be prepared 2 hours ahead.)*

Black, brine-cured olives, available at Greek and Italian markets and some supermarkets.

LEG OF LAMB WITH MINT PESTO

This do-ahead dish of roast lamb (below) served at room temperature with a mint-and-parsley pesto makes an impressive main course. 50 SERVINGS

LAMB

4 6-pound legs of lamb, boned, butterflied
16 tablespoons (about) vegetable oil

PESTO

4½ cups packed fresh mint leaves
2 cups packed fresh parsley leaves
1 cup walnuts
4 garlic cloves
3 cups olive oil
¾ cup fresh lime juice
10 teaspoons sugar
1 tablespoon salt

Additional olive oil (optional)

FOR LAMB: Preheat oven to 350°F. Cut ¼- to ½-inch slits in thick portions of legs of lamb. Cover with plastic wrap. Pound to uniform thickness. Pat lamb dry with paper towels. Cut each leg of lamb in half crosswise. Season lamb generously with salt and pepper. Heat 2 tablespoons vegetable oil in heavy large skillet over medium-high heat until very hot. Add 1 lamb piece and cook until brown on 1 side, about 2 minutes. Arrange lamb browned side up in heavy large roasting pan. Brown remaining lamb pieces in remaining vegetable oil in 7 more batches. Divide 4 lamb pieces between 2 large roasting pans. Set remaining 4 lamb pieces aside. Transfer lamb in roasting pans to oven; roast to desired doneness, about 15 minutes for medium-rare. Remove lamb from pans. Repeat with remaining lamb. Cool completely. Cover and refrigerate lamb until well chilled. *(Can be prepared 1 day ahead; keep chilled.)*

FOR PESTO: Combine half of mint leaves, parsley leaves, walnuts and garlic cloves in processor and blend to paste. Gradually add 1½ cups olive oil through feed tube and blend until smooth. Blend in half of fresh lime juice, sugar and salt. Transfer to large bowl. Repeat with remaining half of pesto ingredients. *(Can be prepared 1 day ahead. Pour ½-inch layer of olive oil over pesto, if desired. Cover; chill. Bring pesto to room temperature.)*

Cut lamb into ¼-inch-thick slices. Arrange on platter and serve with pesto.

CORN SALAD WITH CILANTRO-JALAPEÑO DRESSING

Make this colorful salad (opposite) the day before the big event and refrigerate. 50 SERVINGS

DRESSING

8 bunches fresh cilantro, stemmed
2⅔ cups vegetable oil
1⅓ cups white wine vinegar
6 tablespoons fresh lime juice
3 jalapeño chilies, stemmed, coarsely chopped
2 shallots, halved
2 teaspoons salt

SALAD

36 fresh ears corn, husked

1 cup corn oil
2 large onions, finely chopped
6 tablespoons finely chopped peeled fresh ginger
4 red bell peppers, cut into ¼-inch pieces
4 green bell peppers, cut into ¼-inch pieces

Fresh cilantro sprigs

FOR DRESSING: Working in 2 batches, combine all ingredients in blender and puree. Transfer to large bowl. Cover and refrigerate. *(Can be prepared 2 days ahead.)*

FOR SALAD: Working in batches, cook corn in large pot of boiling water until tender, 5 minutes. Drain; cool. Cut kernels off cobs.

Heat ½ cup oil in each of 2 heavy large saucepans over medium heat. Add half of onions to each pan and sauté until translucent, about 10 minutes. Add half of ginger to each pan and sauté 2 minutes. Divide red and green bell peppers between pans and sauté until slightly softened, about 5 minutes. Divide corn between pans and sauté until heated through. Transfer corn mixture to 2 bowls. Immediately pour dressing over, dividing equally. Toss to combine. Cover and chill until cold. *(Can be prepared 1 day ahead.)*

Toss salads. Garnish with cilantro sprigs.

GREEN VEGETABLE SALAD WITH ORANGE-HAZELNUT DRESSING

Sugar snap peas, green beans, broccoli and asparagus are tossed with an orange-flavored vinaigrette in this make-ahead salad (opposite). 50 SERVINGS

SALAD

3 pounds sugar snap peas, stemmed, strings removed
3 pounds green beans, cut into 1-inch-long pieces
4 large broccoli bunches, stemmed, cut into florets
4 pounds asparagus, trimmed, cut into 1-inch-long pieces

DRESSING

3 cups olive oil (preferably extra-virgin)
1⅓ cups red wine vinegar
1⅓ cups orange juice
¼ cup grated orange peel
1 teaspoon salt
1½ cups hazelnuts, toasted, husked, chopped

Peel (orange part only) from 2 oranges, cut into thin strips

FOR SALAD: Bring large pot of salted water to boil. Working in batches, add sugar snap peas and cook until bright green and crisp, about 1 minute. Using slotted spoon, transfer peas to bowl of ice water and cool. Drain peas. Return water in pot to boil. Working in batches, add green beans and cook until crisp-tender, about 5 minutes. Using slotted spoon, transfer beans to bowl of ice water and cool. Drain beans. Return water in pot to boil. Working in batches, add broccoli and asparagus and cook until crisp-tender, about 3 minutes. Drain well. Transfer to bowl of ice water and cool. Drain broccoli and asparagus well. Combine all vegetables in 2 large bowls. *(Can be prepared 1 day ahead. Cover and chill.)*

FOR DRESSING: Whisk first 5 ingredients in large bowl. *(Can be prepared 1 day ahead. Cover and refrigerate.)* Mix in hazelnuts.

Pour dressing over vegetables and toss gently. Garnish with orange peel strips and serve.

CHEESECAKES WITH FRESH BERRY TOPPING

These cheesecakes (opposite) have no crust, making them a snap to prepare. MAKES TWO 9-INCH CHEESECAKES

10   8-ounce packages cream cheese, room temperature
2   cups sugar
2   tablespoons Grand Marnier, other orange liqueur or orange juice
8   large eggs
2   cups sour cream
¾   cup plus 2 tablespoons fresh lemon juice
4   tablespoons grated lemon peel

2   6-ounce baskets raspberries
2   6-ounce baskets blackberries
½   cup apricot preserves
3   tablespoons water

Preheat oven to 300°F. Butter two 9-inch-diameter springform pans with 2¾-inch-high sides. Using electric mixer, beat 5 packages cream cheese in large bowl until light. Add 1 cup sugar and 1 tablespoon Grand Marnier and beat until thoroughly combined. Add four eggs 1 at a time, beating well after each addition. Fold in 1 cup sour cream, half of lemon juice and 2 tablespoons peel. Transfer batter to 1 prepared pan. Repeat with remaining cream cheese, sugar, Grand Marnier, eggs, sour cream, lemon juice and peel to make another cake. Bake cheesecakes until outsides are set but centers still move slightly when pans are shaken, about 1 hour 15 minutes. Transfer cheesecakes to racks to cool. Cover with plastic; chill overnight. *(Can be made up to 3 weeks ahead and frozen.)*

Run small sharp knife around pan sides to loosen cheesecakes if necessary. Release pan sides. Transfer cheesecakes to platters. Toss berries gently in large bowl. Mound berries on cheesecakes, leaving 1-inch border. Heat preserves with 3 tablespoons water in heavy small saucepan over medium heat, stirring until melted. Brush warm glaze over berries. *(Can be made 1 day ahead. Cover loosely; chill.)*

TOASTED COCONUT BARS

Make these attractive, coconut-topped bars (opposite) two days before the party. MAKES ABOUT 50

CRUST

4½   cups sifted all purpose flour
1   cup sifted powdered sugar
2   cups (4 sticks) chilled unsalted butter, cut into pieces

TOPPING

2   cups (packed) golden brown sugar
1   cup sugar
6   large eggs
¼   cup cream of coconut (such as Coco Lopez)*
2   tablespoons milk
2   tablespoons all purpose flour
2   teaspoons vanilla extract
6   tablespoons unsalted butter, melted

3   cups sweetened shredded coconut

FOR CRUST: Preheat oven to 325°F. Mix flour and powdered sugar in processor. Add chilled butter and cut in using on/off turns until mixture begins to come together. Press dough evenly over bottom of two 13 x 9 x 2-inch baking pans. Refrigerate 15 minutes. Bake until golden brown, about 25 minutes. Cool. Reduce oven temperature to 300°F.

FOR TOPPING: Combine golden brown sugar, sugar, eggs, cream of coconut, milk, flour and vanilla extract in large bowl and whisk just until blended. Fold in melted butter.

Sprinkle coconut over crusts. Pour topping evenly over coconut, dividing equally between pans. Bake until toppings are set and golden brown, about 45 minutes. Transfer to rack and cool. Cut into squares. *(Can be prepared 2 days ahead. Store in airtight container.)*

Cream of coconut is available in the liquor department of most supermarkets.

CHOCOLATE-RASPBERRY BARS

To add to the selection on the dessert table, here are dense chocolaty brownies (below) topped with fresh raspberries. MAKES ABOUT 50

BROWNIES

12	ounces unsweetened chocolate, chopped
1½	cups (3 sticks) unsalted butter
1	cup seedless raspberry jam
8	large eggs
4	cups sugar
1	tablespoon vanilla extract
½	teaspoon salt
2	cups all purpose flour

TOPPING

1	cup whipping cream
½	cup seedless raspberry jam
2	tablespoons (¼ stick) butter
16	ounces bittersweet (not unsweetened) or semisweet chocolate, chopped
6	6-ounce baskets raspberries

Powdered sugar

FOR BROWNIES: Preheat oven to 350°F. Line two 13 x 9-inch baking pans with foil; butter foil. Combine chocolate, butter and jam in heavy large saucepan. Stir over low heat until smooth. Remove from heat. Whisk eggs in large bowl until foamy. Add sugar, vanilla and salt; whisk until thoroughly incorporated. Stir in chocolate mixture. Add flour; mix just until blended. Spread batter in prepared pans. Bake just until springy to touch and tester inserted into centers comes out with a few moist crumbs attached, about 30 minutes. Cool brownies in pans on racks. *(Can be prepared ahead. Cover with foil. Place in plastic bag and freeze 2 weeks. Thaw at room temperature.)*

FOR TOPPING: Combine cream, jam and butter in large saucepan. Bring to simmer, stirring until jam and butter melt. Remove from heat. Add chocolate; stir until smooth. Let stand until cool but spreadable, about 40 minutes.

Spread topping over brownies. Immediately top with raspberries, arranging in rows. Chill until cold. *(Can be prepared 1 day ahead.)*

Using foil as aid, remove brownies from pans. Fold down foil sides. Trim edges. Cut into bars. Sift powdered sugar over.

Options

These recipes expand or change the menu to suit your individual needs.

SUN-DRIED TOMATO AND HERB-CHEESE STRUDELS

These are a little more work than the cheese straws, but if you have the time, they could be substituted, making a nice addition to the appetizer selection. (Assemble the strudels two days ahead. Bake just before your guests arrive or four hours ahead and serve at room temperature.) MAKES 60 SLICES

9 ounces soft fresh goat cheese (such as Montrachet), room temperature
9 ounces cream cheese, room temperature
¼ cup plus 2 tablespoons minced drained oil-packed sun-dried tomatoes
2 tablespoons minced fresh parsley
2 tablespoons minced fresh oregano or 1½ teaspoons dried

12 frozen phyllo pastry sheets, thawed
⅓ cup olive oil

1 large plum tomato, seeded, diced
Fresh oregano sprigs

Stir first 5 ingredients in bowl until smooth. Season filling with pepper.

Place 1 phyllo sheet on work surface (keep remainder covered). Brush lightly with oil and season with pepper. Top with 1 more sheet. Brush lightly with oil; season with pepper. Repeat with 1 more sheet. Fold stacked phyllo in half lengthwise. Brush top with oil.

Spoon ¼ of filling in 1-inch-wide log down 1 long side of sheet, leaving 1-inch borders. Fold each short end over filling. Brush edges with oil. Roll up into log, starting at long side. Wrap strudel tightly in plastic. Refrigerate seam side down. Repeat with remaining phyllo and filling, forming 4 strudels total. *(Can be prepared ahead. Refrigerate up to 2 days or freeze up to 2 weeks.)*

Preheat oven to 375°F. Lightly oil cookie sheets. Place strudels on prepared sheets, seam sides down. Using serrated knife, score each strudel (cutting through phyllo only), making 14 diagonal cuts in each. Brush strudels with oil. Bake until golden, about 15 minutes. Cool 10 minutes.

Cut through score lines, forming slices. Arrange cut side up on platter. Garnish slices with tomato and oregano.

GRILLED CHICKEN WITH OLIVE PUREE

A simple main-course option. The versatile, easy-to-make puree in this recipe also adds terrific flavor to sandwiches, pizzas and pastas. 50 SERVINGS

10 cups pitted black brine-cured olives (such as Kalamata) or 4½ cups olivada*
1½ cups (or more) olive oil
50 boneless chicken breast halves with skin
4 tablespoons minced fresh rosemary or 4 teaspoons dried

Puree olives with 1 cup olive oil in processor. Gently slide hand under skin of chicken breasts to loosen, forming pocket and keeping skin attached. Spread about 1½ tablespoons olive puree under skin of each chicken breast. Fasten skin with toothpicks to hold olive filling in place. Brush chicken breasts with ½ cup olive oil and sprinkle with minced rosemary. Place chicken in shallow dishes. Cover; chill at least 3 hours or overnight.

Prepare barbecue (medium-high heat). Season chicken with salt and pepper. Working in batches, grill chicken until golden and cooked through, turning frequently and brushing chicken with more olive oil if necessary to prevent sticking, about 20 minutes. Serve hot or at room temperature.

*An olive spread, sometimes called black olive cream, available at Italian markets, specialty foods stores and some supermarkets.

DOUBLE-LEMON WEDDING CAKE

*Many of this classic cake's components can be
made ahead, and once the tiers are filled (with a
luscious lemon cream studded with berries) and
decorated, they can be refrigerated up to two days
or frozen up to two weeks before the wedding. To
prevent discoloration of the filling, use a saucepan
with a nonreactive interior, such as enamel or
stainless steel. (The lemon-juice acid will adversely
affect the filling if it's made in an unlined iron or
aluminum saucepan.)* 50 SERVINGS

CAKE

13   large eggs
5½   cups sugar
2⅔   cups vegetable oil
2¾   cups part-skim ricotta cheese
     (about 21 ounces)
¼   cup orange juice
¼   cup grated lemon peel
     (from about 8 lemons)
3   tablespoons orange liqueur
2½   tablespoons fresh lemon juice
1   tablespoon vanilla extract
8¾   cups all purpose flour
2   tablespoons baking powder
1   teaspoon salt

LEMON FILLING

5   large eggs
1¼   cups (2½ sticks) unsalted butter,
     room temperature
1¼   cups sugar
¾   cup fresh lemon juice (from about 5 lemons)
1   tablespoon grated lemon peel

3   cups chilled whipping cream
6   tablespoons sugar

LEMON SYRUP

1½   cups water
¾   cup fresh lemon juice
¾   cup sugar

PRELIMINARY ASSEMBLY

1   8-inch-diameter cardboard cake round*
3½   cups fresh raspberries
3½   cups fresh small blackberries or
     boysenberries

1   12-inch-diameter cardboard cake round*

FROSTING

11   large egg yolks
3¼   cups plus 7 tablespoons sugar
1   cup plus 2 tablespoons milk
     (do not use low-fat or nonfat)
1½   tablespoons grated lemon peel
1   tablespoon vanilla extract
3   pounds unsalted butter, cut into large pieces,
     room temperature

¾   cup water

7   large egg whites

FINAL ASSEMBLY AND DECORATION

3   12-inch-long, ¼-inch-diameter
     wooden dowels*

2   3-foot-long peach and/or
     cream-colored ribbons
2   4-foot-long peach and/or
     cream-colored ribbons

Assorted nonpoisonous flowers
(such as roses, freesias and tulips)

FOR CAKE: Position rack in center of oven and preheat to 350°F. Butter bottom of 12-inch-diameter cheesecake pan (not springform) with 3-inch-high sides and removable bottom.* Butter bottom of 8-inch-diameter cheesecake pan (not springform) with 3-inch-high sides and removable bottom.* Line bottom of pans with parchment paper.*

Beat eggs, sugar and oil in large bowl of heavy-duty mixer at medium-low speed 5 minutes. Increase speed to medium and beat until mixture is very thick and falls in heavy ribbon when beater is lifted, about 5 minutes. Whisk cheese, orange juice, lemon peel, liqueur, lemon juice and vanilla in medium bowl until well blended. Add cheese mixture to egg mixture; beat at low speed just until blended. Transfer to extra-large bowl (at least 6-quart capacity). Sift flour, baking powder and salt into large bowl. Sift dry ingredients over batter in 5 additions, whisking to blend after each addition. Transfer about 11 cups batter to 12-inch prepared pan and about 5 cups batter to 8-inch prepared pan (batter should be of equal depth in both pans).

Bake cakes until golden brown and firm (tops may crack) and tester inserted into center comes out clean, rotating pans occasionally for even baking and covering cakes loosely with foil if browning too quickly, about 1 hour 30 minutes. Transfer to racks; cool completely.

FOR LEMON FILLING: Whisk eggs to blend in medium bowl. Combine butter, 1¼ cups sugar, lemon juice and peel in heavy medium saucepan. Stir over medium heat until butter melts, sugar dissolves and mixture comes to boil. Gradually whisk lemon mixture into eggs. Return to same pan. Stir over medium heat until curd thickens and just begins to bubble, about 3 minutes. Strain curd into large bowl. Chill until cold and thick, stirring occasionally, about 4 hours.

Beat cream and 6 tablespoons sugar in medium bowl until firm peaks form. Fold into curd in 4 additions. Chill filling until very cold, about 2 hours.

FOR LEMON SYRUP: Stir all ingredients in heavy medium saucepan over medium heat until sugar dissolves. Increase heat; bring to boil. Chill syrup until cold, about 1 hour. *(Cakes, filling and syrup can be made 1 day ahead. Cover cakes; store at room temperature. Cover filling and syrup; keep refrigerated.)*

FOR PRELIMINARY ASSEMBLY: Cut around sides of cakes to loosen. Push up pan bottoms, releasing cakes from pan. If necessary, cut between parchment and pan bottoms to loosen cakes. Invert cakes onto surface. Peel off parchment. Wash and dry pans and reassemble.

Using long serrated knife, cut off domed top of 8-inch cake to level. Cut cake horizontally into 3 equal layers. Place bottom cake layer, cut side up, on 8-inch cardboard. Place cake on cardboard back into pan. Brush bottom layer with ¼ cup lemon syrup. Spread with 1½ cups lemon filling. Sprinkle with 1½ cups raspberries. Place top cake layer atop raspberries; press cake lightly to compact. Brush with ¼ cup syrup. Spread with 1½ cups filling. Sprinkle with 1½ cups blackberries. Top with middle cake layer. Press cake lightly to compact. Brush with ¼ cup syrup. (Assembled cake may be higher than pan sides.) Cover tightly with plastic wrap.

Using long serrated knife, cut off domed top of 12-inch cake to level. Cut cake horizontally into 3 equal layers. Place bottom layer, cut side up, on 12-inch cardboard. Place cake on cardboard back in pan. Brush with ½ cup lemon syrup. Spread with 3 cups lemon filling. Sprinkle with 2 cups raspberries. Using 10- or 11-inch-diameter tart pan bottom as aid, slide top layer onto raspberries. Press cake lightly to compact. Brush with ½ cup syrup. Spread with 3 cups lemon filling.

Sprinkle with 2 cups blackberries. Using tart pan bottom as aid, slide middle layer onto blackberries. Press cake lightly to compact. Brush with ½ cup syrup. (Assembled cake may be higher than pan sides.) Cover tightly with plastic wrap. Refrigerate both cakes at least 8 hours or overnight.

FOR FROSTING: Whisk yolks and 1 cup plus 2 tablespoons sugar in large bowl to blend. Bring milk and lemon peel just to boil in heavy large saucepan. Gradually whisk hot milk into yolk mixture. Return to same saucepan. Stir custard over medium heat until thick, about 3 minutes (do not allow custard to boil). Strain custard into extra-large (6-quart) metal bowl; add vanilla extract. Using handheld electric mixer, beat custard until color lightens and custard cools to room temperature, about 15 minutes. Gradually add butter; beat until well blended, scraping down sides of bowl often. (If buttercream appears curdled at any time, place bowl directly over low heat for several seconds. Remove from heat and beat well; repeat warming and beating as necessary to achieve smooth texture.) Set buttercream aside at room temperature.

Stir 2¼ cups sugar and ¾ cup water in heavy medium saucepan over medium heat until sugar dissolves. Attach clip-on candy thermometer to side of pan. Increase heat and boil syrup without stirring until thermometer registers 240°F, occasionally brushing down sugar crystals from sides of pan with wet pastry brush, about 7 minutes.

Meanwhile, beat egg whites in large bowl of heavy-duty mixer until stiff but not dry. Gradually add 5 tablespoons sugar and beat until firm glossy peaks form. Gradually beat hot sugar syrup into egg whites. Continue to beat 2 minutes longer. Place bowl of meringue in larger bowl filled with ice and water. Using handheld electric mixer with clean beaters, continue to beat until meringue cools to room temperature, about 10 minutes. Gradually add meringue to buttercream, beating until well blended.

Cut around sides of 8-inch cake. Push up pan bottom, releasing cake from pan. Remove pan bottom, leaving cake on cardboard base. If desired, place cake on revolving cake stand.* Using offset spatula, spread thin layer of frosting (about 1 cup) over top and sides of cake to anchor crumbs.

Cut around sides of 12-inch cake. Push up pan bottom, releasing cake from pan. Remove pan bottom, leaving cake on cardboard base. If desired, place cake on revolving cake stand. Using offset spatula, spread thin layer of frosting (about 2⅓ cups) over top and sides of cake to anchor crumbs. Refrigerate cakes on their cardboard bases until frosting is firm, about 1 hour.

Spread enough frosting (about 1½ cups) over top and sides of 8-inch cake to coat. Spread enough frosting (about 3 cups) over top and sides of 12-inch cake to coat. Dip large offset spatula into very hot water to warm blade; wipe dry. Run spatula over sides and tops of cakes, warming spatula repeatedly as necessary, until frosting is smooth. Using pastry bag fitted with small plain round tip, pipe border of small frosting dots around top edge of each cake. Refrigerate both cakes uncovered on their cardboard bases until frosting hardens, about 4 hours. *(Once frosting has hardened, cakes on their bases can be wrapped in plastic and refrigerated up to 2 days or double-wrapped with plastic and frozen up to 2 weeks. Before continuing with recipe, thaw wrapped frozen cakes overnight in refrigerator.)*

FOR FINAL ASSEMBLY AND DECORATION: Insert 1 dowel straight down into center of 12-inch cake to cardboard base. Mark dowel about ¼ inch above top of frosting. Remove dowel and cut with serrated knife at marked point. Cut 2 more dowels to same length. Press 3 cut dowels into cake, positioning about 3½ inches inward from cake edges and spacing evenly. Place 12-inch cake on platter. Using large metal spatula as aid, place 8-inch cake on its cardboard atop dowels in 12-inch cake, centering carefully.

Wrap 3-foot-long ribbons around base of 8-inch cake; cut to fit with slight overlap. Press ribbons gently into frosting to adhere. Wrap 4-foot-long ribbons around base of 12-inch cake; cut to fit with slight overlap. Press ribbons gently into frosting to adhere.

Arrange flowers on top of and around cake. *(Decorated cake can be made 6 hours ahead. Let stand at cool room temperature.)*

Transfer 8-inch cake to work surface; cut cake into 20 slices. Remove dowels from 12-inch cake. Starting 2 inches inward from edge and inserting knife straight down, cut 8-inch-diameter circle in center of cake. Starting 2 inches in from 8-inch-diameter circle and inserting knife straight down, cut 4-inch-diameter circle in center of 8-inch circle. Cut outer portion of cake into 18 slices. Cut middle portion of cake into 8 slices. Cut inner 4-inch portion of cake into 4 wedges. Serve.

*Cake pans, parchment paper, cardboard rounds, revolving cake stand and wooden dowels are available at many cake and candy supply stores.

1

Assemble the cakes in their baking pans, which have removable bottoms. A 10- or 11-inch tart pan bottom is helpful for transferring the cut cake layers. During assembly, the trimmed cake top is placed on the first portion of filling and berries, becoming the middle cake layer.

2

The assembled tiers are chilled until very cold, which makes them easier to frost. To remove from the pans, cut around the sides; gently push up from the bottom.

3

The first coating of frosting, called a crumb coat, is a thin layer that anchors any cake crumbs and provides a smooth surface for the final layer of frosting.

4

The dowels that will support the top cake need to be tall enough to keep the tiers separate, but not so tall that there will be a gap between the tiers. To measure, insert one dowel into the center of the 12-inch cake. Mark the dowel about ¼ inch above the frosting.

5

The elegant finish: First wrap a wide (1- to 1½-inch) ribbon around the base of the cakes. Then wrap a narrower ribbon of contrasting color around the base, placing the second ribbon over the first.

6

To serve the bottom cake, first cut it into three separate sections: a two-inch-wide outside ring; a two-inch-wide ring inside that; and a center four-inch-diameter circle. Cut each section into slices.

As often as not, entertaining is a spur-of-the-moment thing: brunch for the overnight guests whose flight was postponed until later in the day; lunch for your grown kids, stopping by to do their laundry; snacks for the Brownie troop meeting at your house; dinner for those old friends you ran into while antiquing; dessert for the book club, after you've all been to see the movie version of a novel you read a while back. For these kinds of spontaneous get-togethers, a help-yourself buffet of quickly prepared and ready-made foods is the easiest way to go.

This section of the book offers ten different menus for buffet meals that come together in minutes with foods from your pantry, the refrigerator and the market around the corner. Each of the menus is an "idea" as much as it is a meal, and each assumes participation on the part of the guests. Pick an appealing idea—say, an ice cream sundae bar—set out any number (or all) of the menu suggestions and then let your guests do the rest, adding a little of this, some of that and coming up with their own creations.

Every menu here includes recipes for two or three dishes that you might want to make yourself (though in many cases, store-bought versions will work just as well). None of these recipes is complex or time-consuming, and all of the other menu suggestions are easily purchased, readied or assembled.

When time is short, these menus are just the ticket—the ticket to entertaining in an instant.

INSTANT
ENTERTAINING

Breakfast on the Go

- ASSORTED CEREALS

Bagels and Muffins

- ASSORTED BAGELS
- ONE-WEEK BRAN MUFFINS

Toppings

- PRESERVES AND JAM
- CREAM CHEESE
- PEAR BUTTER WITH CARDAMOM AND CINNAMON

Fresh Fruit

- MIXED BERRIES
- SLICED MELON
- ORANGE SEGMENTS

- VANILLA YOGURT

- JUICES, COFFEE, MILK

For a quick and easy breakfast that can expand to feed any number of people, consider a breakfast bar, made up of purchased foods, things you've prepared ahead of time and dishes that require little more than arranging.

If you set out a selection of cereals, bagels and muffins, toppings for the breads and fruit, there will be something for everyone. Offer a couple of different cereals, geared to the ages of the crowd. Send somebody out for bagels while you bake a batch of muffins (the batter in the recipe here can be made a week ahead; the pear butter to spread on the muffins will keep two weeks). For a fruit platter, cantaloupe wedges sprinkled with berries, plus orange segments, are attractive and simple.

This is an ideal menu for overnight guests who may rise early when you'd rather not. Get everything ready, including the coffeemaker, the night before. The cereals and breads can be left out (in plastic bags), and the toppings and fruit can be refrigerated on a single shelf, ready to eat: instant breakfast.

ONE-WEEK BRAN MUFFINS

The batter keeps in the refrigerator up to one week, so it takes almost no time to have freshly baked muffins for breakfast. For variety, add currants, dried cranberries or other dried chopped fruit before baking the muffins. MAKES 18

2½	cups all purpose flour
1½	cups sugar
2½	teaspoons baking soda
1	teaspoon salt
3	cups raisin bran cereal (about 5 ounces)
2	cups buttermilk
½	cup vegetable oil
2	large eggs

Stir flour, sugar, baking soda and salt in large bowl to blend. Mix in cereal. Whisk buttermilk, oil and eggs in medium bowl to blend. Mix into dry ingredients. *(Can be made up to 1 week ahead. Cover and chill. Mixture will thicken.)*

Preheat oven to 425°F. Line 18 muffin cups with foil liners. Spoon ⅓ cup batter into each muffin cup. Bake until tester inserted into center of muffins comes out clean, about 20 minutes. Transfer to rack and cool.

PEAR BUTTER WITH CARDAMOM AND CINNAMON

Delicious with the muffins here; wonderful on toast, too. MAKES ABOUT 3⅔ CUPS

5	pounds ripe pears, peeled, cored, cut into 1-inch pieces
1⅓	cups Johannisberg Riesling wine
⅓	cup fresh lemon juice
1¼	cups sugar
1¼	teaspoons ground cinnamon
1	teaspoon ground cardamom

Combine pears, wine and lemon juice in heavy large pot. Bring mixture to boil. Reduce heat to medium-low; cover and simmer until pears are tender, occasionally stirring and pushing pears into liquid to submerge, about 20 minutes.

Working in batches, transfer mixture to processor; puree. Return to same pot. Add sugar, cinnamon and cardamom. Simmer over low heat until mixture thickens and mounds slightly on spoon, stirring often and partially covering if mixture splatters, about 2 hours. Transfer hot pear butter to clean jars. Cover and cool. Refrigerate. *(Can be made 2 weeks ahead. Keep refrigerated.)*

Help-Yourself Brunch

- BAKED MAPLE AND
  CINNAMON FRENCH TOAST

- BACON

  OR

- POTATO, RED PEPPER, FENNEL AND
  SAUSAGE ROAST

Assorted Breads

- SWEET ROLLS
- BAGELS
- CRISPIES

- FRUIT SALAD

- JUICES AND COFFEE

Brunch offers a wonderful pause in the middle of a busy weekend day, and it doesn't need to be elaborate or time-consuming. The menu here revolves around two simple dishes that can be started about an hour before eating, giving you time to catch up with old friends over coffee.

You might never have thought of making French toast for six, an idea that becomes feasible when the French toast is baked. And to make the dish really special, there's a deliciously easy cinnamon-scented maple syrup to drizzle on top of each serving. Also simple is a side dish of red bell peppers, potatoes and sausage that bakes alongside the main dish. All you need add to the spread is an assortment of breads, maybe bagels and sweet rolls, a fruit salad, juices and freshly brewed coffee.

This versatile menu lends itself to gatherings of all kinds, whether it's everyone back to your house after a charity walk, or home at last after a morning at the swap meet. Ready almost everything ahead of time, then sit down and relax with your guests.

BAKED MAPLE AND CINNAMON FRENCH TOAST

A simpler, baked version of a favorite morning treat. Maple syrup and cinnamon flavor the soaking mixture and top the toast. 6 SERVINGS

FRENCH TOAST

6   1-inch-thick slices whole wheat French bread or other whole wheat bread
4   large eggs
2   cups low-fat milk
½   cup pure maple syrup
1½ teaspoons vanilla extract
½   teaspoon ground cinnamon

SYRUP

¾   cup pure maple syrup
⅜   teaspoon ground cinnamon

FOR FRENCH TOAST: Preheat oven to 425°F. Generously butter large baking pan. Arrange bread slices in single layer in pan. Combine eggs, milk, ½ cup syrup, vanilla and cinnamon in medium bowl and beat to blend. Pour over bread. Let soak until all egg mixture is absorbed, turning bread slices after 10 minutes, about 25 minutes.

Bake bread 15 minutes. Turn; bake until golden, about 10 minutes longer.

MEANWHILE, PREPARE SYRUP: Combine syrup and cinnamon in heavy small saucepan. Bring to simmer. Remove syrup from heat.

Serve French toast with syrup.

POTATO, RED PEPPER, FENNEL AND SAUSAGE ROAST

A one-dish side-dish option. 6 SERVINGS

1¾ pounds small red potatoes, cut into 1-inch pieces
2   large red bell peppers, seeded, cut into 1-inch pieces
1   large fennel bulb, trimmed, cut into 1-inch pieces
1   tablespoon olive oil
1¼ teaspoons fennel seeds, crushed
1   pound chicken or turkey sausage, cut into 1-inch pieces

Preheat oven to 425°F. Combine first 5 ingredients in 2 large baking pans. Mix to coat with oil. Season with salt and generous amount of pepper. Bake 20 minutes. Divide sausages between pans; bake until potatoes are tender with crusty outsides and sausages are cooked through, about 30 minutes more.

Tortilla Wraps

- FLOUR TORTILLAS

Fillings

- LEMON-SAGE CHICKEN FILLING
- GRILLED TUNA FILLING
- STEAK, CORN AND JALAPEÑO FILLING

Toppings

- FRESH TOMATO SALSA
- ROASTED RED PEPPERS
- CRUMBLED GOAT CHEESE
- CHOPPED CILANTRO
- SOUR CREAM

- BEER AND SODAS

- COFFEE SORBET AND COOKIES

A WRAP LITERALLY GIVES YOU A HANDLE ON LUNCH. Start with tortillas, set out a variety of quick-cooking fillings, add a selection of appealing toppings and the meal is as easy as a make-it-yourself sandwich.

Large flour tortillas are the best wraps: Big and soft, they hold a lot and roll up easily. Everything else is strictly a matter of choice. There are three fillings here: a lemon-chicken one and a fresh tuna one that cook up quickly on the grill, and a spicy steak one that can be readied in about 15 minutes. Toppings to roll up with the fillings include fresh salsa, roasted peppers, goat cheese and sour cream, to name just a few. Dessert can be as simple as purchased sorbet and bakery cookies.

LEMON-SAGE CHICKEN FILLING

Be sure to have plenty of warm flour tortillas on hand so that guests can assemble their own "wraps." 8 SERVINGS

4   pounds skinless boneless chicken
    breast halves
¾   cup fresh lemon juice
6   tablespoons olive oil
¼   cup vodka (optional)
¼   cup chopped fresh sage or 1 tablespoon dried
2   teaspoons honey
    Dash of hot pepper sauce

Place 1 chicken breast between sheets of waxed paper. Pound to thickness of ½ inch using meat mallet or rolling pin. Repeat with remaining chicken. Mix lemon juice, oil, vodka, sage, honey and hot pepper sauce in large shallow glass dish. Add chicken; turn to coat. Let stand 15 minutes or up to 1 hour.

Prepare barbecue (medium-high heat). Remove chicken from marinade; reserve marinade. Cook chicken until just springy to touch, brushing frequently with reserved marinade, about 4 minutes per side. Cut chicken into strips and serve.

GRILLED TUNA FILLING

Two ingredients and 10 minutes to a terrific filling. 8 SERVINGS

3   pounds 1½-inch-thick tuna steaks
2   limes, halved

Prepare barbecue (medium-high heat). Place tuna on grill and cook to desired degree of doneness, about 5 minutes per side for medium-rare. Cut tuna into 1-inch-wide strips and place on platter. Squeeze juice from limes over tuna and serve.

STEAK, CORN AND JALAPEÑO FILLING

This quick sauté of steak and vegetables tastes delicious in tortillas. 8 SERVINGS

½   cup olive oil
4   medium red onions, sliced
4   red bell peppers, sliced
2   pounds round, flank or skirt steak, cut into
    ¼-inch-thick, long narrow strips
3   cups frozen whole kernel corn, cooked
    according to package directions, drained
4   jalapeño chilies, minced with seeds
2   teaspoons ground cumin
2   teaspoons chili powder
6   tablespoons minced fresh cilantro

Heat oil in heavy large skillet over medium heat. Add onions and bell peppers and sauté until tender, about 10 minutes. Transfer to plate. Add steak to skillet and stir until no longer pink, about 1 minute. Return onions and peppers to skillet. Add corn, jalapeño, cumin and chili powder and stir until heated through. Season with salt and pepper. Remove from heat and mix in cilantro. Transfer steak mixture to heated bowl and keep warm; serve.

Pita Pockets

- HUMMUS AND FRESH VEGETABLES

- PITA BREAD ROUNDS

Fillings

- GRILLED TOFU AND VEGETABLE FILLING
- GRILLED SAUSAGE AND ONION FILLING

Toppings

- CRUMBLED FETA CHEESE
- SLICED TOMATOES
- SHREDDED ROMAINE LETTUCE

- TABBOULEH IN LETTUCE CUPS

- BEER AND LEMONADE

- ICE CREAM BARS

For something different from burgers on the grill, fire up the barbecue and cook up the fillings for make-your-own pita pockets. It's not the same old thing, and it makes for deliciously creative eating.

While the barbecue is heating, munch on a selection of fresh vegetables—jicama sticks, hearts of palm, carrot sticks and red pepper squares—dipping into hummus, a garlicky chickpea spread available at many markets and Middle Eastern foods stores. While you're there, pick up a pile of pita rounds, then cut them into semicircles. They make tasty holders for a mint-scented tofu and vegetable filling and a mustardy sausage and onion filling. Set out a selection of toppings, including crumbled feta cheese, sliced tomatoes and shredded lettuce. Tabbouleh, that lemony bulgur salad typical of Middle Eastern cooking, makes a quick side dish when spooned into lettuce cups. Dessert might be nut-crusted ice cream bars.

A casual summer's evening party, this menu requires little preparation, just a trip to the market and a 15-minute stint at the grill. Set everything out as a help-yourself buffet, and leave the rest of the "work" to your guests.

GRILLED TOFU AND VEGETABLE FILLING

Both this and the sausage filling take just minutes on the grill. 6 SERVINGS

1½	cups bottled Italian dressing
9	tablespoons finely chopped fresh mint
12	¾-inch-thick slices firm tofu, drained well
6	medium green bell peppers, quartered lengthwise, seeded
24	green onions, all but 3 inches of green tops trimmed

Prepare barbecue (medium heat). Whisk dressing and mint in small bowl to blend. Arrange tofu, peppers and onions on small platter; brush with some of dressing mixture.

Grill vegetables and tofu until lightly charred and heated through, occasionally turning and brushing with dressing, about 8 minutes for vegetables and 5 minutes for tofu.

Cut tofu, peppers and green onions into pieces. Place in serving bowl.

GRILLED SAUSAGE AND ONION FILLING

6 SERVINGS

¾	cup beer
9	tablespoons coarse-grained Dijon mustard
3	tablespoons vegetable oil
3	tablespoons chopped fresh thyme or 1 tablespoon dried
9	½-inch-thick red onion slices
12	links fully cooked bratwurst (about 30 ounces), halved lengthwise

Prepare barbecue (medium heat). Whisk beer, mustard, oil and thyme in small bowl to blend. Brush both sides of onion slices with some of mustard dressing, being careful to keep onion slices intact.

Grill onion slices and bratwurst until onion is tender and slightly charred at edges and bratwurst is golden brown, turning twice, about 10 minutes for onion slices and 6 minutes for bratwurst.

Separate onion slices into rings. Place in large bowl. Cut sausages into bite-size pieces. Add to bowl with onions. Add remaining mustard dressing to bowl with onion slices and sausages and toss to coat.

Snack Bar

- BANANA-ORANGE SMOOTHIES

- RANCH DIP WITH CELERY STICKS,
  BABY CARROTS, JICAMA STICKS,
  SUGAR SNAP PEAS AND
  CHERRY TOMATOES

Munchies

- PRETZELS
- BAGEL CHIPS
- PITA CHIPS
- PEANUTS
- CHUNKS OF CHEESE

- MILK AND APPLE JUICE

- CHOCOLATE CHIP COOKIES WITH
  OATMEAL AND PECANS

AFTER A SOCCER GAME OR A BAND REHEARSAL, gymnastics or the park, it's hard to say who needs a snack more—the young participants or their "chauffeurs." And when everyone's coming home with a friend and you have a rowdy bunch of hungry kids to feed, a help-themselves snack bar can be the easiest way to go. It's entertaining *and* nourishing.

A quickly blended fruit drink (the one here combines yogurt, bananas, oranges, cherries and strawberries, but you can vary the fruit based on what your kids like) is a good start. Children enjoy the dump-and-whir process of making these tasty smoothies (keep a close eye on the younger ones).

From there the kids can go on to a buffet-style snack bar that includes an assortment of all their favorite things: pretzels, bagel chips, pita chips, peanuts and chunks of cheese, to name a few. To up the ante healthwise, set out a selection of raw vegetables with good old-fashioned ranch dip, a favorite with the age group (the older folks present may want something a little more sophisticated, such as an herbed cheese spread).

And if no snack is complete without cookies, there's a terrific recipe here for a chocolate chip version with the added crunch of pecans (but, of course, a local bakery's take on the same will do just fine).

BANANA-ORANGE SMOOTHIES

A refreshing and healthful "drink." 8 SERVINGS

4   8-ounce containers low-fat berry yogurt
4   bananas, peeled, cut into pieces
4   oranges, peeled, white pith removed, cut into segments
32 frozen dark cherries
24 frozen strawberries

Combine 2 containers yogurt, 2 bananas, 2 oranges, 16 cherries and 12 strawberries in blender. Blend on medium speed until smooth. Divide among 4 glasses. Repeat with remaining ingredients.

CHOCOLATE CHIP COOKIES WITH OATMEAL AND PECANS

Old-fashioned "cookie-jar" cookies, these will keep for a week. MAKES ABOUT 4 DOZEN

1   cup (2 sticks) margarine
1   cup (packed) dark brown sugar
½   cup plus 2 tablespoons sugar
2   large eggs
1   teaspoon vanilla extract
2   cups plus 2 tablespoons all purpose flour
¾   teaspoon baking soda
½   teaspoon salt
2½   cups quick-cooking oats
2   cups semisweet chocolate chips (about 12 ounces)
1   cup chopped pecans

Preheat oven to 350°F. Lightly grease 2 heavy large baking sheets. Beat margarine and both sugars in large bowl until fluffy and well blended. Beat in eggs 1 at a time, then vanilla. Sift flour, baking soda and salt over margarine mixture and stir to blend. Mix in oats, then chocolate chips and pecans.

Working in batches, drop dough by rounded tablespoonfuls onto prepared sheets. Bake cookies until golden brown, about 14 minutes. Transfer cookies to racks and cool completely. *(Can be prepared 1 week ahead. Store cookies in airtight container at room temperature.)*

Drinks and Eats

Vegetable Platter

- ROASTED BELL PEPPERS WITH BASIL AND BALSAMIC VINEGAR
- OLIVES WITH FENNEL AND ORANGE
- MARINATED ARTICHOKE HEARTS
- SLICED ITALIAN BREAD

Cheese Platter

- HERBED GOAT CHEESE DIP
- GRAPES
- PEARS
- CRACKERS
- BREADSTICKS

- MIXED NUTS

- PRETZELS

- COCKTAILS, WINE, FLAVORED WATERS

"COME ON OVER FOR A DRINK...." THE INVITATION can cap a busy afternoon with an hour of relaxation. Or it can give an evening out a festive head start.

A cocktail party can also be a surprisingly easy way to entertain a group, requiring much less time and energy than, say, a dinner party. The menu here divides into two quickly assembled yet appealing appetizer platters, a vegetable one and a cheese one. Bread, crackers and breadsticks round things out, and pretzels and nuts offer more to munch on.

If there's no time to spare, prepare either or both platters with purchased foods; look for the roasted peppers, the olives and the herbed cheese in specialty foods shops and delis. Then, limit your efforts to creative arranging and drink mixing.

ROASTED BELL PEPPERS WITH BASIL AND BALSAMIC VINEGAR

This simple mix of bell peppers, oil and vinegar is delicious on sliced bread. 8 SERVINGS

 3 red bell peppers
 3 yellow bell peppers
4½ tablespoons olive oil
1½ tablespoons balsamic vinegar
 1 tablespoon matchstick-size orange peel strips
12 large fresh basil leaves

Char bell peppers over gas flame or in broiler until blackened on all sides. Wrap in paper bag; let stand 10 minutes. Peel and seed. Cut into ¾-inch-wide strips. Place in bowl. Mix in oil, vinegar and orange peel. Season with salt and pepper. Let stand 1 hour. *(Can be prepared 1 day ahead. Cover and refrigerate. Bring to room temperature before serving.)* Chop basil; mix into peppers and then serve.

OLIVES WITH FENNEL AND ORANGE

Fennel seeds bring out the richness of the olives; orange peel and dried red pepper flakes enliven them. MAKES ABOUT 6 CUPS

 6 cups assorted black and green olives (preferably imported, such as Kalamata, Sicilian, garlic-stuffed), drained
 ¼ cup olive oil (preferably extra-virgin)
 ¼ cup fresh lemon juice
 ¼ cup fresh orange juice
 2 tablespoons minced orange peel (orange part only)
 1 tablespoon fennel seeds, crushed
 ½ teaspoon dried crushed red pepper

Combine all ingredients in large bowl. Cover and refrigerate overnight, stirring occasionally. *(Can be prepared up to 5 days ahead.)*

Bring olives to room temperature; serve.

HERBED GOAT CHEESE DIP

A homemade version of an herb- and garlic-flavored cheese spread. MAKES ABOUT 2½ CUPS

28 large garlic cloves (unpeeled)
16 ounces soft fresh goat cheese (such as Montrachet)
 ½ cup minced fresh basil or 1 tablespoon dried
 ¼ cup olive oil
 ¼ cup chopped fresh chives or green onion tops
 2 tablespoons minced fresh cilantro
 4 teaspoons minced fresh rosemary or 1 teaspoon dried
 Cayenne pepper

Cook garlic in medium saucepan of simmering water until very soft, about 20 minutes. Drain; cool. Peel garlic. Transfer garlic to processor. Add goat cheese and blend well. Transfer to bowl. Mix in next 5 ingredients. Season with salt, pepper and cayenne. *(Can be made 3 days ahead. Cover and refrigerate.)*

Top a Potato

- Baked Potatoes

Toppings
- Cheesy Ratatouille
- Sun-dried Tomato and Olive Pesto

Garnishes
- Sour Cream
- Chopped Chives
- Chopped Olives
- Chopped Red Onions
- Grated Parmesan Cheese
- Crumbled Bacon

- Mixed Green Salad

- Beer and Wine

- Lemon Bars

CHILDREN WILL LOVE THE IDEA; SO WILL THEIR PARENTS. The smallest ones may insist, "Only bacon" or "Just butter," but everyone else can bring to the all-American Idaho baker a cook's tour of tastes. It's a potato bar, and it's a quick and clever way to whip up lunch or supper for a group of families.

Only the potatoes themselves should be served straight from the oven. The toppings can be made ahead and reheated as needed. Everyone will have a hard time deciding whether to go with the ratatouille with goat cheese or the sun-dried tomato pesto; many may opt for a spoonful of each. The kids will set their sights on the bacon, olives, sour cream and grated Parmesan, with the adventurous ones adding chives and chopped red onion.

To complete the spread, include a big salad, and round out the meal with purchased lemon bars or another easy-eating dessert.

CHEESY RATATOUILLE

This simple do-ahead ratatouille gets topped with goat cheese and baked briefly just before serving. MAKES ABOUT 3 CUPS

2 tablespoons olive oil
4 large garlic cloves, chopped
1 large eggplant (unpeeled), diced
2 green bell peppers, diced
2 large tomatoes, chopped
1 onion, cut into 1-inch pieces
1 large zucchini, cut into ½-inch pieces
½ cup chopped fresh basil or
    1 tablespoon dried
2 tablespoons red wine vinegar

4 ounces soft fresh goat cheese
    (such as Montrachet) or Muenster cheese
    or a mixture of the two, diced

Heat oil in heavy large pot over medium heat. Add garlic; stir 1 minute. Add eggplant, green bell peppers, tomatoes, onion, zucchini and basil. Sauté 5 minutes. Cover and simmer until all vegetables are tender, stirring occasionally, about 25 minutes. Uncover pot and simmer until juices thicken, stirring occasionally, about 10 minutes. Mix in vinegar; season to taste with salt and pepper. *(Can be prepared 2 days ahead. Cover and refrigerate.)*

Preheat oven to 350°F. Spread ratatouille in 9-inch-diameter pie dish. Sprinkle with cheese. Bake until heated, about 20 minutes.

SUN-DRIED TOMATO AND OLIVE PESTO

You might also spread this tangy, versatile sauce on toasted baguette slices for an easy appetizer, or use it as a topping for homemade pizza. It is delicious with grilled steaks, chicken or fish, too, or over polenta. MAKES ABOUT 2 CUPS

⅔ cup oil-packed sun-dried tomatoes
    Olive oil
¾ cup (packed) stemmed fresh parsley
⅔ cup drained canned pitted black olives
½ cup pine nuts (about 2¾ ounces)
2 shallots, coarsely chopped
2 garlic cloves
1 tablespoon red wine vinegar

Place strainer over 1-cup glass measuring cup. Pour tomatoes with their oil into strainer to drain. Add enough olive oil to glass cup to measure ¼ cup oil total, if neccesary. In processor, blend drained tomatoes, parsley, olives, pine nuts, shallots and garlic with vinegar until finely chopped. With machine running, gradually add ¼ cup oil; process mixture until well blended. If pesto is dry, mix in more oil by spoonfuls. Season with salt and pepper. *(Can be made ahead. Press plastic wrap onto surface of pesto. Cover; refrigerate for 2 days or freeze for 1 week. Bring to room temperature before using.)*

Pasta Bar

Pastas

- FETTUCCINE
- PENNE
- ROTELLE

Sauces

- TOMATO-SAUSAGE SAUCE
- WILD MUSHROOM SAUCE

Toppings

- GRATED PARMESAN CHEESE
- TOASTED BREADCRUMBS

- MIXED GREEN SALAD

- GARLIC BREAD

- RED AND WHITE WINES

- FRUIT SORBET AND BISCOTTI

YOU WOULDN'T CALL IT A FANCY MEAL, BUT FOR PASTA lovers, it's the best: a sampler of noodles and sauces to mix and match as they wish.

There's a thick sausage-tomato sauce to toss with corkscrews, shells, wagon wheels or any pasta shape that will hold the chunky sauce. There's a deliciously woodsy mushroom sauce (a mix of wild mushrooms underscored by dried porcini) to ladle over flat or tube-shaped noodles. Both sauces and roughly two pounds of dried pasta will serve eight to ten people. The sequence of preparations is easy on a cook, because the tomato sauce can be frozen and the mushroom sauce will hold for an hour or so.

Invite friends into the kitchen to help cook the pasta and toss a salad of mixed greens. Add grated Parmesan and toasted breadcrumbs to the buffet, then keep dessert as simple as sorbet and biscotti.

TOMATO-SAUSAGE SAUCE

An all-purpose sauce that can be made up to one week ahead. MAKES ABOUT 8 CUPS

½   cup olive oil
2   pounds sweet Italian sausages,
    casings removed
2   large onions, chopped
¼   cup chopped garlic
1   6-ounce can tomato paste
2   28-ounce cans Italian-style tomatoes
1   cup water
1   cup chopped fresh basil
    (about 4 large bunches)

Heat oil in heavy large pot over high heat. Add sausage; sauté until brown, breaking up with back of spoon, about 6 minutes. Add onions and garlic to pot; sauté until onions are translucent, about 8 minutes. Mix in tomato paste. Add tomatoes with their juices, 1 cup water and basil. Bring sauce to simmer, breaking up tomatoes with back of spoon. Reduce heat to medium and simmer until sauce is thickened to desired consistency, stirring occasionally, about 45 minutes. Season with salt and pepper. *(Can be prepared ahead. Refrigerate up to 1 day or freeze up to 1 week. Rewarm over medium-low heat before serving.)*

WILD MUSHROOM SAUCE

For best results, make this flavorful sauce in two skillets. 8 SERVINGS

4   cups hot water
2   ounces dried porcini mushrooms

4   tablespoons olive oil
2   pounds assorted mushrooms (such as
     oyster, crimini and stemmed shiitake), sliced
8   large garlic cloves, chopped
6   tablespoons unsalted butter
2   tablespoons chopped fresh thyme
1½   cups canned low-salt chicken broth
½   cup freshly grated Parmesan cheese

Combine 4 cups hot water and porcini in medium bowl. Let stand until porcini soften, about 40 minutes. Drain; reserve soaking liquid. Chop porcini coarsely.

Heat 2 tablespoons oil in each of 2 heavy large skillets over medium-high heat. Add fresh mushrooms and garlic, dividing equally; sauté until brown, about 6 minutes. Add half of porcini to each skillet and sauté until fragrant, about 4 minutes. Add half of butter and thyme to each skillet; stir 1 minute. Add broth and 2½ cups reserved mushroom soaking liquid to skillets, dividing equally. Boil until sauce thickens slightly, about 5 minutes. *(Can be prepared up to 1 hour ahead. Let sauce stand at room temperature.)* Stir ¼ cup cheese into each skillet and serve.

Salad Bar

- Mixed Greens

Dressings

- Creamy Dill Dressing
- Pesto Vinaigrette

Mix-ins

- Cooked Chicken
- Cooked Shrimp
- Marinated Artichoke Hearts
- Garbanzo Beans
- Sliced Mushrooms
- Chopped Hard-boiled Eggs
- Asparagus Spears
- Red Onion Rings
- Olives

Toppings

- Crumbled Bacon
- Toasted Pine Nuts
- Onion Bagel Croutons

- Crusty Rolls

- Iced Tea and White Wine

- Ice Cream and Mixed Berries

IT MAY NOT BE A NEW IDEA, BUT THE SALAD BAR remains one of the most versatile entertaining concepts around. Beginning with the basic components—lettuce, mix-ins and dressings—it can expand to feed almost any number of people. It doesn't require a large dining room; set up a salad bar on the kitchen island, atop the sideboard or on the patio table. And it's a wonderfully appealing lunch or supper, especially on a hot summer's day.

Put your signature on the spread with two dressings of contrasting flavors and colors: a creamy herb dressing, accented with dill, Parmesan, lemon and garlic, and a lighter vinaigrette, flavored with ingredients typical of pesto. The croutons here, quickly made from onion bagels, provide the crunch that really makes a good salad.

The rest of the salad bar you can leave to serendipity: It's brought together in minutes from what looked good at the market plus what you have on hand, which may range from chopped leftover ham or sliced cooked chicken to steamed broccoli or crisp asparagus spears. Crusty rolls make the buffet a meal, while ice cream and fresh berries for dessert are, at the same time, rich and light.

CREAMY DILL DRESSING

For best flavor, make this dill-accented dressing ahead. MAKES ABOUT 2 CUPS

1¼	cups mayonnaise
½	cup sour cream
⅓	cup chopped fresh dill
¼	cup freshly grated Parmesan cheese
3	tablespoons fresh lemon juice
4	teaspoons grated onion
3	garlic cloves, minced
2	teaspoons Worcestershire sauce

Whisk mayonnaise and sour cream in medium bowl until smooth. Stir in remaining ingredients. Season with salt and pepper. Cover; chill 1 hour to blend flavors.

PESTO VINAIGRETTE

A processor-fast dressing. MAKES ABOUT 2 CUPS

2	cups coarsely chopped fresh parsley leaves
2	cups (packed) fresh basil leaves
6	tablespoons fresh lemon juice
6	garlic cloves, chopped
4	teaspoons Dijon mustard
4	teaspoons grated lemon peel
1½	cups olive oil

Combine first 6 ingredients in processor and process until finely chopped. With machine running, gradually add oil and blend well. Transfer to serving bowl. Season with salt and pepper. *(Can be prepared 2 hours ahead. Cover and chill. Bring to room temperature before using.)*

ONION BAGEL CROUTONS

Crunchy and quick-to-make, these are a terrific addition to the "bar." MAKES ABOUT 4 CUPS

3	tablespoons butter
1½	tablespoons olive oil
2	small garlic cloves, minced
3	onion bagels, each cut into 2 semicircles

Preheat oven to 325°F. Combine first 3 ingredients in heavy small saucepan over medium heat. Stir until butter melts. Remove from heat. Slice bagels into ¼-inch-thick rounds. Place on baking sheet. Brush with butter mixture. Bake until crisp and brown, about 30 minutes. Cool. *(Can be prepared 1 week ahead. Store in airtight container at room temperature.)*

Do-It-Yourself Sundaes

- Assorted Ice Creams

Sauces
- Strawberry-Orange Compote
- Bittersweet Chocolate Sauce
- Hot Caramel Sauce

Toppings and Mix-ins
- Crumbled Brownies
- Crumbled Cookies
- M & M's
- Chocolate Chips
- Peanut Butter Chips
- Chopped Nuts
- Sliced Strawberries
- Chopped Dried Fruit

Garnishes
- Whipped Cream
- Cherries
- Candy Sprinkles
- Grated Chocolate
- Grated Coconut

- Coffee and Milk

A SUNDAE BAR IS A PARTY IN ITSELF, THE THEME, the activity and the food all rolled into one—one deliciously messy, fun-to-make dessert. It's a help-yourself buffet that begins with an assortment of different ice creams and includes several sauces as well as toppings limited only by the scope of your imagination (use the list here as a jumping-off point; excess is the name of the game).

A sundae bar can be readied ahead of time, making it a very versatile party. Scoop the ice cream into paper muffin cups and freeze. Make the sauces ahead (or purchase them, if time is running short) and just rewarm. All of the toppings can be chopped or grated or simply put into small bowls.

This is an ideal way to entertain kids of almost any age, from preschoolers to high schoolers. Set up a sundae bar to celebrate a team's win, to entertain a group of friends after the movies, to feed the troop that's meeting at your house. Whatever the occasion, a sundae bar will make it special.

STRAWBERRY-ORANGE COMPOTE

Sweetened fresh fruit makes a delicious ice cream topping. 8 SERVINGS

2   12-ounce baskets strawberries, hulled, sliced
4   oranges, peel and white pith removed
2   tablespoons honey
½   teaspoon ground cardamom

Place sliced strawberries in large bowl. Using small sharp knife, hold oranges over same bowl and cut between membranes to release segments, allowing juice and segments to fall into bowl. Squeeze orange membranes over same bowl to release any juice. Mix in honey and ground cardamom. *(Can be made 2 hours ahead. Cover and refrigerate.)*

BITTERSWEET CHOCOLATE SAUCE

A rich, homemade version of a classic sundae topper. MAKES ABOUT 1¾ CUPS

1   cup whipping cream
2   tablespoons honey
1   tablespoon brandy (optional)
Pinch of salt
8   ounces bittersweet (not unsweetened) or semisweet chocolate, finely chopped
2   teaspoons vanilla extract

Combine cream, honey, brandy (if desired) and salt in medium saucepan. Stir over high heat until mixture comes to boil. Remove from heat. Add chocolate and whisk until melted. Whisk in vanilla. Let stand until cool but still pourable. *(Can be made 3 days ahead. Cover and chill. Before serving, stir over low heat until just liquid but not warm.)*

HOT CARAMEL SAUCE

Make this sauce a day ahead and rewarm before serving. MAKES ABOUT 2 CUPS

1¼ cups (packed) golden brown sugar
⅔   cup light corn syrup
⅔   cup whipping cream
¼   cup (½ stick) unsalted butter
⅛   teaspoon salt

Stir brown sugar, corn syrup, whipping cream, butter and salt in heavy medium saucepan over low heat until sugar dissolves, about 4 minutes. Increase heat to medium-high and boil without stirring until deep amber color, brushing down sides of pan with wet pastry brush and swirling pan occasionally, about 11 minutes. Cool slightly. *(Can be prepared 1 day ahead. Cover and refrigerate. Reheat sauce over low heat, stirring constantly.)*

DURING THE WEEK, IT'S ALL ANYONE CAN DO TO JUGGLE work, homework and housework; it's only on the weekend that we have time to cook (which, when it's really fun, involves more than simply reheating) and sit around the table longer than it takes just to eat. With this in mind, the last section of the book includes a weekend's worth of menus that point up all of the opportunities, Friday night through Sunday evening, to entertain family and friends.

Consider Friday night. Instead of staying late on the job to finish the project that has to be done before the calendar turns over to Monday, invite colleagues back to your house for a "working" dinner. Or make a date with the kids, and get the weekend off to a fun start with a "family night at the videos." Fast-forward to Sunday, which holds all kinds of possibilities, from a quick-cooking breakfast or a brunch with friends to a family supper in the dining room. In between, there are menus for an easy and tasty breakfast, a portable lunch, cocktails for a crowd, an elegant dinner party and a come-as-you-are potluck.

The weekend is full of potential get-togethers. Hang your hat on one of them, reacquaint yourself with your kitchen and get ready to enjoy an old-fashioned pleasure: the company of friends and family over a home-cooked meal.

GET-TOGETHERS

Friday Dinner with Co-Workers

WHETHER YOU'RE CELEBRATING THE END OF A work week or bringing the project and your colleagues home with you, a casual dinner with co-workers is a welcome break, a chance to relax or refuel. It's also an opportunity to get to know the people you work with, a chance to talk about families and hobbies instead of profits and losses.

If everyone's set to meet at your house, avoid a kitchen rush hour by doing a few things the night before. Stop by the grocery on your way home Thursday. Make the dressing for the watercress salad and the blueberry sauce for the dessert later that same evening. On Friday, slip out an hour or so early and put the swordfish steaks in to marinate while you have a glass of wine, set the table and change.

From there on, it's a simple matter of chopping the salsa ingredients and mixing them together, grilling the swordfish and asparagus (which takes less than 10 minutes), marinating the mushrooms and tossing the salad. Dessert is that refreshing sauce you made last night spooned over lemon sorbet and topped with fresh blueberries.

This menu serves six but could be doubled easily. To offer a choice of meat or fish (or to serve steak to a meat-loving crowd), there's a recipe for beef tenderloin steaks (in the Option section) that can grill alongside the swordfish. Make the mango salsa (a spicy mix of mangoes, jalapeño and red pepper) that accompanies the steak ahead, and dinner will be ready in a matter of minutes.

menu for six

- GRILLED SWORDFISH WITH TOMATO-ORANGE SALSA

- GRILLED ASPARAGUS SPEARS

- WATERCRESS AND MUSHROOM SALAD

- SAUVIGNON BLANC

- LEMON SORBET WITH BLUEBERRIES AND BLUEBERRY SAUCE

menu option

- SPICED BEEF TENDERLOIN STEAKS WITH MANGO SALSA

GRILLED SWORDFISH WITH TOMATO-ORANGE SALSA

In addition to being easy, colorful and delicious, this recipe is also low in calories—but no one will know if you don't tell them. (Let the fish marinate while everyone makes their way from the office, then winds down.) Pour a crisp Sauvignon Blanc throughout the meal. 6 SERVINGS

SALSA

3   oranges, peeled, white pith removed, seeded, diced
1½ cups chopped seeded tomatoes
¼   cup minced red onion
¼   cup chopped fresh parsley
2   tablespoons fresh orange juice
2   teaspoons minced garlic
2   teaspoons balsamic vinegar
1   teaspoon minced peeled fresh ginger
½   teaspoon cayenne pepper

MARINADE

¾   cup bottled teriyaki sauce
⅔   cup dry Sherry
4   teaspoons minced garlic
2   teaspoons minced peeled fresh ginger
1   teaspoon oriental sesame oil

6   5- to 6-ounce swordfish steaks (1 inch thick)

FOR SALSA: Toss all ingredients in large bowl. Season to taste with salt and pepper. Let stand at least 1 hour. *(Can be prepared 4 hours ahead. Cover; chill. Bring to room temperature.)*

FOR MARINADE: Combine first 5 ingredients in small saucepan. Bring to boil. Set aside; cool.

Place swordfish in single layer in shallow glass baking dish. Pour marinade over swordfish; turn to coat evenly. Cover and refrigerate fish 1½ hours, turning often.

Prepare barbecue (medium-high heat). Remove fish from marinade. Grill until opaque in center, about 4 minutes per side. Transfer to platter. Serve with salsa.

GRILLED ASPARAGUS SPEARS

The grill—and a dash of roasted garlic oil—gives the asparagus terrific flavor. Flavored olive oils are becoming more readily available, and garlic oil can be found at most specialty foods stores and some supermarkets. 6 SERVINGS

4   cups water
2   teaspoons olive oil
1½ teaspoons roasted garlic oil or olive oil
1½ pounds large asparagus, trimmed

2   tablespoons chopped fresh Italian parsley

Prepare barbecue (medium-high heat). Combine 4 cups water, olive oil and roasted garlic oil in large bowl. Add asparagus to water mixture and toss to coat. Let stand 5 minutes. Drain. Season with salt and pepper.

Grill asparagus until crisp-tender, turning frequently, about 6 minutes. Transfer to platter. Sprinkle with chopped parsley.

WATERCRESS AND MUSHROOM SALAD

To retain the crispness of the watercress, toss it with the remaining salad ingredients right before you're ready to serve the meal. 6 SERVINGS

2   tablespoons balsamic vinegar
1½ teaspoons grated orange peel
½   teaspoon Dijon mustard
¼   cup canned low-salt chicken broth
1   tablespoon oriental sesame oil
1   tablespoon olive oil

1¼ pounds large mushrooms, stems trimmed, caps thinly sliced
½   cup thinly sliced green onions

2   large bunches watercress, trimmed

Combine vinegar, orange peel and mustard in small bowl. Gradually whisk in broth, sesame oil and olive oil. Season dressing to taste with salt and pepper. *(Can be prepared 1 day ahead. Cover and refrigerate.)*

Place mushrooms and green onions in large bowl. Pour ¼ cup dressing over mushroom mixture. Toss to coat well. Let stand 45 minutes at room temperature. *(Can be prepared 4 hours ahead. Cover; chill.)*

Add watercress and remaining dressing to mushroom mixture and toss. Season salad to taste with salt and pepper.

LEMON SORBET WITH BLUEBERRIES AND BLUEBERRY SAUCE

If you make the sauce on Thursday night, dessert will require a minimum of effort. 6 SERVINGS

SAUCE

4   cups fresh blueberries or
    1 pound frozen, thawed
1   cup water
3   tablespoons fresh lemon juice
2   tablespoons cornstarch
3   tablespoons sugar

3   half-pints lemon sorbet or sherbet
2   cups fresh blueberries
    Thinly sliced lemon peel (yellow part only)
    Fresh lemon balm or mint sprigs

FOR SAUCE: Combine first 4 ingredients in heavy large saucepan. Stir over medium-high heat until mixture boils and thickens. Cool slightly. Puree mixture in processor or blender until smooth. Mix in sugar. Chill until cold, about 3 hours. *(Can be prepared 2 days ahead. Keep refrigerated.)*

Scoop sorbet into goblets. Spoon sauce over. Top with fresh berries. Garnish with lemon peel and lemon balm.

Option

This recipe expands or changes the menu to suit your individual needs.

SPICED BEEF TENDERLOIN STEAKS WITH MANGO SALSA

This recipe would work well in place of the fish, though you will want to substitute a red wine (a Zinfandel would be nice). 6 SERVINGS

SALSA

½   cup hot jalapeño jelly
3   tablespoons fresh lime juice
2½   cups chopped peeled pitted mango
1¼   cups chopped red bell pepper
¾   cup chopped red onion
⅓   cup chopped fresh cilantro
1   jalapeño chili, minced

BEEF

1   tablespoon ground cinnamon
1   tablespoon ground coriander
1   tablespoon sugar
1   tablespoon paprika
1½   teaspoons salt
½   teaspoon cayenne pepper
12   4-ounce beef tenderloin steaks
     Olive oil

FOR SALSA: Whisk jelly and lime juice in large bowl. Mix in all remaining ingredients. Season to taste with salt and pepper. *(Can be made 2 hours ahead. Cover; chill.)*

FOR BEEF: Mix first 6 ingredients in small bowl. Brush both sides of steaks with olive oil. Sprinkle ½ teaspoon spice mixture over each side of each tenderloin steak.

Prepare barbecue (medium-high heat). Grill steaks to desired doneness, 2 minutes per side for medium-rare. Pass salsa separately.

Friday Dinner with the Kids

IN NOT A FEW HOUSEHOLDS, DINNER TOGETHER is a rare and wonderful thing. When it does happen, celebrate, because this is "company" at its best—noisy, loving, hungry, and clamoring, "What's for dinner?"

"Spaghetti and meatballs" is a good answer. Not only do kids like this all-time classic, but it's a dish you can make ahead of time. Refrigerate the meatballs and sauce overnight, or freeze them, together, for up to a month. Make the Italian dressing ahead, too, so that tossing the salad and boiling the pasta are all that remain to be done once everyone's assembled.

In anticipation of a Friday night family dinner, grab the kids one evening during the week (after their homework's done, of course) and let them help you make dessert: old-fashioned peanut butter cookies with chunks of chocolate added to sweeten the deal. In this simple recipe, the dough is rolled into balls—something even the youngest cook can do—then baked.

If it happens, much to your surprise, that everyone's home and hungry, and the cupboard is almost bare, reach for the canned tuna, some breadcrumbs, a loaf of bread and a few other ingredients typically on hand, and whip up the tuna burgers in the Option section, another kid-pleaser.

menu for four

- SPAGHETTI WITH MEATBALLS AND TOMATO SAUCE

- GARLIC BREAD

- MIXED GREENS SALAD WITH ITALIAN DRESSING

- RED WINE AND MILK

- PEANUT BUTTER COOKIES WITH CHOCOLATE CHUNKS

menu option

- OPEN-FACE TUNA BURGERS

SPAGHETTI WITH MEATBALLS AND TOMATO SAUCE

The whole family is sure to love this version of spaghetti and meatballs. Have some garlic bread on the side, and serve red wine for the grown-ups and milk for the kids. This recipe makes enough meatballs and tomato sauce to use for sandwiches the next day. 4 SERVINGS

SAUCE

3	tablespoons olive oil
1½	large onions, chopped
3	garlic cloves, chopped
1	tablespoon chopped fresh rosemary or parsley
1½	28-ounce cans crushed tomatoes with added puree (about 4½ cups)
1	cup canned beef broth

MEATBALLS

4	slices English muffin toasting bread or white sandwich bread with crusts, torn into pieces
2	cups milk
¾	pound ground veal
¾	pound sweet Italian sausages, casings removed
¾	cup freshly grated pecorino Romano cheese
3	large eggs
1	tablespoon chopped fresh rosemary or parsley
1	teaspoon salt
1	teaspoon pepper

Olive oil (for frying)

1	pound spaghetti
	Additional freshly grated pecorino Romano cheese

FOR SAUCE: Heat olive oil in heavy large pot over medium-high heat. Add onions and garlic; sauté until tender, about 8 minutes. Add rosemary; stir 30 seconds. Add tomatoes and beef broth. Bring to boil. Reduce heat; simmer sauce for 20 minutes.

MEANWHILE, PREPARE MEATBALLS: Place bread in medium bowl. Pour milk over. Let stand until bread is very soft, about 15 minutes. Squeeze milk from bread; place bread in large bowl. Add veal, sausage, ¾ cup cheese, eggs, rosemary, salt and pepper. Using hands, blend veal mixture thoroughly.

Pour oil into heavy large skillet to depth of ¼ inch; heat over medium-high heat. Working in batches, form veal mixture into 1½-inch balls; add to skillet. Cook until brown, about 4 minutes. Using slotted spoon, transfer meatballs to papers towels; drain.

Add meatballs to tomato sauce. Simmer until sauce thickens and meatballs are just cooked through, about 10 minutes. Season to taste with salt and pepper. *(Can be prepared 1 day ahead. Cover and refrigerate. Before using, bring to simmer, stirring frequently.)*

Cook pasta in pot of boiling salted water until just tender but still firm to bite, stirring occasionally. Drain. Transfer to platter. Spoon sauce and meatballs over. Serve, passing additional grated cheese separately.

MIXED GREENS SALAD WITH ITALIAN DRESSING

This dressing is great for turning mixed greens into a delicious salad. Add in sticks of cucumber, carrot and celery, if you like. 4 SERVINGS

6	tablespoons olive oil
2	tablespoons white wine vinegar
2	tablespoons chopped fresh parsley
1	tablespoon fresh lemon juice
2	garlic cloves, chopped
1	teaspoon dried basil
	Pinch of dried oregano
	Assorted mixed greens

Combine first 7 ingredients in small bowl and whisk to blend. Season to taste with salt and pepper. *(Can be prepared 1 day ahead. Cover and refrigerate.)* Toss with mixed greens and serve.

PEANUT BUTTER COOKIES WITH CHOCOLATE CHUNKS

Peanut butter cookies are an all-American classic, and the inclusion of honey, oats and chocolate chunks in this recipe makes for a terrific interpretation. MAKES ABOUT 27

1½ cups unbleached all purpose flour
⅓   cup old-fashioned oats
1   teaspoon baking soda
¼   teaspoon salt
1   cup old-fashioned chunky peanut butter (about 9 ounces)
1   cup (packed) golden brown sugar
½   cup (1 stick) unsalted butter, room temperature
¼   cup honey
1   large egg
1   teaspoon vanilla extract
5   ounces semisweet chocolate, coarsely chopped

Mix flour, oats, baking soda and salt in medium bowl. Using electric mixer, beat peanut butter, brown sugar, butter, honey, egg and vanilla in large bowl until well blended. Stir dry ingredients into peanut butter mixture in 2 additions. Stir in chopped chocolate. Cover and refrigerate until dough is firm and no longer sticky, about 30 minutes.

Preheat oven to 350°F. Butter 2 heavy large baking sheets. With hands, roll 1 heaping tablespoonful of dough for each cookie into 1¾-inch-diameter ball. Arrange cookies on prepared baking sheets, spacing 2½ inches apart. Bake cookies until puffed, beginning to brown on top and still very soft to touch, about 12 minutes. Cool cookies on baking sheets for 5 minutes. Using metal spatula, transfer cookies to rack and cool completely. *(Can be made 2 days ahead. Store in airtight container at room temperature.)*

Option

This recipe expands or changes the menu to suit your individual needs.

OPEN-FACE TUNA BURGERS

An easy main-course alternative. For kids who like tuna sandwiches, these quick-cooking burgers will be a real hit. 4 SERVINGS

1   12-ounce can solid white tuna packed in water, drained well
½   cup finely chopped green onions
⅓   cup (packed) fresh breadcrumbs
¼   cup yellow cornmeal
8   tablespoons mayonnaise
1   large egg, beaten to blend
1½ tablespoons Dijon mustard

4   slices rye, whole wheat or sourdough bread, toasted
4   small lettuce leaves
4   large slices tomato

1   tablespoon olive oil

Place tuna in large bowl; break up finely with fork. Mix in green onions, breadcrumbs, cornmeal, 4 tablespoons mayonnaise, egg and mustard. Season with salt and pepper. Shape mixture into four ¾-inch-thick patties.

Arrange bread on 4 plates. Spread each slice with 1 tablespoon mayonnaise; then top each with lettuce and tomato.

Heat oil in heavy large skillet over medium-high heat. Add tuna patties and cook until firm to touch and heated through, about 4 minutes per side. Place tuna on tomato slices and serve sandwiches immediately.

Saturday Morning Breakfast

THE TEMPTATION IS TO HIT THE GROUND running on Saturday, grabbing a cup of coffee and maybe a banana on your way out the door to the hockey game, the grocery store, the cleaners, the mall and any of the thousands of other things that seem to consume the day. But your energy will go a lot further, and your mood will be much brighter, if you take a little time for a hearty, yet still easy, family breakfast.

The toasty-rich smell of griddle cakes or pear muffins will make the day feel like a holiday, yet the griddle cakes take just minutes to make and the muffins (in the Option section) can be baked weeks ahead and frozen. Both recipes feature the flavor and nutrition of whole wheat flour, and either goes well with a melting pat of orange-flavored butter (another do-ahead recipe that's also very versatile, adding terrific flavor to any number of foods, from raisin toast to baked sweet potatoes).

To go with either the griddle cakes or the muffins, there are skillet-glazed plums, spiced with cinnamon and topped with a honey cream that's actually half and half, buttermilk and honey thickened overnight (one less thing to do in the morning). For a rich and warming drink, try the cinnamon-scented hot chocolate. Sausages, orange juice and coffee round out the meal and get things off to a leisurely start. Not that you'll be able to maintain that pace over the course of the day.

menu for four

- WALNUT GRIDDLE CAKES WITH ORANGE BUTTER

- SAUSAGES

- WARM SPICED PLUMS WITH HONEY CREAM

- MOCHA-CINNAMON HOT CHOCOLATE

- COFFEE AND ORANGE JUICE

menu option

- PEAR AND GRANOLA WHOLE WHEAT MUFFINS

WALNUT GRIDDLE CAKES WITH ORANGE BUTTER

Team the pancakes with sausages, and offer coffee and fresh orange juice. 4 SERVINGS

ORANGE BUTTER

½ cup (1 stick) unsalted butter, room temperature
1 tablespoon grated orange peel
2 teaspoons orange juice

GRIDDLE CAKES

¾ cup all purpose flour
¾ cup whole wheat flour
2 tablespoons brown sugar
1¾ teaspoons baking powder
½ teaspoon salt
2 to 2¼ cups low-fat milk
1 large egg
1 large egg white
2 tablespoons (¼ stick) unsalted butter, melted
⅔ cup chopped walnuts

Nonstick vegetable oil spray
Warm maple syrup

FOR ORANGE BUTTER: Mix all ingredients in small bowl; set aside. *(Can be prepared 1 day ahead. Cover and refrigerate. Bring to room temperature before using.)*

FOR GRIDDLE CAKES: Sift first 5 ingredients into medium bowl. Whisk 2 cups milk, egg, egg white and butter in large bowl to blend. Whisk in dry ingredients. Thin with remaining ¼ cup milk if too thick. Mix in walnuts.

Preheat oven to 200°F. Spray nonstick griddle or skillet with oil spray. Heat over medium heat. Working in batches, pour batter onto griddle by scant ¼ cupfuls. Cook until bubbles appear and bottoms of griddle cakes are golden, about 3 minutes. Turn and cook until bottoms are golden, about 2 minutes. Transfer to baking sheet. Keep warm in oven. Serve with orange butter and maple syrup.

WARM SPICED PLUMS WITH HONEY CREAM

The honey cream in this dish is also nice on oatmeal, waffles or fresh fruit. (Make it the night before to give it time to thicken.) 4 SERVINGS

1½ cups half and half
3 tablespoons low-fat buttermilk
3 tablespoons honey

2 pounds ripe plums, halved, pitted, cut into ¾-inch-thick wedges
½ cup sugar
½ teaspoon (scant) ground cinnamon

Whisk first 3 ingredients in medium glass bowl to blend. Let stand, uncovered, in warm place until thick, at least 6 hours or overnight. Refrigerate until ready to serve.

Heat large skillet over medium-high heat. Add plums and sugar; stir until sugar dissolves and forms glaze and plums are tender, about 8 minutes. Sprinkle cinnamon over. Spoon into bowls. Pour honey cream over.

MOCHA-CINNAMON HOT CHOCOLATE

This rich and chocolaty drink is a comforting breakfast treat. 4 SERVINGS

4 cups milk
2 3-inch-long cinnamon sticks, broken in half
6 tablespoons (packed) dark brown sugar
5 tablespoons instant espresso powder
¼ cup unsweetened cocoa powder
3 ounces milk chocolate, chopped
Ground nutmeg

Bring milk and 2 cinnamon sticks to simmer in heavy large saucepan over medium-high heat. Add brown sugar, espresso powder and cocoa powder. Whisk to blend. Add chocolate and whisk until melted and smooth. Discard cinnamon sticks. Ladle hot chocolate into 4 mugs. Sprinkle with nutmeg.

Option

This recipe expands or changes the menu to suit your individual needs.

PEAR AND GRANOLA WHOLE WHEAT MUFFINS

Nourishing muffins that are nice for a snack or a quick breakfast. Have them instead of the pancakes, if you like. MAKES 10

¾ cup pear nectar
2 large eggs
2 tablespoons vegetable oil
1 tablespoon fresh lemon juice
1 teaspoon grated lemon peel
1 cup whole wheat flour
1 cup all purpose flour
⅔ cup (packed) golden brown sugar
½ cup low-fat granola
1 tablespoon baking powder
½ teaspoon ground nutmeg
½ teaspoon salt
1¼ cups finely chopped unpeeled pear (about 1 medium)

Preheat oven to 350°F. Line ten ⅓-cup muffin cups with foil muffin papers. Whisk first 5 ingredients in large bowl to blend. Stir both flours and sugar in medium bowl until no sugar lumps remain. Mix in granola, baking powder, nutmeg and salt. Add pear; toss to coat. Stir flour mixture into egg mixture just to blend (batter will be thick). Divide among prepared muffin cups, mounding in center.

Bake muffins until golden brown and tester inserted in center comes out clean, about 20 minutes. Transfer muffins to rack and cool. *(Can be prepared ahead. Cover and keep 2 hours at room temperature or wrap tightly in plastic and freeze up to 2 weeks. If frozen, rewarm muffins in foil in 350°F oven for 12 minutes.)*

All in the Family

It's the rare family that regularly eats dinner together anymore. But as difficult as it is to get everyone to the table at the same time, you don't want to give up on the idea, even if it's only once a week. Here are some tips on making the family meal a reality in the face of hectic schedules, finicky eaters, heavy homework loads, etc.

•

Make a standing weekend date with the family: dinner on Friday night, an early breakfast on Saturday morning or supper on Sunday evening.

•

Pick a dish that everyone likes, maybe pancakes, tacos or roast chicken, and make it your family's specialty.

•

If your kids are young, bring them into the kitchen with you. Give them pads of heavy paper and crayons and let them design the "place mats" while you whip up something to eat.

•

When the kids have to wait for a parent who's running late, stave off hunger with baby carrots, peas in the pod and bean sprouts, none of which will ruin their appetites before dinner.

•

When you do get some time in the kitchen, prepare a double batch of something that keeps well. Store the extra "instant dinner" in the freezer, ready for that night when everyone's home but there's no time to cook.

•

For children who like their food the plainer the better, try serving dinner "add-on" style. Start with plain pasta, simple grilled chicken breasts or burgers, then set out a variety of toppings, sauces and mix-ins, encouraging the kids to create their own dishes.

Saturday Portable Lunch

As often as not, Saturday's plans will include a picnic lunch, whether at the beach, on a hike, or in the bleachers at a game. Or a picnic may *be* the plan, a good excuse to get out of town and enjoy the day. (Such an outing can also be an ideal way to entertain weekend guests for a few hours.)

Soup and a sandwich is a classic lunchtime combo, one that works in cool weather as well as warm. If the day is chilly, pack a thermos of tomato-dill soup, warming and appealing with its topping of melting white cheddar cheese. If it's hot, fill a chilled jug with the mint-scented cucumber-potato soup in the Option section, a smooth, refreshing puree served cold. Add an easy accompaniment: chicken sandwiches with watercress and chive butter (made with purchased roast chicken).

Brownies are always an easy picnic dessert. In the recipe here, they're still easy, but they're more delicious than ever, baked like a cake, glazed with bittersweet chocolate and topped with chopped pecans and bits of toffee. For serving ease, wrap individual slices separately. And while you're packing up, don't forget to include, as needed, a bottle opener and cups for the iced tea, mugs for the soup, plates, napkins and spoons, along with a large blanket and a trash bag. And a map, if unknown territory is your destination.

menu for six

- Tomato, Dill and White Cheddar Soup
- Chicken Sandwiches with Chive Butter
- Iced Tea
- Chocolate-Toffee Brownie Cake

menu option

- Cold Cucumber, Potato and Mint Soup

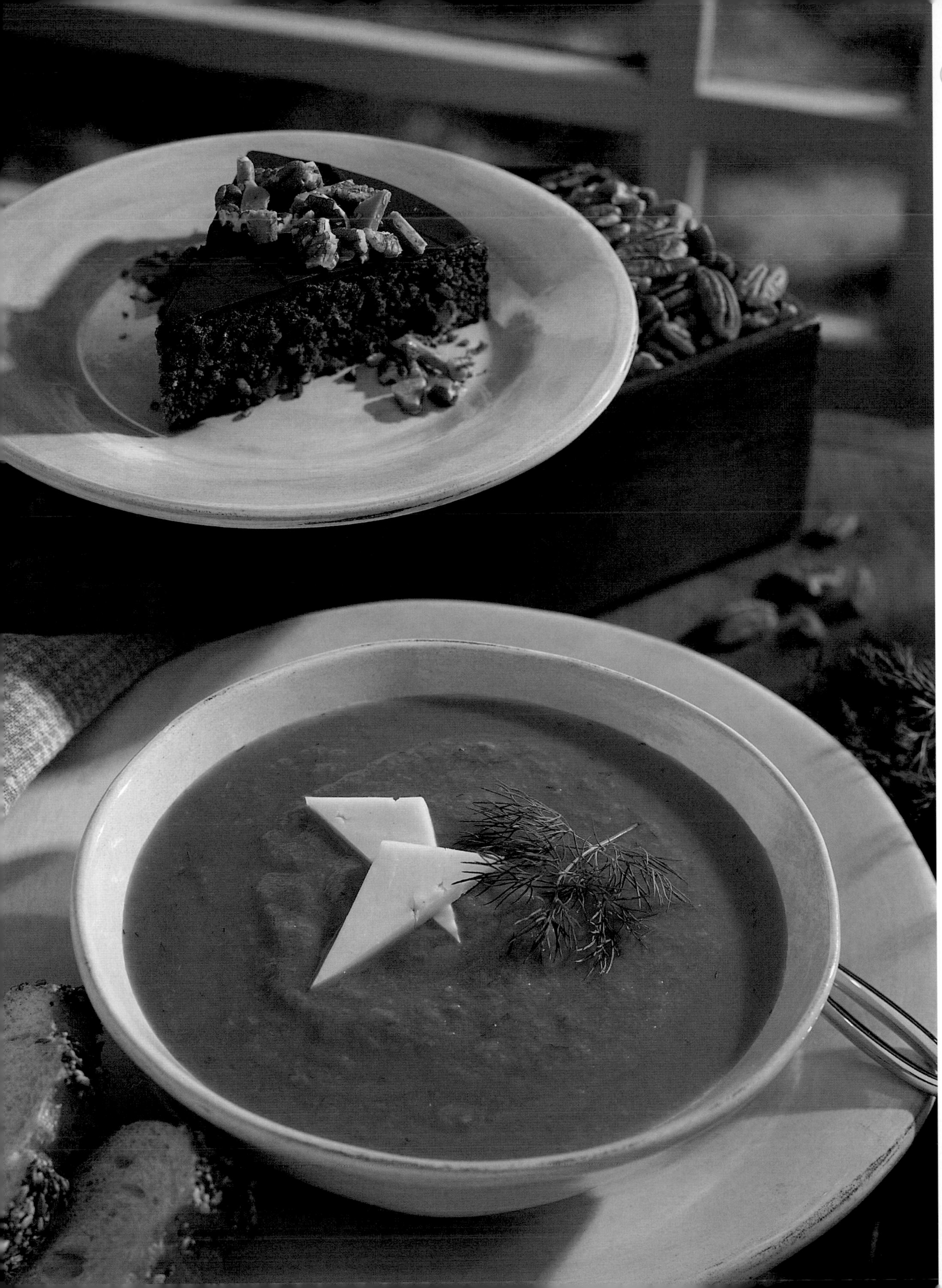

TOMATO, DILL AND WHITE CHEDDAR SOUP

This easy-to-make soup is a terrific Saturday lunch, especially when accompanied by the chicken sandwiches here and iced tea. If you're serving people who don't like spicy foods, eliminate the cayenne pepper. (To keep this warm for a cool-weather picnic, transport it in a thermos, then pour into mugs and top with cheese.) 6 SERVINGS

2 tablespoons olive oil
3 cups chopped leeks (white and pale green parts only)
4 28-ounce cans diced tomatoes with juices
4½ cups canned low-salt chicken broth
6 tablespoons (packed) chopped fresh dill or 2 tablespoons dried dillweed
¼ teaspoon cayenne pepper

½ cup light sour cream

4 ounces chilled sharp white cheddar cheese, sliced
Fresh dill sprigs

Heat oil in heavy large pot over medium heat. Add leeks and sauté until tender, about 6 minutes. Add tomatoes and their juices, broth, chopped dill and cayenne and bring to boil. Reduce heat and simmer uncovered until tomatoes are very soft, about 20 minutes.

Working in batches, puree soup in processor until smooth. Return to same pot. *(Can be made 1 day ahead. Cover and chill.)* Bring to simmer over medium-low heat. Season with salt and pepper. Gradually whisk in light sour cream (do not boil).

Transport soup in thermos. Pour into mugs and place cheese atop each. Garnish with dill sprigs and serve hot.

CHICKEN SANDWICHES WITH CHIVE BUTTER

Just the thing for a soup-and-sandwich lunch. Take bottles of iced tea along to drink. 6 SERVINGS

9 tablespoons butter, room temperature
4½ tablespoons minced fresh chives or green onion tops
1½ teaspoons Dijon mustard
Generous pinch of cayenne pepper

12 large slices whole wheat sandwich bread
1½ pounds purchased roast chicken, thinly sliced
2 small bunches watercress, thick stems trimmed

Combine butter, chives, mustard and cayenne in medium bowl; blend well. Season to taste with salt and pepper. *(Butter can be made 1 day ahead. Cover and refrigerate. Bring to room temperature before continuing.)*

Spread chive butter on 1 side of each bread slice. Place thinly sliced chicken on buttered side of 6 bread slices. Top chicken with some watercress. Press remaining 6 bread slices, buttered side down, onto watercress. Cut each sandwich into 4 pieces. Wrap in plastic. *(Can be made 4 hours ahead. Keep chilled.)*

CHOCOLATE-TOFFEE BROWNIE CAKE

English toffee enhances both the cake and the topping of this delicious treat. 6 TO 8 SERVINGS

CAKE

3½ tablespoons unsweetened cocoa powder

¾ cup all purpose flour
½ teaspoon baking powder
¼ teaspoon salt
½ cup (1 stick) unsalted butter, cut into small pieces

2 large eggs
⅔ cup sugar
¼ cup hot water

1¾ cups pecans, coarsely ground
(about 6 ounces)
½ cup English toffee bits (such as Heath's Bits)
½ cup semisweet chocolate chips

GLAZE

4 ounces bittersweet (not unsweetened) or
semisweet chocolate, chopped
3 tablespoons unsalted butter
1 tablespoon honey

¼ cup chopped pecans
½ cup English toffee bits

FOR CAKE: Position rack in center of oven and preheat oven to 350°F. Butter 9-inch-diameter cake pan with 2-inch-high sides. Sprinkle pan with ½ tablespoon cocoa powder; tilt pan to coat bottom and sides. Shake out excess.

Mix flour, baking powder and salt in small bowl. Stir butter and remaining 3 tablespoons cocoa in heavy small saucepan over medium-low heat until butter melts and mixture is smooth. Remove from heat.

Using electric mixer, beat eggs and sugar in large bowl until thick and fluffy. Mix in ¼ cup hot water and cocoa mixture. Mix in flour mixture. Stir in pecans, toffee bits and chocolate chips.

Transfer batter to prepared pan; smooth top. Bake cake until top is firm and tester inserted into center comes out with moist crumbs still attached, about 25 minutes. Cool in pan on rack 15 minutes. Run knife around pan sides to loosen cake. Turn cake out onto platter. Cool completely.

FOR GLAZE: Stir chocolate, butter and honey in small saucepan over medium-low heat until mixture is smooth. Cool until mixture thickens slightly but is still pourable, 10 minutes.

Pour glaze over top of cake, allowing some to run down sides. Spread glaze over top and sides of cake. Sprinkle top of cake with pecans and toffee bits. Chill until glaze is set, about 1 hour. (Can be made 1 day ahead. Keep chilled.) Cut cake into slices.

Option

This recipe expands or changes the menu to suit your individual needs.

COLD CUCUMBER, POTATO
AND MINT SOUP

Here's a cooling alternative for a warm-weather picnic. Transport it in a thermos; pour into mugs to serve. 6 SERVINGS

¼ cup (½ stick) unsalted butter
1 large onion, chopped
4 large cucumbers (about 2¾ pounds), peeled, seeded, chopped
1 pound boiling potatoes, peeled, chopped
4 cups canned low-salt chicken broth

½ cup plus 2 tablespoons half and half
¼ cup finely chopped fresh mint
3 tablespoons red wine vinegar
½ teaspoon white pepper
Fresh mint sprigs

Melt butter in heavy large saucepan over low heat. Add chopped onion; cover and cook until translucent, stirring occasionally, about 15 minutes. Increase heat to high. Add cucumbers, potatoes and broth and bring to boil. Reduce heat, cover and simmer until potatoes are tender, about 30 minutes. Cool. Puree soup in batches in blender or processor until smooth. Strain soup into large bowl. Cover and chill until cold, about 8 hours.

Stir half and half, chopped mint, vinegar and white pepper into soup. Season with salt. *(Can be prepared 1 day ahead. Cover and refrigerate.)* Transport soup in thermos. Pour into mugs. Garnish with mint sprigs.

Saturday Cocktails and Appetizers

THE COCKTAIL PARTY IS MORE POPULAR NOW than ever, as a new generation has discovered just how easy this kind of thing is to pull off, especially when the guest list is a long one. A cocktail party is neither a whole-dinner nor a whole-evening commitment for host or guests. And the cook can prepare things as time allows, filling in as needed with purchased items.

Cocktails, though, aren't necessarily what they used to be—many people now opt for wine, beer or water, instead. And guests have also come to appreciate party fare that's lower in fat. For that reason, the main menu here features five appetizers as healthful as they are delicious. But because a bite or two of something sinful is the key to balance in any diet, the offerings in the Options section bring greater richness to the spread and a feeling of indulgence.

Every dish here can be made ahead, at least in good part. You can start the day before with the roasted red pepper salsa (which gets spooned into endive leaves); the deviled eggs (with mashed potato substituting for some of the yolks); and the pastry-wrapped Brie. Other dishes, like the shrimp in snow peas, the canapés and the vegetable rolls, are easily made the morning of the party, leaving you plenty of time to put the finishing touches on the remaining hors d'oeuvres, clean the house and dress up a bit. After all, it is a cocktail party.

menu for ten to twelve

- COCKTAILS, WINE, BEER, BOTTLED WATER

- SPICY SHRIMP WRAPPED IN SNOW PEAS

- ENDIVE LEAVES WITH ROASTED RED BELL PEPPER SALSA

- CRUNCHY VEGETABLE ROLLS WITH SOY DIPPING SAUCE

- DEVILED EGGS WITH SMOKED SALMON AND GREEN ONIONS

- PUREED BROCCOLI AND ROASTED GARLIC CANAPÉS

menu options

- HERBED BRIE EN CROÛTE

- POTATOES TOPPED WITH SOUR CREAM AND CAVIAR

- SPINACH-BACON SPIRALS

- BLACK PEPPER ALMONDS

SPICY SHRIMP WRAPPED IN SNOW PEAS

Asian flavors accent this low-fat do-ahead appetizer. MAKES 20

20 uncooked large shrimp, peeled, deveined
1 tablespoon minced fresh ginger
2 teaspoons vegetable oil
1 large garlic clove, pressed
½ teaspoon Chinese five-spice powder*

20 large snow peas, stringed
1 teaspoon oriental sesame oil
½ teaspoon sesame seeds, toasted

2 tablespoons reduced-sodium soy sauce

20 small wooden skewers or toothpicks

Combine shrimp, ginger, vegetable oil, garlic and five-spice powder in medium bowl; toss to blend. Cover mixture and refrigerate at least 1 hour and up to 4 hours.

Bring medium pot of salted water to boil. Add snow peas; cook just until crisp-tender, about 45 seconds. Drain. Rinse with cold water. Drain; pat dry. Transfer peas to bowl. Drizzle sesame oil and sesame seeds over; toss to coat. Set aside.

Heat large nonstick skillet over medium-high heat. Add shrimp mixture and sauté 3 minutes. Add soy sauce; stir until shrimp are just opaque in center and liquid evaporates, about 1 minute. Transfer to plate and cool completely.

Wrap 1 snow pea lengthwise around each shrimp from head to tail. Secure with skewers. *(Can be prepared 6 hours ahead. Cover and refrigerate.)* Serve chilled or at room temperature.

A blend of ground anise, cinnamon, star anise, cloves and ginger; available in the spice section of most supermarkets nationwide.

ENDIVE LEAVES WITH ROASTED RED BELL PEPPER SALSA

In this healthful salsa, fennel, olives and rosemary combine with roasted bell peppers. MAKES 24

2 large red bell peppers

½ cup minced fresh fennel bulb
2 tablespoons chopped brine-cured black olives (such as Kalamata)
1 tablespoon olive oil (preferably extra-virgin)
1 tablespoon red wine vinegar
¾ teaspoon minced fresh rosemary or ½ teaspoon dried
½ teaspoon minced garlic

24 Belgian endive leaves (from about 3 large heads), ends trimmed

Char red bell peppers over gas flame or in broiler until blackened on all sides. Enclose in paper bag; let stand 10 minutes. Peel, seed and chop peppers.

Mix fennel, olives, oil, vinegar, rosemary, garlic and peppers in medium bowl. Season with salt and pepper. *(Can be made 1 day ahead. Cover and refrigerate.)*

Arrange endive leaves on platter. Spoon 1 tablespoon salsa onto each endive leaf.

CRUNCHY VEGETABLE ROLLS WITH SOY DIPPING SAUCE

These rolls are baked instead of deep-fried, making them a healthful, satisfying alternative to traditional egg rolls. 12 SERVINGS

Nonstick vegetable oil spray
6 teaspoons oriental sesame oil
9 tablespoons chopped green onions
3 tablespoons finely chopped garlic
3 tablespoons finely chopped peeled fresh ginger
9 cups (packed) coarsely chopped fresh spinach
12 fresh shiitake mushrooms, stemmed, caps thinly sliced
6 small zucchini, cut into matchstick-size strips
3 carrots, cut into matchstick-size strips
13 tablespoons low-sodium soy sauce

12 6-inch egg roll wrappers

9 tablespoons rice vinegar

Preheat oven to 375°F. Spray 2 heavy baking sheets with vegetable oil spray. Heat 1½ teaspoons sesame oil in each of 2 heavy large nonstick woks or skillets over high heat. Add green onions, garlic and ginger, dividing equally; stir-fry 1 minute. Add spinach, mushrooms, zucchini and carrots, dividing equally; stir-fry until vegetables are crisp-tender and spinach wilts, about 3 minutes. Add 2 tablespoons soy sauce to each wok and stir to coat vegetables, about 30 seconds. Combine vegetables in colander and drain off liquid. Cool vegetables completely.

Place egg roll wrappers on work surface. Spoon filling in 4 x 2-inch rectangle in center of each wrapper, dividing equally. Fold in short sides, then roll up tightly. Arrange seam side down on prepared sheets. *(Can be made 6 hours ahead. Cover with plastic wrap; refrigerate. Remove plastic before continuing.)* Bake until wrappers are crisp and filling is heated through, turning once, about 10 minutes.

Meanwhile, mix vinegar and remaining 3 teaspoons sesame oil and 9 tablespoons soy sauce in small bowl.

Transfer vegetable rolls to platter. Serve warm with dipping sauce.

DEVILED EGGS WITH SMOKED SALMON AND GREEN ONIONS

Smoked salmon enhances this innovative version of a classic. Potato stands in for half of the yolks to cut fat and cholesterol. MAKES 12

1 8- to 9-ounce russet potato, peeled, cut into ½-inch pieces

6 large eggs
1 tablespoon olive oil (preferably extra-virgin)
1 tablespoon fresh lemon juice
2 teaspoons whole-grain Dijon mustard
4 tablespoons minced smoked salmon (about 1 ounce)
3 tablespoons finely chopped green onions

Cook potato in pot of boiling salted water until very tender, 10 minutes. Drain; cool.

Meanwhile, place eggs in medium saucepan; cover with water. Bring to boil. Cover; remove from heat and let stand 15 minutes. Drain. Rinse eggs with cold water until cool. Peel off shells. Halve eggs lengthwise. Reserve 3 egg yolks for another use. Combine remaining 3 yolks, potato, oil, lemon juice and mustard in medium bowl. Mash with fork until well blended. Stir in 2 tablespoons salmon and 1½ tablespoons green onions. Season to taste with salt and pepper.

Divide potato-and-yolk mixture among hard-boiled egg white halves, mounding slightly. *(Eggs can be made 1 day ahead. Cover with plastic; chill.)* Garnish eggs with 2 tablespoons salmon and 1½ tablespoons green onions.

PUREED BROCCOLI AND ROASTED GARLIC CANAPÉS

This appetizer takes the idea of cheese and crackers around a few corners, and the detour is worth every gram of fat that's left behind. Here, toasted baguette slices are spread with a bright broccoli, white bean and garlic puree. MAKES 16

4 garlic cloves, peeled
2 tablespoons olive oil (preferably extra-virgin)
⅛ teaspoon dried crushed red pepper
16 ½-inch-thick baguette slices

2 cups broccoli florets plus ½ cup peeled thinly sliced stalks (from about 8 ounces broccoli)
1 cup canned cannellini (white kidney beans), rinsed, drained
2 tablespoons fresh lemon juice

Preheat oven to 350°F. Combine garlic, oil and red pepper in small custard cup. Cover tightly with foil. Bake until garlic is tender, about 35 minutes. Cool slightly. Arrange baguette slices in single layer on baking sheet. Bake until lightly toasted, about 15 minutes. Set aside.

Steam broccoli florets and stalks until very tender, 8 minutes. Rinse with cold water. Drain. Transfer to processor. Add cannellini, lemon juice and oil-and-garlic mixture. Process until smooth. Season puree with salt and pepper. *(Toasts and broccoli puree can be made up to 6 hours ahead. Store toasts airtight at room temperature. Cover and chill puree.)*

Spread broccoli puree atop toasts. Transfer canapés to platter and serve.

Options

These recipes expand or change the menu to suit your individual needs.

HERBED BRIE EN CROÛTE

An indulgent alternative to the canapés. Make two of these pastry-wrapped cheeses, bringing out the second one later in the evening. Serve with a selection of fruit and crackers. 10 TO 12 SERVINGS

2 17.6-ounce wheels ripe Brie, chilled
⅔ cup minced shallots (about 4 large)
¼ cup chopped fresh chives or green onions
4 teaspoons dry white vermouth
½ teaspoon white pepper

1 17¼-ounce package frozen puff pastry sheets, thawed

1 egg, beaten to blend (for glaze)

Cut off top rind of cheeses and discard. Combine shallots, chives, vermouth and pepper in small bowl and mix until blended. Press shallot mixture firmly over top of each cheese wheel.

Roll out 1 pastry sheet on lightly floured surface to 11-inch square. Lay pastry over 1 wheel of cheese. Fold dough under cheese, enclosing completely. Turn cheese over; press pastry seams together, sealing tightly. Turn cheese right side up and place on baking sheet. Wrap in plastic and refrigerate at least 30 minutes. Repeat with remaining pastry and cheese. *(Can be prepared 1 day ahead; keep refrigerated.)*

Preheat oven to 400°F. Brush top and sides of pastry with egg glaze. Bake both cheeses until pastry is golden brown, about 25 minutes. Let stand 30 minutes before serving.

POTATOES TOPPED WITH SOUR CREAM AND CAVIAR

Add these to the menu for that touch of elegance. When you use caviar of different colors, they make a lovely presentation. Get bite-size potatoes for ease of eating. 10 TO 12 SERVINGS

24 baby red-skinned potatoes
1½ tablespoons olive oil
½ cup (about) sour cream
Salmon caviar
Black caviar

Preheat oven to 425°F. Using small sharp knife, cut small slice off bottom of each potato so that potato will stand upright. Toss potatoes with olive oil in large bowl. Place on baking sheet. Bake potatoes until tender, about 30 minutes. Cool slightly. Using melon baller, scoop out small amount from top of each potato. Sprinkle inside of potatoes with pepper. *(Can be prepared 2 hours ahead. Let stand at room temperature. Reheat potatoes in 425°F oven 15 minutes.)* Place teaspoon of sour cream in center of each potato. Garnish potatoes with small scoop of caviar.

SPINACH-BACON SPIRALS

A rich alternative to the vegetable rolls, and a perfect accompaniment to cocktails. Most of the prep work here can be done ahead. Then just slice, bake and serve. MAKES ABOUT 30

6 bacon slices
1 10-ounce package frozen chopped spinach, thawed, squeezed dry
4 ounces cream cheese, room temperature
¼ cup mayonnaise
1 teaspoon salt
½ teaspoon pepper
½ cup chopped green onions

3 9-inch-diameter flour tortillas

Cook bacon in heavy large skillet over medium heat until crisp; drain. Crumble bacon into medium bowl; stir in chopped spinach and then next 5 ingredients.

Heat 1 tortilla in large skillet over high heat until warm and pliable, about 1 minute per side. Transfer to work surface. Spread ⅓ of filling over tortilla, leaving ½-inch border. Roll up tightly, enclosing filling. Wrap in plastic. Repeat with remaining 2 tortillas and spinach filling. Chill rolls until filling is firm, at least 1 hour or up to 4 hours.

Preheat oven to 400°F. Remove plastic; slice off unfilled ends. Cut rolls crosswise on slight diagonal into ¾-inch-thick slices. Arrange slices on large baking sheet. Bake slices until heated through, about 7 minutes.

BLACK PEPPER ALMONDS

Brown sugar and black pepper make these almonds sweet and spicy. MAKES 2⅔ CUPS

1 tablespoon pepper
2 teaspoons salt
¼ cup (½ stick) butter
¾ cup (packed) golden brown sugar
4 teaspoons water
2⅔ cups blanched whole almonds

Preheat oven to 350°F. Line large baking sheet with foil. Lightly butter foil. Mix pepper and salt in small bowl. Melt butter in large nonstick skillet over medium-low heat. Add sugar and 4 teaspoons water; stir until sugar dissolves. Add almonds; toss to coat. Cook over medium heat until syrup thickens and almonds are well coated, stirring occasionally, about 5 minutes. Sprinkle half of pepper mixture over almonds.

Transfer almonds to baking sheet. Using spatula and working quickly, separate almonds. Sprinkle remaining pepper mixture over. Bake until deep golden brown, about 10 minutes. Transfer sheet to rack; cool. *(Can be made 4 days ahead. Store airtight at room temperature.)*

Saturday Elegant Dinner Party

THE SATURDAY NIGHT DINNER PARTY HAS evolved, in recent years, from an elaborate and costly affair that featured complex, time-consuming dishes into a relaxed, lower-key meal of appealing foods that don't require the better part of your weekend to make. The pressure is off; now the goal is to get together with friends and enjoy their company *and* a good meal.

One way to ensure that you'll be relaxed come the arrival of the first guest is to prepare almost everything ahead of time, taking the pressure off in terms of last-minute timing and serving. This menu is ideal in that both the first course and all of the main-course offerings are served either chilled or at room temperature. Gazpacho, this one with shrimp and a garden's worth of vegetables, makes a refreshing start to the meal—and comes straight out of the refrigerator. It's followed by crisp, sesame seed-coated chicken that you bake a day ahead, refrigerate overnight and bring to room temperature before serving. The chicken is served with couscous mixed with toasted pistachios and dried apricots, and a spinach salad with grilled red onions.

For dessert, delicate "purses" of phyllo with a banana and hazelnut filling look impressive but are, in fact, a breeze to make. Put them in the oven as you sit down to dinner. Or to continue in the "make ahead" vein, prepare the mocha tart in the Options section.

menu for ten

- SHRIMP GAZPACHO

- ORANGE CHICKEN WITH SESAME AND GINGER

- COUSCOUS WITH DRIED APRICOTS AND PISTACHIOS

- SPINACH SALAD WITH GRILLED ONIONS AND TAHINI VINAIGRETTE

- CHARDONNAY

- CARAMELIZED BANANA PURSES WITH WHITE CHOCOLATE SAUCE

menu options

- GRILLED LAMB KEBABS WITH CORIANDER AND CUMIN

- MARBLEIZED MOCHA TART

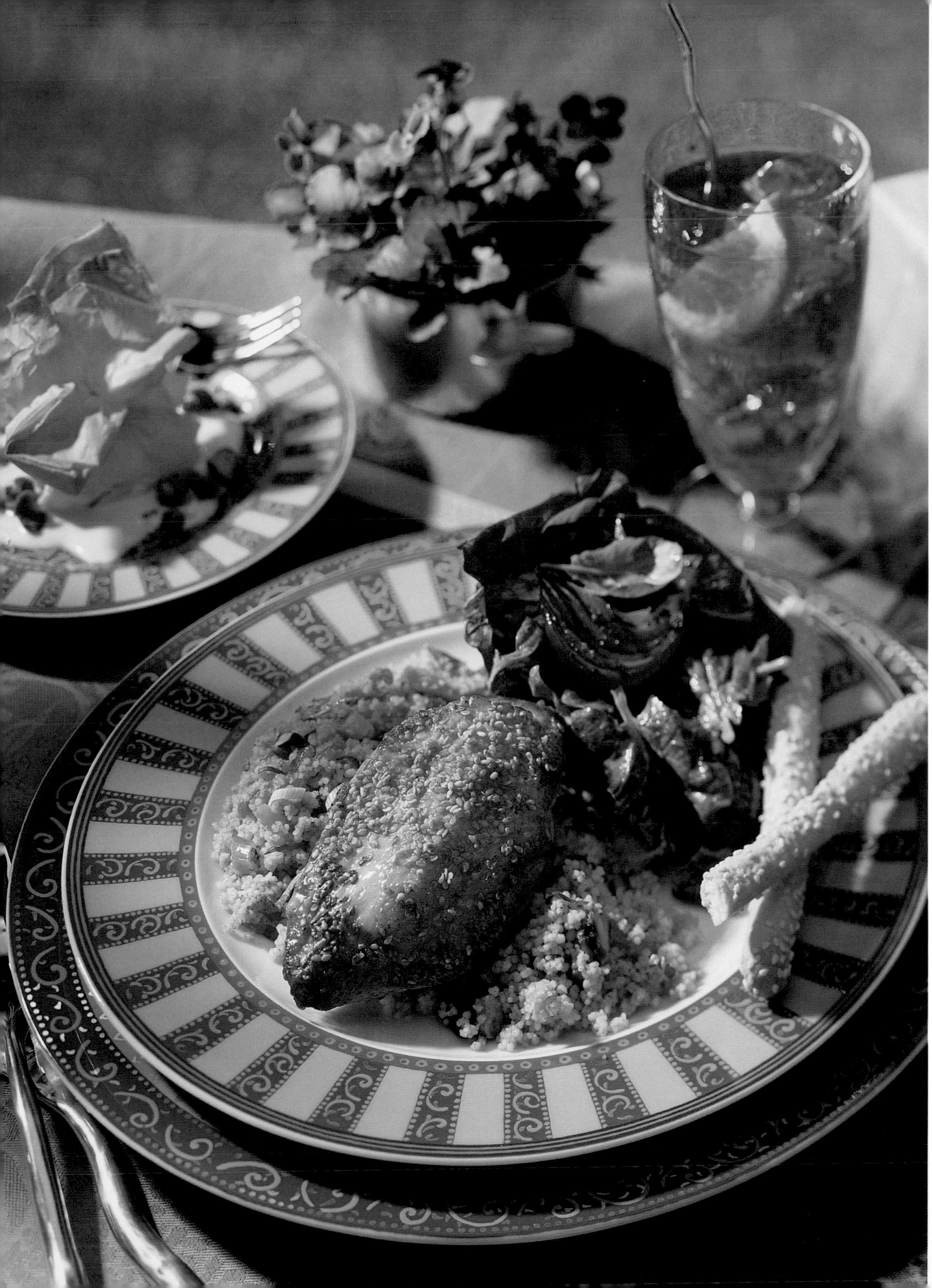

SHRIMP GAZPACHO

This refreshing start to the meal can be prepared Saturday morning and refrigerated until you're ready to serve it. 10 SERVINGS

3 garlic cloves, chopped
3 tablespoons olive oil
3 tablespoons red wine vinegar
3 tablespoons fresh lemon juice
¾ pound cooked large shrimp, peeled, deveined

1 pound large plum tomatoes (about 9), seeded, chopped
1½ green bell peppers, chopped
1½ red bell peppers, chopped
1 medium cucumber, peeled, seeded, chopped
1½ bunches green onions, chopped
1 small bunch fresh cilantro leaves, chopped
1½ large jalapeño chilies, minced
6¾ cups tomato juice, chilled
Lemon wedges

Combine first 4 ingredients in medium bowl. Add shrimp. Cover mixture and refrigerate 1 to 2 hours.

Combine tomatoes, both bell peppers, cucumber, green onions, cilantro and jalapeños in large bowl. Add tomato juice. Stir in shrimp mixture. Season to taste with salt and pepper. *(Can be prepared 6 hours ahead. Cover and refrigerate.)* Ladle soup into bowls. Garnish with lemon wedges and serve.

ORANGE CHICKEN WITH SESAME AND GINGER

Make this on Friday evening so that the cooked chicken can marinate overnight. Take the dish out of the refrigerator about an hour before dinner, and serve it at room temperature with a crisp Chardonnay. 10 SERVINGS

1 cup fresh orange juice
½ cup fresh lemon juice
⅓ cup mango chutney
¼ cup chopped peeled fresh ginger
3 tablespoons seasoned rice vinegar*
3 tablespoons grated orange peel
1 tablespoon oriental sesame oil
½ teaspoon dried crushed red pepper

¼ cup sesame seeds
10 boneless chicken breast halves with skin

6 tablespoons (¾ stick) butter

Combine first 8 ingredients in medium bowl. Whisk until well blended. Pour mixture into 13 x 9 x 2-inch glass baking dish.

Preheat oven to 400°F. Place sesame seeds in small bowl. Sprinkle chicken breast halves with salt and pepper. Place skin side down on seeds, coating skin.

Melt 3 tablespoons butter in large nonstick skillet over high heat. Add 5 chicken breasts, skin side down, to skillet and cook until golden brown, about 3 minutes. Turn chicken over; cook 2 minutes longer. Place chicken, skin side up, in marinade in baking dish. Wash skillet. Repeat with remaining 3 tablespoons butter and 5 chicken breasts.

Cover chicken with foil; bake until cooked through, about 20 minutes. Remove foil; let chicken cool 1 hour in marinade. Cover; chill overnight. Let chicken stand 1 hour at room temperature before serving.

*Also known as sushi vinegar; available in Asian markets and in some supermarkets.

COUSCOUS WITH DRIED APRICOTS AND PISTACHIOS

Toasted pistachios, apricots, cinnamon and all-spice bring great flavor to this accompaniment to the chicken. 10 SERVINGS

3 cups water
4½ tablespoons extra-virgin olive oil
2 teaspoons salt
1½ 10-ounce boxes couscous (about 2¼ cups)
1¼ cups (about 7 ounces) dried apricots, thinly sliced
2¼ teaspoons ground cinnamon
½ teaspoon ground allspice

1¼ cups (about 4 ounces) unsalted pistachios, toasted, chopped
¾ cup chopped green onions
6 tablespoons thinly sliced fresh basil

Combine 3 cups water, oil and salt in medium saucepan; bring to boil. Combine couscous, apricots and spices in large bowl. Add boiling liquid. Cover immediately; let stand until water is absorbed, about 5 minutes. Uncover; fluff with fork. Cool. *(Can be made 6 hours ahead. Cover; refrigerate. Bring to room temperature before continuing.)*

Mix nuts, green onions and basil into couscous. Season with salt and pepper.

SPINACH SALAD WITH GRILLED ONIONS AND TAHINI VINAIGRETTE

Tahini, a creamy sesame seed paste, adds a nice twist to the dressing for the salad. 10 SERVINGS

VINAIGRETTE

½ cup water
¼ cup white wine vinegar
3 tablespoons tahini (sesame seed paste)*
2 tablespoons coarse-grained mustard
1 teaspoon honey
1 small garlic clove, minced
¾ cup vegetable oil

SALAD

2 large red onions

12 cups (packed) baby spinach, trimmed
10 large radicchio leaves

FOR VINAIGRETTE: Combine all ingredients except oil in blender and blend well. Gradually blend in oil. Season to taste with salt and pepper. *(Can be made 2 days ahead. Cover and chill. Bring vinaigrette to room temperature before using.)*

FOR SALAD: Cut onions lengthwise into ½-inch-thick wedges, leaving root ends intact. Place onions in 15 x 10-inch glass baking dish. Pour 1 cup vinaigrette over onions, coating evenly. Let marinate 3 hours. Chill remaining dressing. *(Can be made 1 day ahead. Chill onions.)*

Prepare barbecue (medium-high heat) or preheat broiler. Sprinkle onions with salt and pepper. Grill or broil onions until golden, turning occasionally, about 12 minutes. *(Can be made 6 hours ahead. Keep at room temperature.)*

Place spinach in large bowl. Toss with enough vinaigrette to coat. Season with salt and pepper. Fill radicchio leaves with spinach. Top with grilled onions. Pass remaining vinaigrette.

*Tahini is available at Middle Eastern and natural foods stores and some supermarkets.

CARAMELIZED BANANA PURSES WITH WHITE CHOCOLATE SAUCE

A real winner: Delicate "purses" of phyllo pastry hold a banana and hazelnut filling. They're served with a rich white chocolate sauce and a crunchy hazelnut crumble. 10 SERVINGS

CRUMBLE

1	cup (packed) golden brown sugar
½	cup (1 stick) unsalted butter
1½	cups all purpose flour
1	cup hazelnuts (about 5 ounces), coarsely chopped
	Pinch of salt

FILLING

¾	cup sugar
6	tablespoons (¾ stick) unsalted butter
¼	cup fresh lime juice
6	medium bananas (about 2 pounds), peeled, cut into ¾-inch-thick slices
2	tablespoons Frangelico (hazelnut liqueur) or amaretto

10	sheets fresh phyllo pastry or frozen, thawed
¾	cup (1½ sticks) unsalted butter, melted

White Chocolate Sauce (see recipe at right)

FOR CRUMBLE: Preheat oven to 300°F. Stir sugar and butter in medium saucepan over low heat until butter melts. Remove from heat. Mix in flour, nuts and salt. Spread on baking sheet. Bake until dry and golden, about 30 minutes. Cool. Break into small pieces. *(Can be made 1 day ahead. Store in airtight container at room temperature.)*

FOR FILLING: Stir sugar, 6 tablespoons butter and lime juice in large nonstick skillet over low heat until sugar dissolves. Increase heat to high and stir until butter melts and mixture begins to brown around edges, about 5 minutes. Add bananas and liqueur; stir until bananas are coated with butter mixture, about 2 minutes. Transfer to large bowl; cool.

Mix 1 cup hazelnut crumble into banana mixture. Place 1 phyllo sheet on work surface (keep remaining phyllo covered with plastic wrap, then damp towel). Brush phyllo with melted butter. Fold phyllo in half crosswise, brush with butter, then fold in half again, forming square; brush with butter. Place generous ¼ cup filling in center of phyllo square. Bring all edges of phyllo square up toward center and squeeze firmly at top, forming purse. Place on baking sheet. Repeat with remaining phyllo sheets, melted butter and filling, forming total of 10 purses. *(Can be prepared 6 hours ahead. Chill.)*

Preheat oven to 350°F. Cover phyllo purses loosely with foil. Bake until purses begin to color, about 30 minutes. Remove foil and continue baking until phyllo is golden, about 15 minutes longer.

Place 1 purse on each of 10 plates. Spoon 3 tablespoons warm White Chocolate Sauce around each. Sprinkle remaining hazelnut crumble over sauce and serve.

WHITE CHOCOLATE SAUCE

You can prepare this delicious sauce during the week and then rewarm it before serving. MAKES ABOUT 2 CUPS

6	ounces good-quality white chocolate (such as Lindt or Baker's), chopped
1½	cups whipping cream

Place chocolate in small bowl. Bring cream to boil in heavy small saucepan. Pour cream over chocolate; whisk until smooth. *(Can be made 2 days ahead. Cool; cover and chill. Before serving, rewarm over low heat, stirring.)*

GRILLED LAMB KEBABS WITH CORIANDER AND CUMIN

This easy main-course recipe would lend a heartier feel to the menu but goes equally well with all of the other dishes. 10 SERVINGS

7½ tablespoons olive oil
3 tablespoons red wine vinegar
5 large garlic cloves, minced
1½ tablespoons ground cumin
1½ tablespoons ground coriander
1 teaspoon cayenne pepper
1¼ teaspoons salt
7 to 7½ pounds lamb shoulder (round-bone) chops, trimmed, boned, cut into 1-inch pieces
20 bamboo skewers, soaked in water 10 minutes

Prepare barbecue (medium-high heat) or preheat broiler. Whisk first 7 ingredients in large bowl to blend. Add lamb; toss to coat. Let stand 5 minutes or cover and chill overnight. Thread lamb on skewers, leaving ½-inch space between each piece.

Grill or broil lamb until crusty brown outside but still pink inside, turning occasionally, about 8 minutes. Arrange skewers on plates.

MARBLEIZED MOCHA TART

This would be a good replacement for the "purses" if you'd rather make one dessert. 16 SERVINGS

CRUST

2 cups all purpose flour
⅔ cup powdered sugar
¼ teaspoon salt
½ cup plus 2 tablespoons (1¼ sticks) chilled unsalted butter, cut into pieces
1 large egg yolk
¼ cup (about) ice water

MOCHA GANACHE

15 ounces semisweet chocolate, chopped
1 cup whipping cream
1½ tablespoons instant espresso powder

WHITE CHOCOLATE GANACHE

3 ounces good-quality white chocolate (such as Lindt or Baker's), finely chopped
3 tablespoons whipping cream

FOR CRUST: Blend flour, powdered sugar and salt in processor 5 seconds. Add butter and cut in using on/off turns until mixture resembles coarse meal. Mix in yolk and enough water to form moist clumps. Knead dough briefly on work surface to combine; flatten into disk. Wrap in plastic and chill until firm, at least 2 hours and up to 1 day.

Preheat oven to 375°F. Roll out dough on lightly floured surface to 16-inch round (scant ⅛ inch thick). Transfer dough to 11-inch-diameter tart pan with removable bottom. Press dough into pan; trim excess. Freeze crust 15 minutes.

Place tart pan on baking sheet. Bake crust 10 minutes; pierce with toothpick if crust bubbles. Continue to bake until pale golden, 12 minutes. Transfer to rack; cool.

FOR MOCHA GANACHE: Stir chocolate, cream and espresso powder in heavy medium saucepan over low heat just until chocolate melts and mixture is smooth (mixture will be warm, not hot). Pour into crust.

FOR WHITE CHOCOLATE GANACHE: Stir white chocolate and cream in heavy small saucepan over very low heat just until chocolate melts and mixture is smooth. Drizzle over mocha ganache. Using tip of small knife or toothpick, swirl fillings together to marbleize. Refrigerate tart until filling is firm, at least 3 hours and up to 2 days.

Saturday Potluck Party

IT'S NOT THAT YOU DON'T WANT TO HAVE friends over for dinner, it's just that there doesn't seem to be the time to shop and cook and clean on top of everything else that fills most Saturdays. Here's a solution: a menu of easy Tex-Mex favorites that you can parcel out for a no-stress potluck party.

The centerpiece dish here is chili based on ground turkey and canned white beans with just the right mix of spices and herbs. If you have the time to make it on Friday, know that it will only taste better come Saturday night. To expand the party, add the enchilada casserole in the Options section, another delicious do-ahead dish. That's also where you'll find a terrific make-ahead corn bread, flecked with jalapeño chilies.

For the first person who asks, "So what can I bring?" there's guacamole, everyone's favorite dip. Double up on the recipe to have enough to top the chili, too. Rice mixed with peas, corn and carrots is a quick and colorful side dish that can be made a couple of hours ahead, toted to the party and then rewarmed.

A dessert that features either pineapple or chocolate is well suited to food that moves to a south-of-the-border beat. So if the dessert volunteer likes to bake, there's a pineapple upside-down cake here that's light, easy and do-ahead. Easier still, but just as delicious, is chocolate fondue (in the Options), a communal dessert that everyone gathers around to enjoy, dipping chunks of pound cake and bites of fruit into the creamy melted chocolate.

menu for eight

- GUACAMOLE WITH FRESH VEGETABLES
- TURKEY CHILI WITH WHITE BEANS
- MEXICAN CONFETTI RICE
- BEER AND LIMEADE
- PINEAPPLE UPSIDE-DOWN CAKE WITH DRIED CHERRIES

menu options

- LAYERED ENCHILADA CASSEROLE
- TOASTED JALAPEÑO CORN BREAD
- CHOCOLATE-ORANGE FONDUE

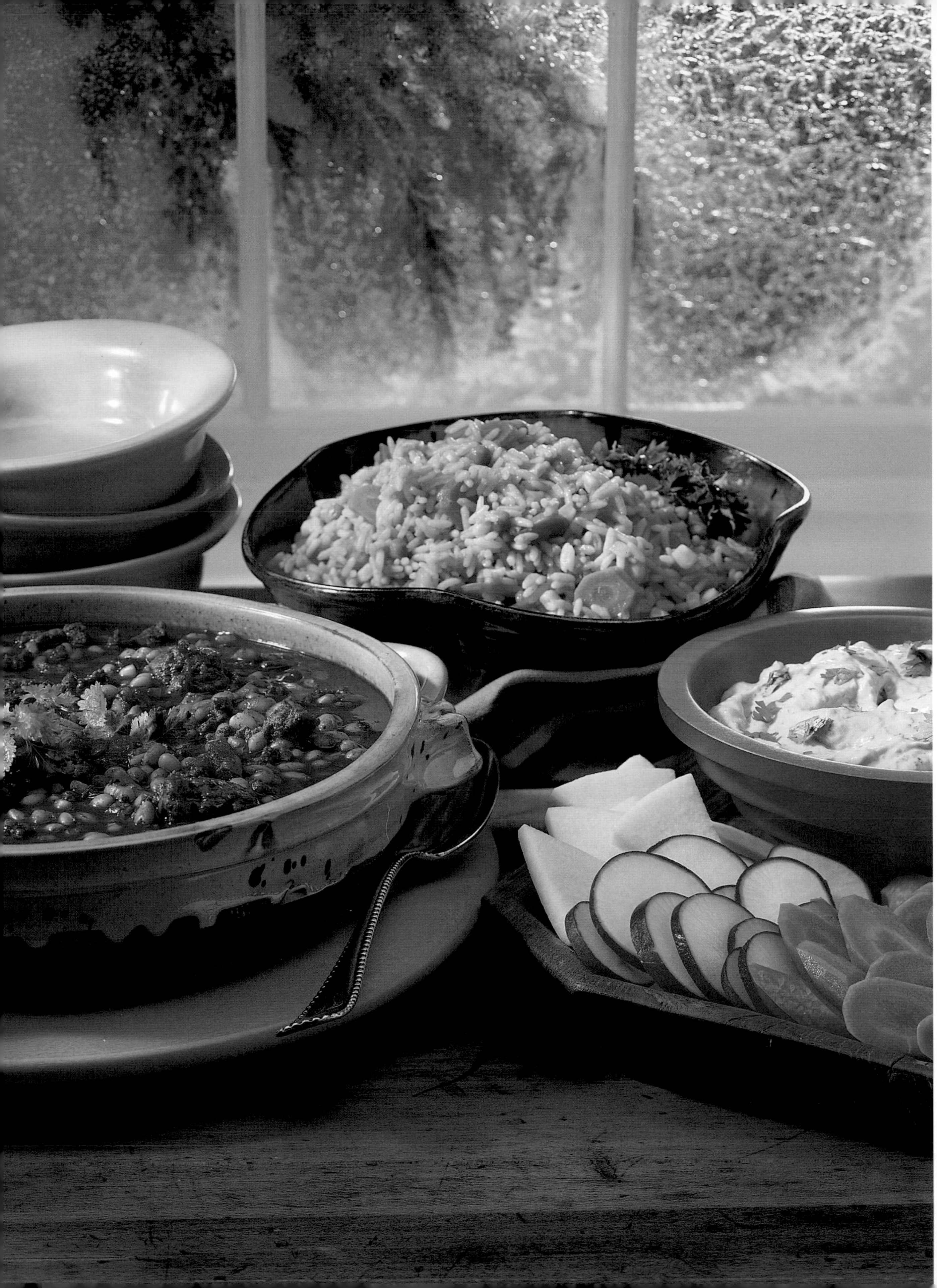

GUACAMOLE WITH FRESH VEGETABLES

Plain nonfat yogurt lightens the traditional recipe and heightens the texture of this easy dip while adding a nice tang. To thicken the yogurt properly, it needs to be drained, so begin preparing the guacamole at least two hours (and up to two days) ahead of time. MAKES ABOUT 1¾ CUPS

1½ cups plain nonfat yogurt

1 large ripe avocado, peeled, pitted, diced
¼ cup chopped green onions
¼ cup chopped fresh cilantro
1 teaspoon fresh lemon juice
¼ teaspoon ground cumin

3 carrots, peeled, sliced diagonally
1 small jicama, peeled, cut into ¼-inch-thick triangles
1 bunch radishes, trimmed, sliced
  Fresh cilantro sprigs

Line strainer with double layer of cheese-cloth. Set strainer over bowl. Add yogurt to strainer. Let drain in refrigerator until yogurt is very thick, at least 2 hours or overnight. Discard liquid. *(Can be made 2 days ahead. Cover and refrigerate.)*

Place yogurt in processor. Add avocado and next 4 ingredients to processor. Puree until smooth. Season with salt and pepper. Transfer to bowl. *(Can be prepared 6 hours ahead. Cover and refrigerate.)*

Place guacamole in center of platter. Surround with carrots, jicama and radishes. Garnish with cilantro sprigs and serve.

TURKEY CHILI WITH WHITE BEANS

Made with ground turkey and white beans, this chili is a nineties version of the typically heavier-weight model. Serve with ice-cold beer and, for the kids, limeade. 8 SERVINGS

1 tablespoon vegetable oil
2 medium onions, chopped
1½ teaspoons dried oregano
1½ teaspoons ground cumin
1½ pounds lean ground turkey
¼ cup chili powder
2 bay leaves
1 tablespoon unsweetened cocoa powder
1½ teaspoons salt
¼ teaspoon ground cinnamon
1 28-ounce can whole tomatoes
3 cups beef stock or canned beef broth
1 8-ounce can tomato sauce

3 15-ounce cans small white beans, rinsed, drained

Chopped red onion
Chopped fresh cilantro
Plain low-fat yogurt or light sour cream

Heat oil in heavy large pot over medium heat. Add onions; sauté until light brown and tender, about 10 minutes. Add oregano and cumin; stir 1 minute. Increase heat to medium-high. Add turkey; stir until no longer pink, breaking up with back of spoon. Stir in chili powder, bay leaves, cocoa powder, salt and cinnamon. Add tomatoes with their juices, breaking up with back of spoon. Mix in stock and tomato sauce. Bring to boil. Reduce heat; simmer 45 minutes, stirring occasionally.

Add beans to chili and simmer until flavors blend, about 10 minutes longer. Discard bay leaves. *(Can be prepared ahead. Cover and refrigerate 1 day or freeze up to 2 weeks. Thaw overnight in refrigerator. Rewarm chili over medium-low heat before continuing.)*

Ladle chili into bowls. Pass red onion, cilantro and yogurt separately.

MEXICAN CONFETTI RICE

Carrots, corn and peas add color and texture to this make-ahead side dish. 8 SERVINGS

1   tablespoon vegetable oil
1½ cups long-grain white rice
1   medium onion, chopped
2   teaspoons minced garlic
3   cups canned low-salt chicken broth
¼   cup tomato sauce
1   teaspoon salt

1½ cups thinly sliced peeled carrots
1   cup frozen corn kernels
½   cup frozen green peas

Heat oil in heavy large pot over medium heat. Add rice; stir 5 minutes. Add onion and garlic; sauté until onion is slightly softened, about 5 minutes. Add broth, tomato sauce and salt; bring to boil over medium-high heat. Boil uncovered until about half of broth is absorbed, stirring often, about 10 minutes.

Mix carrots, corn and peas into rice. Cover pot tightly with lid. Reduce heat to low; cook until rice is tender and liquid is absorbed, about 10 minutes longer. Remove from heat. Let stand covered 10 minutes; serve. *(Can be made 2 hours ahead. Cover with paper towel and let stand. Rewarm rice over low heat.)*

PINEAPPLE UPSIDE-DOWN CAKE WITH DRIED CHERRIES

Made with a fraction of the butter used for most upside-down cakes, this dessert has the texture of angel food cake—and it tastes so good nobody will know it has been streamlined. 8 SERVINGS

1   20-ounce can unsweetened whole pineapple slices in juice

2½ tablespoons unsalted butter
¼   cup (packed) dark brown sugar
¼   cup dried tart cherries

¾   cup all purpose flour
1   teaspoon baking powder
3   large egg whites
⅛   teaspoon salt
½   cup sugar
2   large egg yolks
⅓   cup low-fat (1%) milk
1   teaspoon vanilla extract

Preheat oven to 350°F. Drain pineapple, reserving 5 tablespoons juice. Set aside 1 whole pineapple slice; cut 4 slices in half (reserve remainder for another use).

Melt butter in 9-inch-diameter cake pan with 2-inch-high sides over low heat. Transfer 1½ tablespoons butter to small bowl and reserve; leave remaining butter in pan. Add brown sugar and 3 tablespoons pineapple juice to pan. Stir over medium heat until mixture boils and thickens slightly, about 45 seconds. Remove from heat. Place whole pineapple slice in center of pan atop sugar mixture. Surround with halved pineapple slices, rounded side toward pan edge. Sprinkle cherries in hollows of pineapple slices.

Mix flour and baking powder in small bowl. Using electric mixer, beat egg whites and salt in large bowl until soft peaks form. Gradually add ¼ cup sugar; beat until stiff peaks form. Using same beaters, beat yolks and remaining ¼ cup sugar in another large bowl until well blended. Mix in milk, vanilla extract and reserved 1½ tablespoons butter. Beat in flour mixture just until blended. Fold egg whites into batter in 3 additions. Spread cake batter evenly over pineapple slices in pan.

Bake cake until golden and tester inserted into center comes out clean, about 30 minutes. Cool in pan 5 minutes. Place platter over cake; invert cake onto platter. Remove pan; rearrange any fruit that may have become dislodged. Cool cake on platter 30 minutes. Brush 2 tablespoons pineapple juice over pineapple. Cool completely. *(Can be made 8 hours ahead. Cover; keep at room temperature.)*

Options

LAYERED ENCHILADA CASSEROLE

Here's a hearty and satisfying "Mexican lasagna" that comes together quickly. This could substitute for the chili. 8 SERVINGS

2	pounds lean ground beef
1	large onion, chopped
¼	cup chili powder
1	jalapeño chili, chopped

12	5- to 6-inch-diameter corn tortillas
1	15-ounce can chili beans
1½	cups (packed) grated sharp cheddar cheese
2	14½-ounce cans Mexican-style stewed tomatoes

Preheat oven to 350°F. Butter 13 x 9 x 2-inch glass baking dish. Sauté beef and onion in heavy large pot over high heat until brown, about 10 minutes. Reduce heat to low. Mix in chili powder and jalapeño and sauté 5 minutes. Season mixture with salt and pepper.

Overlap 6 tortillas on bottom of prepared dish, covering completely. Spoon beef mixture, then beans evenly over tortillas. Cover with remaining 6 tortillas. Sprinkle cheese over. Pour tomatoes with their juices over cheese. *(Can be prepared 1 day ahead. Cover with foil and refrigerate.)* Bake uncovered until casserole is heated through and bubbling at edges, approximately 1 hour.

TOASTED JALAPEÑO CORN BREAD

Jalapeño chilies give this bread a nice spicy kick. Add it to the menu (it's a good do-ahead) or have it instead of the rice. MAKES 20 SQUARES

3	tablespoons olive oil
1½	cups chopped onions
¼	cup minced seeded jalapeño chilies

1½	cups yellow cornmeal
1½	cups all purpose flour
1	tablespoon baking powder
2	teaspoons salt
¾	teaspoon baking soda
1½	cups buttermilk
3	large eggs, separated
¼	cup (½ stick) unsalted butter, melted

1	tablespoon plus 1 teaspoon sugar

Preheat oven to 400°F. Generously butter 13 x 9 x 2-inch glass baking dish. Heat oil in medium skillet over medium heat. Add onions and jalapeños; sauté until onions are tender, about 5 minutes.

Mix cornmeal, flour, baking powder, salt and baking soda in large bowl. Whisk buttermilk, yolks and butter in medium bowl to blend. Mix buttermilk mixture into dry ingredients just until blended. Stir in onion mixture.

Using electric mixer, beat egg whites in another large bowl until soft peaks form. Add sugar and beat until whites are stiff but not dry. Stir ⅓ of whites into batter to lighten. Fold in remaining whites. Transfer batter to prepared pan. Bake until corn bread is golden and tester inserted into center comes out clean, about 25 minutes. *(Can be prepared up to 8 hours ahead. Cool; cover with foil and store at room temperature. Rewarm covered in 350°F oven for 10 minutes before serving.)* Cut into 20 squares and serve warm.

CHOCOLATE-ORANGE FONDUE

Grand Marnier and grated orange peel add a touch of elegance to this simple indulgence (much deserved at the end of a light meal). Prepare the fondue just before serving, and keep it warm while dipping so that it will remain smooth. Use a traditional fondue pot, or place the pan of fondue on an electric hot plate. Either way, be sure the heat is low; too much heat will cause the chocolate to burn. Angel food cake, pound cake and fresh and dried fruits make great accompaniments. 8 SERVINGS

⅔ cup whipping cream
1 tablespoon (packed) grated orange peel
16 ounces bittersweet (not unsweetened) or semisweet chocolate, finely chopped
6 tablespoons Grand Marnier or other orange liqueur

16 1-inch pieces pound cake
16 1-inch pieces angel food cake
16 fresh strawberries, hulled
4 kiwis, peeled, each cut into 4 rounds
2 small pears, cored, cut into 1-inch pieces
2 large bananas, each cut into 8 rounds
2 oranges, peel and white pith removed, cut into sections
16 dried Calimyrna figs
16 dried apricot halves

Bring whipping cream and grated orange peel to simmer in heavy large saucepan. Reduce heat to low. Add chopped chocolate and 2 tablespoons Grand Marnier; whisk until mixture is smooth. Remove fondue from heat; blend in remaining Grand Marnier.

Transfer fondue to fondue pot. Place over candle or canned heat burner. Serve with cake pieces and fruit for dipping.

A Drinks Bar for Kids

When there are children at a party, make them feel special with a beverage bar set up just for them. Here are some ideas for kid-pleasing drinks.

BIT OF THE BUBBLY. Taking a cue from the classic Champagne cocktail, pour chilled sparkling apple cider or white grape juice into plastic flutes and add any of the following: a fresh strawberry, pureed fresh or canned peaches, some fresh-squeezed orange juice.

FRENCH SODAS. Mix any of the many flavored syrups available—including mint, raspberry, lemon, vanilla and orange—with soda water and pour over ice.

DIY SMOOTHIES. Set out ice, apple juice, yogurt, bananas, berries and sliced peaches with a blender and let kids create (with supervision) their own cooling concoctions.

HOT CHOCOLATE. Embellish this favorite with any of the following: marshmallows and/or whipped cream; cinnamon and vanilla, with an orange peel garnish; chopped peppermint candies and a candy cane swizzle stick.

PARLOR FAVORITES. Kids will love "drinking" their dessert when you offer root beer floats, chocolate malts and super-thick vanilla shakes (with red licorice straws).

Sunday Family Breakfast

THE ANYTIME-IS-BREAKFAST-TIME OF A LAZY Sunday can recommend dishes hearty enough to be called lunch, but not as fancy as brunch. The menu here comprises everybody's favorite breakfast foods—eggs, muffins and fruit—simply dressed up a bit to make them Sunday-best.

A sunny-looking skilletful of scrambled eggs with a generous helping of sausage is a good place to start. Use a fully cooked smoked sausage, like kielbasa, for its rich flavor, then brown it with green onions. That mixture gets stirred into creamy eggs scrambled with cheese for a dish that takes minutes but tastes wonderful. (If it's an oatmeal kind of day, there's an equally fast recipe in the Option section.)

To go with the eggs there are muffins flavored with almond paste and dried tart cherries, which you can find in most supermarkets now. These can be baked up to two weeks ahead and frozen.

The kids will want to help with the breakfast preparations, no doubt, so assign them the task of chopping the fruit for the fruit salad (even the youngest children will do fine with butter knives, bananas and some supervision). The light poppy seed dressing that gets tossed with the fruit takes this side dish out of the ordinary (and it can be made during a free moment on Saturday).

menu for four

- SCRAMBLED EGGS WITH SAUSAGE AND THYME

- ALMOND AND CHERRY MUFFINS

- FRUIT SALAD WITH POPPY SEED DRESSING

- COFFEE AND ORANGE JUICE

menu option

- OLD-FASHIONED OATMEAL WITH APPLES AND RAISINS

SCRAMBLED EGGS WITH SAUSAGE AND THYME

Neufchâtel cheese (reduced-fat cream cheese) gives this dish a nice texture. Pour coffee and orange juice to drink. 4 SERVINGS

8 large eggs
1 tablespoon coarse-grained mustard
½ teaspoon salt
½ teaspoon pepper
3 tablespoons butter
4 ounces fully cooked smoked turkey sausage (such as kielbasa), quartered lengthwise, thinly sliced crosswise
¾ cup chopped green onions
2 teaspoons dried thyme

4 ounces Neufchâtel cheese (reduced-fat cream cheese), cut into small pieces
Fresh thyme sprigs (optional)

Whisk eggs, mustard, salt and pepper in large bowl to blend. Melt 1 tablespoon butter in 12-inch-diameter nonstick skillet over medium heat. Add sausage; stir until brown, about 3 minutes. Add green onions and thyme; stir 1 minute. Transfer mixture to bowl.

Add 2 tablespoons butter to same skillet; melt over medium heat. Add eggs and cheese; stir until eggs are softly set and cheese begins to melt, 3 minutes. Add sausage; stir until eggs are just set, 2 minutes longer. Transfer to platter. Garnish with thyme sprigs, if desired.

ALMOND AND CHERRY MUFFINS

The almond paste in these muffins adds wonderful flavor and keeps them moist. Make them ahead and rewarm just before serving. MAKES 10

6 tablespoons orange juice
¾ cup dried tart cherries (about 4 ounces)

1 cup plus 2 tablespoons all purpose flour
½ cup sugar
1½ teaspoons baking powder
¼ teaspoon salt
1 7-ounce package almond paste, crumbled
6 tablespoons (¾ stick) unsalted butter, melted, hot
3 large eggs
1½ teaspoons grated orange peel

Position rack in center of oven and preheat to 375°F. Butter ten ⅓-cup metal muffin cups. Bring juice to simmer in small saucepan. Remove from heat. Add cherries; let stand until softened, about 10 minutes.

Mix flour, sugar, baking powder and salt in medium bowl. Using electric mixer, beat almond paste and melted butter in large bowl until well blended (mixture will still have some small pieces of almond paste). Add eggs 1 at a time, beating well after each addition. Mix in cherry mixture and orange peel. Add flour mixture and mix just until blended.

Divide batter among prepared muffin cups. Bake until tester inserted into center of muffins comes out clean but slightly moist to touch, about 20 minutes. *(Can be prepared ahead. Cool. Wrap muffins in foil and store at room temperature 2 days or freeze in airtight container up to 2 weeks. Thaw in refrigerator overnight. Rewarm in foil in 350°F oven 5 minutes.)* Serve muffins warm.

FRUIT SALAD WITH
POPPY SEED DRESSING

*Here, chunks of cantaloupe and pineapple, straw-
berries, grapes and banana slices are tossed with
a slightly sweet, creamy dressing enlivened with
crystallized ginger. (The dressing can be made
up to a day ahead.)* 4 SERVINGS

⅓ cup mayonnaise
⅓ cup sour cream
3 tablespoons chopped crystallized ginger
2 tablespoons honey
2 teaspoons distilled white vinegar
1¼ teaspoons poppy seeds

2 cups diced cantaloupe
1½ cups diced fresh pineapple
1½ cups sliced hulled strawberries
1 cup seedless grapes, halved
1 banana, peeled, sliced

Combine mayonnaise, sour cream, ginger,
honey, vinegar and poppy seeds in small
bowl; whisk to blend. Season dressing to taste
with salt and pepper. *(Dressing can be made
1 day ahead. Cover and refrigerate.)*

Combine all fruit in large bowl. Add dressing
and toss to coat. Refrigerate until cold, about
1 hour. Serve chilled.

Option *This recipe expands or
changes the menu to suit
your individual needs.*

OLD-FASHIONED OATMEAL
WITH APPLES AND RAISINS

*This homey, comforting cereal is like warm
granola, especially with the crunchy honey-toasted
walnut topping. It could replace the scrambled
eggs, if you like.* 4 SERVINGS

¼ cup coarsely chopped walnuts
1 tablespoon honey

3 cups water
2 cups old-fashioned oats
1 teaspoon salt
1 cup unsweetened apple juice
1 cup finely chopped peeled apple
¼ cup (packed) golden brown sugar
¼ cup raisins
½ teaspoon ground cinnamon

½ cup nonfat vanilla yogurt

Stir chopped walnuts in small nonstick skillet
over medium heat until lightly toasted, about
3 minutes. Drizzle honey over and stir until
honey thickens and coats nuts, about 2 minutes. Remove skillet from heat. Stir to loosen
nuts from skillet and cool.

Bring 3 cups water to boil in heavy medium
saucepan. Add oats and salt and stir over
medium heat until oats are softened and very
thick, about 5 minutes. Stir in apple juice,
chopped apple, brown sugar, raisins and
cinnamon. Reduce heat to low, cover and
cook until apples are tender, about 5 minutes.

Divide cereal among 4 bowls. Top with vanilla
yogurt and honey-toasted walnuts and serve.

Sunday Brunch with Friends

WHEN THERE ISN'T A FREE NIGHT IN COMMON for months to come but you want to get together, a leisurely Sunday brunch with friends can be an excellent option. It's easier to schedule and easier still to pull off, as you can dispense with formal courses and focus instead on one great dish.

The phyllo strudels here are an excellent candidate for that "one great dish." Golden and crispy, they slice to reveal a creamy ricotta filling seasoned with Parmesan, basil and prosciutto, with fresh asparagus added for crunch and color. Make the filling the day before and you won't have to rush in the morning. If you don't have a day-before hour, make the simpler quiche in the Option section. Every bit as tasty as the classic quiche Lorraine, this one is made easier with purchased puff pastry.

For a side dish that's elegant *and* easy, sauté wild and button mushrooms with garlic, fennel and mint and serve them in radicchio leaves arranged to resemble cups.

Round out the flavors of the meal with sliced melon; choose crenshaw, casaba or pink-fleshed honeydew for light sweetness, or substitute sliced papaya, or even avocado and oranges.

It's nice to start things off on a bubbly note, with a Bellini or other Champagne cocktail. And it's wonderful to while away the afternoon with coffee, cookies and friendly conversation.

menu for eight

- BELLINIS
- ASPARAGUS AND PROSCIUTTO STRUDELS
- MUSHROOM SALAD IN RADICCHIO CUPS
- SLICED MELON
- CHOCOLATE-ESPRESSO COOKIES

menu option

- PUFF PASTRY QUICHE LORRAINE

ASPARAGUS AND PROSCIUTTO STRUDELS

These savory brunch pastries are terrific with the mushroom salad here and assorted melons. Bellinis would make an occasion of the meal. 8 SERVINGS

1   15-ounce container whole milk ricotta cheese
¾   cup freshly grated Parmesan cheese
    (about 3 ounces)
½   cup chopped fresh basil or
    2½ tablespoons dried
3   ounces prosciutto, chopped
2   egg yolks, beaten to blend
3   tablespoons chopped fresh chives
3   tablespoons chopped fresh Italian parsley
¾   pound asparagus, trimmed
2   teaspoons unsalted butter
2   green onions, chopped
2   large garlic cloves, minced

10 frozen phyllo pastry sheets, thawed
1   cup (2 sticks) unsalted butter, melted
6   tablespoons dry breadcrumbs

Stir first 7 ingredients in large bowl to combine. Cook asparagus in large pot of boiling salted water until just crisp-tender, about 2 minutes. Drain asparagus. Transfer to large bowl of ice water to cool. Drain. Pat dry. Cut asparagus on diagonal into ½-inch-long pieces. Add to ricotta mixture. Melt 2 teaspoons butter in heavy small skillet over medium-high heat. Add green onions and garlic and sauté until just tender, about 2 minutes. Stir into ricotta mixture. Season ricotta mixture to taste with salt and pepper. *(Can be prepared 1 day ahead. Cover and refrigerate.)*

Butter heavy large baking sheet; set aside. Place 1 phyllo sheet on work surface. (Keep remaining phyllo covered with plastic wrap and damp cloth to prevent drying.) Brush phyllo lightly with melted butter. Top with second phyllo sheet. Brush with butter and sprinkle with 1 tablespoon crumbs. Place third phyllo sheet atop crumbs; brush with melted butter. Sprinkle with 1 tablespoon crumbs. Top with fourth phyllo sheet; brush with butter and sprinkle with 1 tablespoon crumbs. Place fifth phyllo sheet atop crumbs and brush with butter.

Spoon half of ricotta mixture along 1 short side of pastry in 3-inch-wide strip, beginning 1½ inches in from short side and leaving 2-inch borders on long sides. Fold long sides in over filling. Brush folded borders with melted unsalted butter. Starting at filled side, gently roll up pastry jelly-roll style, forming strudel. Brush tops, ends and sides of strudel with melted butter. Transfer to prepared baking sheet, seam side down. Form second strudel with remaining 5 phyllo sheets, 3 tablespoons breadcrumbs, melted butter and filling. *(Can be made 4 hours ahead. Cover loosely with plastic wrap; chill.)*

Preheat oven to 375°F. Bake strudels until golden brown, about 25 minutes. Cool 10 minutes. Slice with serrated knife; serve.

MUSHROOM SALAD IN RADICCHIO CUPS

This elegant side dish combines button and wild mushrooms, tosses them with olive oil flavored with mint and fennel, and serves them in "cups" of radicchio leaves. 8 SERVINGS

2   ounces dried porcini mushrooms
2   cups hot water

1   cup olive oil
8   large garlic cloves, chopped
2   teaspoons fennel seeds
2   pounds large button mushrooms, sliced
½   cup chopped fresh mint
¼   cup white wine vinegar
16 large radicchio leaves

Combine porcini and 2 cups hot water in medium bowl. Let stand until porcini soften, about 40 minutes. Pour mixture into strainer set over small bowl. Press porcini to release excess liquid. Coarsely chop porcini. Pour soaking liquid into measuring cup, leaving any sediment behind; reserve soaking liquid.

Heat oil in heavy large skillet over high heat. Add garlic and fennel seeds; sauté 30 seconds. Add button mushrooms and porcini; sauté until beginning to brown, about 10 minutes. Add porcini soaking liquid; boil until evaporated, scraping up browned bits, about 10 minutes. Remove from heat. Mix in mint and vinegar. Season with salt and pepper. Let cool. Spoon salad into radicchio leaves; arrange 2 leaves on each of 8 plates.

CHOCOLATE-ESPRESSO COOKIES

Because they contain so little flour, these cookies have a brownie-like texture. MAKES ABOUT 30

  6   tablespoons all purpose flour
 ¼   teaspoon baking powder
 ¼   teaspoon salt
  8   ounces bittersweet (not unsweetened) or semisweet chocolate, chopped
 ½   cup (1 stick) unsalted butter
  2   large eggs
 ¾   cup sugar
 2¼ teaspoons instant espresso powder
 2¼ teaspoons vanilla extract
  1   cup semisweet chocolate chips
  1   cup coarsely chopped walnuts

Preheat oven to 350°F. Mix flour, baking powder and salt in small bowl. Stir bittersweet chocolate and butter in heavy large saucepan over low heat until melted. Remove from heat. Using electric mixer, beat eggs, sugar, espresso powder and vanilla in medium bowl until well blended. Stir egg mixture into warm chocolate mixture. Stir in dry ingredients (batter will be loose). Stir in chocolate chips and chopped walnuts.

Immediately spoon dough by heaping tablespoonfuls onto nonstick baking sheets, spacing 1½ inches apart. Bake until tops crack but cookies are still soft inside, about 12 minutes. Transfer baking sheets to racks; cool 5 minutes. Transfer cookies to racks; cool completely. *(Can be prepared 1 day ahead. Store cookies in airtight container at room temperature.)*

Option

This recipe expands or changes the menu to suit your individual needs.

PUFF PASTRY QUICHE LORRAINE

This version of the brunch classic (which, by the way, is making a comeback) uses puff pastry rather than the usual pie crust. 8 SERVINGS

 10   ounces thick bacon slices, cut into ½-inch pieces

  1   sheet frozen puff pastry (half of 17¼-ounce package), thawed
  2   cups whipping cream
  5   large eggs
 ¼   teaspoon salt
 ¼   teaspoon pepper
 ¼   teaspoon ground nutmeg
 1½ cups grated Gruyère cheese

Preheat oven to 425°F. Sauté bacon in heavy large skillet over medium heat until brown, about 12 minutes. Using slotted spoon, transfer bacon to paper towels.

Roll out pastry on floured surface to 12-inch square. Transfer to 9-inch-diameter glass pie dish. Trim edges; crimp. Whisk cream, eggs, salt, pepper and nutmeg in bowl to blend. Add bacon and cheese. Pour into pastry.

Bake quiche until edges puff, top is deep golden brown and center is softly set, about 40 minutes. *(Can be prepared 1 day ahead. Cool quiche; cover and chill. Reheat uncovered in 375°F oven until heated through, about 15 minutes.)* Let stand 15 minutes; serve.

Sunday Dinner with the Family

THE WEEK BRINGS WITH IT ANY NUMBER OF obstacles to a family dinner, from late nights at work to school meetings to heavy home-work loads. It may, in fact, be Sunday before the family is guaranteed the time to sit down, catch up and enjoy a good meal.

Roast chicken is classic Sunday night fare, and a favorite with young and old alike. Here, it's flavored with a delicious parsley butter and served with a creamy mushroom gravy. To go with the big, golden brown bird, there's a salad of cucumbers, red onion and radishes and a side dish of roasted potato and carrot wedges.

The kids may laugh at the notion of having pancakes for dessert, but they'll probably be intrigued enough to want to help make them, and they'll love the taste. There are eggs to break (always a favorite "job" with the youngest cooks), berries to mix for the topping and pancakes to flip (something the older kids will enjoy). The participation turns the dessert into a family activity— a delicious diversion on a cold or wet day.

If you're planning a busy Sunday and want to come home to a quicker-cooking meal, opt for the rosemary-scented pork chops in the Option section, marinating the chops and making the sauce in advance. The pancake batter and fruit topping can be made ahead, too. So the family's weekend can still end with the pleasure of sharing good food together.

menu for four

- CUCUMBER, RED ONION AND RADISH SALAD

- PARSLEY ROAST CHICKEN WITH MUSHROOM CREAM GRAVY

- ROASTED POTATOES AND CARROTS

- SAUVIGNON BLANC AND MILK

- SWEDISH PANCAKES WITH BERRY-CARDAMOM TOPPING

menu option

- ROSEMARY PORK LOIN CHOPS

CUCUMBER, RED ONION
AND RADISH SALAD

*This sweet and sour slaw-like salad could be
either a first course or a side dish.* 4 SERVINGS

1   medium cucumber, peeled, thinly sliced
1   cup thinly sliced red onion
4   large red radishes, thinly sliced

¼   cup vegetable oil
2   tablespoons white wine vinegar
1   teaspoon sugar
½   teaspoon dried crushed red pepper

Combine first 3 ingredients in large bowl.
(Can be prepared 3 hours ahead. Cover; chill.)

Whisk oil, vinegar, sugar and red pepper to
blend in small bowl. Season with salt and
pepper. Pour dressing over vegetables; toss.

PARSLEY ROAST CHICKEN
WITH MUSHROOM CREAM GRAVY

*That Sunday night favorite, roast chicken, is
flavored with parsley butter and served with a rich
and creamy mushroom gravy. Pour a Sauvignon
Blanc and milk.* 4 SERVINGS

2¼   cups chopped fresh parsley
      (about 2 large bunches)
¼   cup (½ stick) butter, room temperature
1   7½-pound roasting chicken,
      excess fat discarded

1⅓   cups canned low-salt chicken broth

2   large shallots, chopped
1   pound mushrooms, sliced
2   tablespoons all purpose flour
⅓   cup whipping cream

Position rack in center of oven and preheat
to 450°F. Mix 1½ cups chopped fresh parsley
and butter in medium bowl. Set chicken in
large roasting pan. Sprinkle inside and
outside with salt and pepper. Spoon parsley
butter into cavity. Tie legs together to hold
shape. *(Can be prepared 6 hours ahead. Cover
and refrigerate.)* Place chicken in oven, legs
toward back. Roast 20 minutes. Slide spatula
under chicken to free from pan bottom.
Continue to roast until juices run clear when
chicken is pierced in thickest part of thigh,
about 1 hour 10 minutes longer.

Transfer chicken to platter. Pour drippings
from roasting pan into cup. Pour canned
chicken broth into roasting pan. Bring to
boil over high heat, scraping up browned
bits. Remove from heat.

Pour 3 tablespoons reserved drippings into
heavy large skillet. Heat over medium-high
heat. Add chopped shallots and stir to coat.
Add sliced mushrooms and sauté until just
starting to soften, about 3 minutes. Add flour
and stir 1 minute. Add broth from roasting
pan and bring to boil, stirring frequently.
Mix in whipping cream and boil until sauce
thickens slightly, about 3 minutes. Season
gravy to taste with salt and pepper. Add
remaining ¾ cup chopped parsley.

Serve chicken with mushroom gravy.

ROASTED POTATOES AND CARROTS

A simple dish to go with the chicken. 4 SERVINGS

3   medium russet potatoes (about 2¼ pounds),
      each cut lengthwise into 8 wedges
3   large carrots, halved lengthwise and crosswise
3   tablespoons butter
1¼   cups chopped fresh parsley

Preheat oven to 450°F. Combine potato
wedges and carrots in large roasting pan.
Dot with butter. Sprinkle with 1 cup chopped
fresh parsley, salt and pepper. Roast until
tender and beginning to brown, stirring occasionally, about 1 hour 25 minutes. Sprinkle
with remaining ¼ cup chopped parsley.

SWEDISH PANCAKES WITH BERRY-CARDAMOM TOPPING

In keeping with the subtly Swedish menu theme, serve that country's famous little pancakes with a berry topping for dessert. 4 SERVINGS

PANCAKES

2 large eggs
1 cup milk
⅔ cup all purpose flour
¾ teaspoon ground cardamom
¼ teaspoon salt
⅓ cup half and half
3 tablespoons unsalted butter, melted

TOPPING

1 6-ounce basket raspberries
1 6-ounce basket blackberries
¼ cup sugar
½ teaspoon ground cardamom

Additional unsalted butter, melted

FOR PANCAKES: Blend eggs and ⅓ cup milk in processor until smooth. Add flour, cardamom and salt; process until mixture is thick and smooth. With machine running, add remaining ⅔ cup milk, half and half and 3 tablespoons melted unsalted butter; mix batter until smooth.

FOR TOPPING: Combine raspberries, blackberries, sugar and ground cardamom in medium bowl. Mix together gently. Let mixture stand until berries are juicy, stirring occasionally, at least 30 minutes. *(Batter and topping can be prepared 8 hours ahead. Cover and chill.)*

Preheat oven to 200°F. Place ovenproof platter in oven. Heat heavy large griddle or skillet over medium-high heat. Brush griddle with melted butter. Working in batches, add batter to griddle, using 1 tablespoonful for each pancake. Cook until pancakes are brown, about 1 minute per side. Transfer to platter in oven to keep warm. Repeat with remaining batter, brushing with more butter as needed.

Place pancakes on plates. Spoon berry topping over and then serve.

Option *This recipe expands or changes the menu to suit your individual needs.*

ROSEMARY PORK LOIN CHOPS

These would fit right in to the menu. 4 SERVINGS

MARINADE

½ cup olive oil
2 tablespoons finely chopped garlic
1½ tablespoons chopped fresh rosemary
4 fresh thyme sprigs
4 bay leaves, crumbled
2 teaspoons pepper
4 5-ounce (1-inch-thick) boneless pork loin chops

SAUCE

2⅔ cups canned low-salt chicken broth
1 teaspoon tomato paste
2 tablespoons olive oil
2 tablespoons minced shallots
1 teaspoon finely chopped garlic
¼ cup Sherry wine vinegar
4 tablespoons (½ stick) chilled butter

FOR MARINADE: Combine first 6 ingredients in shallow glass baking dish. Add pork; turn to coat. Cover; chill 3 hours or up to 1 day.

FOR SAUCE: Whisk chicken broth and tomato paste in heavy medium saucepan to blend. Boil until reduced to ¾ cup, about 18 minutes. *(Can be prepared 1 day ahead; chill.)*

Scrape off excess marinade from pork. Heat oil in heavy large skillet over medium-high heat. Add pork and sauté until cooked through, about 5 minutes per side. Transfer pork to platter; tent with foil to keep warm. Add shallots and garlic to same skillet; sauté 30 seconds. Add vinegar; boil until reduced to glaze, whisking constantly, about 1 minute. Add reduced broth mixture. Bring sauce to boil. Reduce heat to medium. Whisk in butter 1 tablespoon at a time. Simmer until thickened, 3 minutes. Spoon sauce onto plates; top with chops.

Index

Page numbers in italic indicate color photographs.

Shopping Directory

OCCASIONS

Celebration Dinner: *"Blue Fluted" plates by Royal Copenhagen from Georg Jensen, 212-759-6457. "Fairfax" sterling silverware by Gorham; call 800-635-3669 for nearest store location. Flowers by Charles R. Case, The Flower Basket of Westport, Connecticut, 203-222-0206. Place card holders from Keesal & Mathews, 212-410-1800. Antique ironstone compote, Italian handblown glass hurricane candleholder and all other items privately owned.*

Elegant Shower: *Table, chairs and wire stand with presents from Clementine, 800-983-0022. Mother-of-pearl flatware by R&B Imports; call 561-392-9942 for nearest store location. Napkins and tablecloth by Archipelago; call 212-334-9460 for nearest store location. Gold "Roman Antique" plates by Annieglass; call 800-347-6133 for nearest store location. "Forma" bowl (chicken salad) and platter (peppers) by The Cyclamen Collection, 510-597-3640. Wine bucket by S. Browne & Co., 203-966-2403. Tent from Abbey Richmond Inc., 800-637-2789. Stacked glass cake stands and all other items privately owned.*

Romantic Dinner: *"Dieulefit" octagonal plates (style number MI-14/03; soufflés), platter (MI-36/03; caviar pizzas) and chargers (MI-31/03; lobster) from Romancing Provence Ltd.; call 212-481-9879 for nearest store location. Pearwood-handled flatware by Vance Kitera; call 800-646-6360 for nearest store location. Antique monogrammed cup, antique silver tumbler used as vase and all other items privately owned.*

Kid's Birthday Party: *Basket by Simon Pearce; call 800-774-5277 for nearest store location. Checked and striped ribbons by Offray (available at craft stores and floral supply shops nationwide). Restaurant supply-store dishes, vintage quilt, antique graniteware colander, vintage refrigerator containers, vintage English lunch box, Bakelite cake server and all other items privately owned.*

Afternoon Tea: *Candlesticks and antique plates (sandwiches) from Fairground Attraction, 914-241-4433. Antique glass petal plates (jams) from Blithewold, 914-666-7533. Silver tea service, antique ironstone platter (honey tea cake), creamware cup and saucer, antique Wedgwood footed bowl (scones) and all other items privately owned.*

Celebrating a Birthday Milestone: *Silver tray from S. Browne & Co., 203-966-2403. Dessert plates and copper chargers from LCR; call 888-221-9270 or 800-878-9446 for nearest store location. Burlwood cake server and flatware from R&B Imports, 561-392-9942. Paisley throw (style number K7100; on sideboard) from Karavan; call 914-654-0300 for nearest store location. Candlesticks and lamp with beaded shade from Uproar Home, 212-614-8580 or 203-221-9210. Linen napkin by Archipelago; call 212-334-9460 for nearest store location. Gold "Roman Antique" plates by Annieglass; call 800-347-6133 nearest store location. French press coffeemaker from Williams-Sonoma; call 800-541-1262 for nearest store location. Urn with fruit from The Import Collection; call 888-782-4620 for nearest store location. Hemp runner from Zona, 212-925-6750. Horn salt and pepper shakers and paisley throw (on table) from Simon Pearce; call 800-774-5277 for nearest store location. Drabware cups and saucers, agate bowl (peppers), antique wooden pedestal and all other items privately owned.*

Cookout for a Crowd: *"Whipstitch Brights" napkins by Archipelago; call 212-334-9460 for nearest store location. "Conical" flatware by Sabre from Marel Gifts, 800-261-3501. Clear-stemmed glass from Pottery Barn; call 800-922-9934 for nearest store location. Blue-stemmed glasses from Crate&Barrel; call 888-249-4155 for nearest store location. Spiral-stemmed glass from Opus Imports, 800-699-8988. Handled basket with vegetables from Simon Pearce; call 800-774-5277 for nearest store location. Graniteware spattered plate, galvanized metal pail and all other items privately owned.*

Big Anniversary with Family and Friends: *"Cambridge" cake knife from Savoir Vivre International, 212-684-6065. Egyptian cotton napkin from Anichini, La Collezione, 310-657-4292. Cake plate by Home Essentials and "Godinger Silver" cake server from Tesoro, 310-273-9890. Vintage cocktail shaker/strainer, antique silver spoon with beaded edge (potatoes) and all other items privately owned.*

Potluck Housewarming Party: *Aluminum baguette tray (style number DRLT001), pewter spoon (DRMS002), cream footed fruit bowl (DREABO41) and "White Mist Cambridge" flatware from Wolfman Gold & Good Company, 212-431-1888. "Cucina Fresca" plates and bowl (spread), "Cucina Rustica" bowl (carrot salad) and wooden footed bowl used as pedestal from Vietri Inc.; call 800-277-5933 for nearest store location. Pilsner, basket, square plate and tray all from Simon Pearce; call 800-774-5277 for nearest store location. Plaid stitch napkins by XOCHI from Wooden Spoons Ltd., 201-664-5858. All other items privately owned.*

Gala Buffet: *Champagne buckets (used as vases) and "Heartland" stemware from Simon Pearce; call 800-774-5277 for nearest store location. "Saumur" serving fork and spoon, "Mouchete" plate (frittata) and "Quattro" stainless steel flatware from the Blachere Group, 800-641-4808. "Casserole" bowl (style number DRLAPC001; corn salad) and "Melange Parchment" plate (DRASP007; green vegetable salad) from Wolfman Gold & Good Company, 212-431-1888. Cotton damask napkins from Ad Hoc Softwares, 212-925-2652. "Satin Center" ribbon (wedding cake) from Midori; call 206-282-3595 for nearest store location. All other items privately owned.*

INSTANT ENTERTAINING

Breakfast on the Go: *Linen "Voile" napkin by Necessities; call 718-797-0530 for nearest store location. Antique ironstone pedestal privately owned.*

Tortilla Wraps: *Antique wire basket, privately owned.*

Pita Pockets: *Curly maple cutting board from Simon Pearce; call 800-774-5277 for nearest store location. Skillet privately owned.*

Drinks and Eats: *French wicker tray privately owned.*

Salad Bar: *Place mat, Simon Pearce; call 800-774-5277 for nearest store location. Other items privately owned.*

Do-It-Yourself Sundaes: *Antique linen napkin and "Candlewick" antique glass plate privately owned.*

GET-TOGETHERS

Friday Dinner with the Kids: *"Dinerware" plate by 10 Strawberry Street (available with blue rim), from the Pottery Shack, 714-494-1141. Vintage hotel silverware from Pottery Barn; call 800-922-5507 for nearest store location. "Debussy" wineglass by Cassis & Company from Julienne, 818-441-2299. "Cabana Stripe" tablecloth by Necessities from Room with a View, 310-998-5858. All other items privately owned.*

Saturday Morning Breakfast: *Place mat by Angel Zimmick from Barneys New York, 800-777-0087. "Tulipe" flatware by Chambly from Avventura, 212-769-2510. All other items privately owned.*

Saturday Portable Lunch: *Bowl and dessert plate by Aletha Soulé from The Loom Company; call 212-366-7214 for nearest store location. "Houndstooth" napkin by Necessities; call 718-797-0530 for nearest store location. All other items privately owned.*

Saturday Elegant Dinner Party: *"Kusumam" charger, dinner and dessert plates by Rosenthal Studio-Linie from On A Mission, 909-626-4810. "Ispahan Blue" tablecloth by Primrose Bordier for Palais Royal from Bo Danica, 800-654-4674. "Morocco Gold" goblet by Smyers Glass and handmade greeting card by Constance Kay, both from Feast Pasadena, 626-584-0021. "Bronze Sphere" flatware by Izabel Lam International, 718-797-3983.*

Saturday Potluck Party: *Baker (chili) from Beans, 617-244-4468. Wooden platter (guacamole) from Equator, 212-219-3708. Ontano orange wooden platter (cake) by Vietri Inc.; call 800-277-5933 for nearest store location. All other items privately owned.*

Sunday Dinner with the Family: *Antique blue and white table, baskets, bread boards, porcelain and pewter serving platters from Henrik Aarestrup Scandinavian Antiques, 213-655-5565. Mother-of-pearl-handled dessert set, antique carving set and gravy ladle from David Orgell, 213-272-3355. All other items privately owned.*

Instant Entertaining and Get-Togethers menus not referenced above: *All items privately owned.*

Acknowledgments

The following people contributed recipes included in this book: Mary Baker; Mary Barber; Melanie Barnard; Joseph Bastianich; Caroline Belk; Lena Cederham Birnbaum; Carole Bloom; Amy Bond; Charleen Borger; Vicki Lee Boyajian bakery, Needham, Massachusetts; Jean and Walt Boylan; Dan Budd; Leslie Vaughn Burckard; Jonna and John Carls; Janet and Bob Cole; Sara Corpening; Lane Crowther; Brooke Dojny; Beryl Edwards; Janet Fletcher; Jim Fobel; Margaret and Stephen Gadient; Kathy Gunst; Ken Haedrich; Leslie Holliday; Barbara and Charlie O'Reilly Hyland; Inn of the Anasazi, Santa Fe, New Mexico; Nancy Harmon Jenkins; Julienne, San Marino, California; Karen Kaplan; Barbara Karoff; Jeanne Thiel Kelley; Kristine Kidd; Karen Krasne; Dolores laGuardia; La Litote, Abercrombie & Kent, Oak Brook, Illinois; The Lark, West Bloomfield, Michigan; Jan and Basil Liascos; Anna Meshkat Liebling; Diane Lipman; Michael McLaughlin; Chuck and John McNeil; Jinx and Jefferson Morgan; Selma Brown Morrow; Gina and Jeff Mummery; Sandi Nelson; 95 School Street, Bridgehampton, New York; Ellen Ogden; The Picnic Cafe, Nashville, Tennessee; Paul V. Pusateri; Jan Rayfiel; Martha Peyton Reynolds and Rick Reynolds; Mimi Rippee; Betty Rosbottom; Richard Sax; Sue Ann Scarcia-Barry; Jane Seaman; Ilana Sharlin; Marie Simmons; Sylvia Snyder; Stafford in the Field, Chocorua, New Hampshire; Jordan and Dean Stringfellow; Sarah Tenaglia; Susie and Brad Tjossem; Shula Udoff; Vincent Guerithault on Camelback, Phoenix, Arizona; Charlotte Walker; Nancy Faulkner Wiersum; Lucindy Willis; Kathryn Dowling Wrye and Donald Wrye.

The following people contributed photographs included in this book: David Bishop; Beatriz Da Costa; Lannen/Kelly; Brian Leatart; Judd Pilossof.

Original photography, front jacket, pages 2 and 4 through 135 (with the exception of pages 86, 87, 112 and 113) by Deborah Klesinski. Prop stylist: Francine Matalon-Degni. Food stylists: Polly Talbott, William Leland Smith, Tracy Alison Stewart.

Special thanks to
JOHN AND MARY BAUMANN
JILL AND FRANK COHEN
KAREN AND PETER COVENEY
PATTI AND ERIC FAST
TINA AND STEVEN LANG *and*
DAWN AND DONALD SULLIVAN
for graciously sharing their homes and collections with us.

M T W T F

SATURDAY

SUNDAY